# EARLY MODERN
# Genealogy

# EARLY MODERN
# Genealogy

## RESEARCHING YOUR
## FAMILY HISTORY
### *1600–1838*

### PAUL CHAMBERS

SUTTON PUBLISHING

First published in the United Kingdom in 2006 by
Sutton Publishing Limited · Phoenix Mill
Thrupp · Stroud · Gloucestershire · GL5 2BU

British Library Cataloguing in Publication Data
A catalogue record for this book is available from the British Library.

ISBN 0-7509-3688-6

Typeset in 11.5/14pt BemboMono.
Typesetting and origination by
Sutton Publishing Limited.
Printed and bound in England by
J.H. Haynes & Co. Ltd, Sparkford.

For Matthew, Frances, James,
Oliver, Daisy and Sam

# CONTENTS

CONTENTS

# LIST OF ILLUSTRATIONS

# PREFACE

This book has been written for those who have managed to trace their family history back to around 1838 or earlier and who want to take their research further back in time into the early modern era.

Gathered together in this book is a comprehensive list of the best and most accessible records generated between approximately 1603 and 1837 which may be of use to those researching their family tree. As well as showing what records are available, this book also provides information about what these documents mean, where they are to be found (especially published versions of them) and how best they can be interpreted. This book will show that there is a wealth of pre-Victorian material available to the genealogist, much of which can be found in printed volumes; this dispenses with the need to travel to record offices in order to consult original documents.

In writing this guide I have assumed that readers will have a range of experience: from those with little or no knowledge of family history research to those who may be more familiar with historical records and custom. I have also assumed that many readers will be researching their family history from outside Great Britain or will not have regular access to those archives that hold original documents.

As well as serving the general genealogical community, this book will also function as a reference guide for more experienced genealogists, as well as historians and archaeologists who need to trace information about local or national historical figures.

The researching and writing of this book were by no means a solo process, and my profound thanks go to all those people who were kind enough to offer me their time, advice and knowledge. In particular I would like to thank the staff at the following institutions for allowing me access to their records and for their patience when answering my many questions: Bodleian Library; British Library; Cambridge County Record Office; Cambridge University Library; Family Records Centre (The National Archives); Guildhall Library (London); Historical Manuscripts Commission (The National Archives); Institute of Historical Research; Norfolk Record Office; Public Record Office (The National Archives); Royal Historical Society; Society of Genealogists; Somerset Record Office and University College London. I would also like to thank Steve Birks of www.thepotteries.org and Dr John Symonds for allowing me to use examples of their own genealogical research.

A big thank you must go to my agent, Sugra Zaman of Watson Little Ltd, for her sterling work on my behalf and to the magnificent staff at Sutton, especially Christopher Feeney and Hilary Walford, whose advice and patience are greatly appreciated. Finally, I must thank my wife, Rachel, and my parents and parents-in-law for their help and support.

It should be noted that this book is a sequel to my volume on *Medieval Genealogy* (Sutton Publishing, 2005) and that, although each book covers a separate time period, a few sections, such as those on manors and some types of legal and court records, have a relevance both to medieval and early modern times. Rather than waste valuable space duplicating what has already been said in *Medieval Genealogy*, I have summarised these chapters while still highlighting their relevance to early modern family history research.

# ABBREVIATIONS

| | |
|---|---|
| CLRO | Corporation of London Record Office |
| CRO | County Record Office |
| LMA | London Metropolitan Archive |
| MDR | Manorial Documents Register |
| PCC | Prerogative Court of Canterbury |
| TNA: PRO | The National Archives: Public Record Office |
| VCH | Victoria County History |

# CHAPTER ONE

# AN INTRODUCTION TO EARLY MODERN GENEALOGY

## 1.1. THE EARLY MODERN ERA

### The Scope of this Book

The early modern era is ill defined, but it is normally said to begin in the sixteenth century and end at the beginning of the nineteenth century. This book covers much of that period and looks at records that were generated between the start of the reign of James I, in 1603, to the death of William IV, in 1837. This timeframe neatly slots in between the more arcane medieval era, where genealogical records are harder to come by (see Chambers, 2005), and the Victorian era, when the nature of many records was changed by new laws and organisations.

The early modern records covered by this book are for the most part those that were generated in England and Wales. This is because, although Scotland, Ireland and other dependencies were joined with England and Wales to form Great Britain during the early modern era, many of their laws and systems remained separate, as do their archives. Thus many of the records discussed in this book will be of limited use to those seeking information about Scotland, Ireland and others; for information on these I recommend using more specific guides such as Grenham (1999).

### A Summary of Early Modern History

By 1603 England and Wales had been ruled as a joint administrative unit for centuries, and shared a majority of the same laws and customs. After the political and religious turbulence of the sixteenth century, England and Wales entered the seventeenth century as a major military and economic power within Europe and quickly began to use their naval prowess to found trading companies, farms and plantations in the New World. These would, in time, expand to form the impressive and sometimes oppressive British Empire.

The start of the early modern era saw the English populace become increasingly discontented with the behaviour of their monarchs, James I and Charles I. Eventually, the latter engineered an argument with the London Parliament that, in

1642, pushed the country into a civil war that lasted until the King's execution in 1649. From 1649, England and Wales were ruled by Parliament until the restoration of Charles II in 1660. This period of Parliamentary rule is known as the Commonwealth era and it has a great significance to family historians.

The Commonwealth era (1649–60) saw the introduction of laws that had an effect on the generation, collection and storage of local and national documents. This means that in some instances, such as with the parish registers (see Section 4.1), there is a break in the record during the Commonwealth while other records were organised differently (e.g. probate records: Section 4.2). It is also generally true to say that before the Civil War record-keeping was not as full and obsessive as it was to become afterwards (although there is still a wealth of material available).

The restoration of Charles II in 1660 also saw the restoration of many of the pre-Commonwealth laws and record-keeping practices, although it marked the end of some types of medieval record (e.g. the inquisitions post mortem: Section 6.3), and the establishment of a permanent army and navy. After the overthrow of James II in 1688, the power of the monarch was curtailed in favour of Parliament, and shortly afterwards, in 1703, Scotland joined England, Wales and Ireland to form the United Kingdom of Great Britain.

The eighteenth century saw a huge change in Britain's society, as the country's wealth swelled from the creation of its empire. Cities and towns expanded, as did the middle classes, creating new careers in trading, finance, transport and so on. People moved in search of work, creating slum districts in the cities that filled with poverty-stricken people. Towards the end of the eighteenth century innovations in manufacturing and engineering, such as the creation of a canal network and turnpikes, saw the beginnings of the Industrial Revolution.

Changes were also taking place in the countryside with the break-up of the once-powerful manorial estates into smaller farmsteads and the transformation of open fields and common land into enclosed fields and pastures. This combination of trade, technology and farming meant that, by the time of Queen Victoria's coronation, in 1837, Britain had become a populous, wealthy and industrialised society. However, many of the laws and customs that were designed to cope with a post-medieval society could not function effectively in this new world. Eventually the pressures generated by this new socio-economic society forced the Victorians to revise and reorganise the administration of Britain and led to the sweeping-away of many of the laws and practices of the early modern era and the laying of a foundation for modern British society.

## 1.2. ADMINISTRATIVE GEOGRAPHY

In early medieval times England was subdivided into a hierarchy of geographic units that were (and in some cases still are) used to facilitate local and national administrative policy. You will encounter the names of these units continuously in documents, and one of the keys to tracing your ancestors is knowing the name(s) of the parish, hundred and county in which they may have been living.

## The County

The counties of England date back to Anglo-Saxon times, and most survived for centuries without interference to either their name or their boundaries. However, in 1972 there was a major reorganisation of the county boundaries, which saw some counties joined with their neighbours (e.g. Huntingdonshire was joined with Cambridgeshire), while others had their boundaries moved, causing parishes, towns and even cities to move from one county to another.

Of course, historical documents refer to the old county system, and it has therefore been common practice among family historians to use the county names as they were before the changes were implemented. This convention will be followed in this book.

## The Hundred

In Anglo-Saxon times the counties were subdivided into small administrative units known as hundreds, each of which contained several parishes. The hundred was based around a meeting place (after which the hundred was normally named) at which a court or other official function would be held.

The hundreds are now defunct as administrative units, with many people unaware of their existence, but they still had a function in the early modern era, especially regarding taxation returns. To find the name of the hundred(s) in which your ancestors lived, consult local historical guides or the Victoria County History (see Section 2.2), which is organised using the old system of hundreds. In northern counties hundreds are sometimes referred to as wapentakes.

## The Parish

The parish system is the most modern of the commonly used administrative units seen in early modern England. The parish boundary system dates to just after the Norman Conquest and was largely the creation of the medieval Church, which wanted to invent a local geographical unit to help with its ecclesiastical courts. Each parish was based around a single church and would normally include only one or two villages (after which the parish would usually be named) containing a few hundred people. Parish names are commonly referred to in local and national records and may be the only location given for a named individual. Parishes are still important administrative units within England.

*The counties of England and Wales as they were before the widespread boundary changes that were implemented in 1974.*

## The Borough

Towns and larger villages could apply to have their status upgraded to that of a borough. This was done by Royal Charter and was highly desirable, as it gave them a degree of autonomy from landlords and local government. In practice, though, boroughs were administered in much the same way as parishes.

## Counties Palatine

After the Norman invasion of 1066 William the Conqueror gave some of his earls special authority to administer their lands semi-autonomously from the Crown. These earls became known as palatines and the counties that they administered as counties palatine. This autonomy meant that the counties palatine were often exempt from some of the administrative actions taking place elsewhere in the kingdom, such as taxations and the courts. This means that some national records (mostly those involving the courts) may not apply to the counties palatine or that they may have been created differently and filed in a separate location.

The traditional counties palatine are those covering Durham and Chester, ruled by the bishops of Durham and earls of Chester respectively since the time of William the Conqueror. In 1351 Lancashire (under the guise of the duchy of Lancaster) became a palatine.

Although not strictly a palatine, the duchy of Cornwall (traditionally administered by the monarch's eldest son) is also usually considered as such. At various times the Isle of Ely, Shropshire and Hexhamshire (Northumberland) have also had autonomy from the Crown. Most of the privileges held by the counties palatine disappeared in the nineteenth century, although some retained their courts until the 1970s.

## 1.3. RESEARCH HINTS

In the chapters that follow you will find a comprehensive list of the most useful and accessible resources available to those researching their early modern family history, together with an explanation of the purpose for which these records were created, where they (or published editions of them) may be found and what relevance they might have to family historians.

It is hoped that the chapter titles will be reasonably self-explanatory and should, together with the index, guide you to the records you need. However, for those who are relatively new to genealogy, I have tried to arrange the chapters in the order that one would perhaps research the life of an individual person, beginning with records that directly concern people's lives (e.g. parish registers, taxation, property and occupational records) before moving on to the more centralised and specialised records of the courts, government and other large institutions. As you research your ancestors' lives, you will be offered little snippets of information (e.g. their place of abode, occupation or a reference to an event such as a court case), which can be further investigated and developed using this book (use the index to guide you to the relevant chapter). Even so, below are some general hints that can help narrow down the hunt for information about your ancestors.

## Start with Local Records

It is always best to search for information about ancestors in the place where they were known to be living. First check the local parish registers (baptisms, marriages and burials: see Section 4.1) and, if unsuccessful, widen your search to include the records of neighbouring parishes. I have had to search through dozens of parish registers when searching for the baptisms, marriages and burials of individual ancestors (do not forget to try the Mormons' online FamilySearch facility: Section 2.1). If that fails, then you will have to start looking at records for the hundred or county or at other local records such as land (or other) taxes, probate courts or parish records. If your parish has a VCH entry, this may give you additional clues as to what records may be available. Should any of these records tell you something about the trade or social status of your ancestor, use this to steer you towards the relevant chapters in this book. Those whose ancestors were landowners or tenants should look at property or manorial records.

Although it is tempting to jump ahead a hundred years or so and search for potential ancestors in older records, it pays to be systematic when researching. This avoids making errors in respect of people who share the same surname as your ancestors but who are from an unrelated family. It is best to work backwards in small steps.

## Use Every Piece of Information

Genealogical records can give you dozens of tiny bits of information that you will be able to use to take your research in new directions. Some of the clues you will be offered are obvious: for example, the 1796 will of Kennedy Deane states that he is a carpenter in the Royal Navy, which put me on to the records described in Chapter 11. Other clues require more work, such as the reference I found in a 1826 poll book to my ancestor George Chambers owning some land in a neighbouring parish, which led me to find a wealth of material in the manorial records there. Other clues I have had to chase up include using a reference to a cousin in a will to find the parents of the testator and using the mention of one person's Nonconformist religion to track down their ancestry. Even the most obvious clues may be missed first time round (I missed a reference to a person's grandfather in one document), so it pays to reread documents. Getting into the discipline of transcribing documents helps one to pay more attention to the words.

## Random Searching

The random searching of published volumes and original records is an acknowledged research technique in genealogy and one that can produce results. A few years ago I ordered up the wrong box of documents in a CRO but, rather than return them, I kept them because I thought they might be worth a look and, as a result, found two title deeds relating to my family history. It is worth checking everywhere for references to your ancestors, even in the most unlikely of places, as you never know what may result. To me part of the fun of genealogy is sitting in libraries and record offices randomly leafing through records, never knowing what nuggets of information they may contain.

## Share Information

Genealogy is a pastime that is undertaken by millions of people worldwide, and the odds are that you will not be the only person who is looking into the history of a particular family. Until a few years ago finding genealogists who were working in the same area as yourself was difficult, but this problem has largely been solved by the Internet (see Section 2.3). Publishing your own website or registering your interest on a bulletin board or newsgroup can alert other people to your research and allow them to get in touch with you. Two heads working on a problem are usually better than one, so sharing research can be beneficial. Conversely, if your research reaches an advanced stage and you are in a position to produce a family tree and/or written family history, do consider making extra copies and depositing them in places commonly accessed by genealogists such as the Society of Genealogists' library or the CRO covering the region where your ancestors lived.

# CHAPTER TWO

# USEFUL RESOURCES

## 2.1. INSTITUTIONS AND SOCIETIES

The majority of useful English and Welsh records are concentrated in a relatively small number of institutions. The following is a list of those institutions and societies whose collections or facilities are likely to be of particular use to the genealogist. Mortimer (1999), Wood (1999) and Gibson and Peskett (2001) provide guides to finding and using record offices within the United Kingdom.

### The National Archives (TNA): Public Record Office (PRO)

Ruskin Avenue, Kew, Richmond, Surrey TW9 4DU
Tel: + 44 (0)20 8876 3444; fax: + 44 (0)20 8392 5286
Website: www.nationalarchives.gov.uk

*General Information*

The National Archives is a public institution that is responsible for looking after the records of central government and the courts of law. Within The National Archives are the Historical Manuscripts Commission (HMC), an advisory body to the government, and the Public Record Office (PRO), which is responsible for the gathering and conservation of documents and making them available for consultation. The HMC and the PRO were separate institutions until April 2003, when they were incorporated into 'The National Archives'. Needless to say, any books printed before 2003 will continue to refer to the HMC and PRO under their old titles.

The National Archives (TNA): Public Record Office (PRO) (hereafter referred to as TNA: PRO) houses the majority of the national records relating to England and Wales, especially those relating to government and the law courts. The documents it holds run from Anglo-Saxon times to the modern day, and for most genealogists TNA: PRO will represent a primary source of information. Fortunately, many of the more useful records have been catalogued, indexed or published (in one form or another), which can lessen the need to visit in person. One of the objectives of this book is to provide a comprehensive list of published sources so that those who cannot gain access to places such as TNA: PRO can still research their ancestry.

The need for TNA: PRO arose because, before 1800, the nation's public records were spread across several dozen buildings, including places such as the Tower of London, various chapels, outbuildings and government buildings. Many of these repositories were entirely unsuited to the purpose of storing physical records, and so documents were being steadily lost to the damp, insects or overuse. To solve the problem an Act of Parliament in 1838 created the groundwork for the Public Record Office and, over the next few decades, the documents of government and the legal system (and others besides) were drawn together under the same roof and, for the first time, were catalogued and classified.

The first Public Record Office was in Chancery Lane, central London, but a lack of space forced it to move to newer premises in Kew, south London, where it remains today. For a comprehensive guide to TNA: PRO and its records see Bevan (2000) or, for the Family Records Centre, Colwell (2002).

*Visiting TNA: PRO*

At the time of writing, TNA: PRO at Kew is open 9.00–17.00 (Monday, Wednesday, Friday); 10.00–19.00 (Tuesday); 9.00–19.00 (Thursday) and 9.30–17.00 (Saturday). Check the TNA: PRO website for details of public holidays and for staff training and other periods of closure.

Unlike visits to some archive centres, a visit to TNA: PRO is a relatively painless process that does not require you to book a seat in advance (although it is sensible to check that it will be open and have the documents you want beforehand). Some TNA: PRO material, such as the Prerogative Court of Canterbury (PCC) wills and death duty registers, is also available on microfilm at the Family Records Centre in central London (1 Myddelton Street, London, EC1R 1UW; tel: + 44 (0)20 8392 5300). Other records are accessible through the TNA: PRO website (see below).

To gain access to the archives you will need to apply for a Reader Ticket. This can be done in advance via the website, but proof of identity will be needed before it will be issued to you. Once you have your Reader Ticket you will be taken on a short tour of the facilities and shown how to find and order the documents you need using The Catalogue, their computer catalogue. A full set of leaflets describing the TNA: PRO's various record types is available in the building or on line through their website (see below).

A comprehensive library, lockers, a café and a stationers-cum-bookshop are all available on site. Children under the age of fourteen are not permitted in the building, and only pencils and non-bulky notebooks are allowed into the document rooms; laptops and tape recorders are usually permitted. Physical copies (on film or paper) or digital scans of original documents can be ordered on site or through the website. TNA: PRO will also allow readers with digital cameras to take photographs of certain documents (see website for details).

*TNA: PRO On Line*

TNA: PRO has fully embraced the Internet revolution and is investing heavily in its online facilities. In fact, the TNA: PRO website (www.nationalarchives.gov.uk) is rapidly becoming a research tool in its own right.

The centrepiece of the website is the TNA: PRO online Catalogue, which is simply called The Catalogue. You can gain access to The Catalogue via the TNA: PRO website and can search it using keywords and by placing restrictions on the dates or class of record to be searched. The Catalogue is a little cumbersome to use but, once mastered, is a very effective research tool.

When searching using keywords, it is often more effective to use the following terms to help restrict the number of documents returned from each search. Placing a phrase in quotes will return only entries containing that exact phrase (e.g. 'Magna Carta'). Linking two search terms with AND, NOT or OR (in capitals) will also restrict what is returned. For example, Chambers AND Cambridge will return only those documents whose descriptions contain these two words. Leave out the AND and The Catalogue will return documents that contain either word. Equally well, Chambers NOT Cambridge will return those documents containing the word Chambers but excluding those with the word Cambridge in them. The Catalogue can also be used to order documents in advance (if you have a Reader Ticket) and for ordering copies of documents via the website.

Only a fraction of the TNA: PRO archive has been entered into The Catalogue but it has a good coverage of documents, some of which have full descriptions. Those classes of document that are searchable on line are indicated in the relevant chapters in this book.

One particularly useful feature associated with The Catalogue is its browse facility which allows you to enter the classification number (department, series and/or sub-series; see below) of a particular document or set of documents so that you can see the associated description. To do this enter a valid number (e.g. C 142 or C 142/772/158) in the top left-hand corner of The Catalogue (where it says 'go to reference'). This should bring up a description of that document or set of documents. To get more information and/or to see surrounding documents, click where it says 'browse from here'. This will bring up a list of documents in the same series or sub-series as the one that you are looking at, which can be very useful when you need to browse through the documents looking for the ones that might particularly apply to your ancestors.

In addition to The Catalogue, the TNA: PRO website also houses a number of other databases that are of use to the genealogist. These include the E 179 database (see Section 5.1) and, as part of its Documents Online service, a facility for searching and ordering copies of PCC wills going back to the fourteenth century (see Section 4.2). Other useful features include the online index of information leaflets, many of which cover topics of relevance to genealogists.

*The TNA: PRO Classification System*

Throughout this book (and when searching The Catalogue) you will continually find references to the TNA: PRO document classification system. At first sight the system of letters and numbers given to each individual document looks complex, but is actually quite logical and allows the staff at TNA: PRO to lay their hands on the material you want quickly and efficiently. Let us take the following entry in The Catalogue as an example:

**C 142/772/158**
Chambers, Robert: Cambridge
17 Charles I.

The location of this document within the PRO is described as C 142/772/158. This is what you will need to quote when ordering up this document (or ordering a copy of it). This code breaks down into department ('C'), series ('142'), sub-series ('772') and piece ('158'). This can tell us the following about the document's location:

DEPARTMENT   The 'C' tells us the 'department' within TNA: PRO within which the document is located. This is a code (up to four letters long) that denotes where the document was either produced or was archived. In this case the 'C' refers to the Chancery, but other examples include 'E' for the Exchequer, 'JUST' for Justices and other court records, etc.

SERIES   The '142' tells that this document is located within series '142' within the Chancery department. The department and series are often collectively referred to as the document's class. Throughout this book you will see groups of documents referred to in this way. In the example above, the document is in 'class C 142', which means that it is within the Early Chancery Proceedings.

SUB-SERIES and PIECES   The sub-series is a subdivision of the series (often based on the document's date), while the piece refers to the exact location of the individual document itself.

A detailed description for most classes (i.e. the department and series) of document is available through The Catalogue. To access this, type in the class (e.g. C 142 or E 179) in the 'go to reference' section of The Catalogue. It is also possible to get a more detailed breakdown of documents held under a particular series by using The Catalogue's 'browse' function.

## County Record Offices (CROs)

For a list of County Record Offices, contact details and websites, see Appendix One.

After TNA: PRO, the next largest collection of useful genealogical documents probably resides in the network of CROs that exist across England and Wales. Within these are many of the records (such as local tax records, manorial documents, maps, title deeds, etc.) that were not routinely collected by central government or which have been donated by local churches, businesses, organisations and private individuals. The hours of opening, accessibility and facilities for each CRO vary; phone ahead or check the website for details. Some CROs have searchable online catalogues or detailed breakdowns of their holdings, and many have placed their catalogues in the Access to Archives online catalogue, which is accessible through the TNA: PRO website. Those documents that are likely to be found in CROs are outlined in the relevant sections of this book.

## National Library of Wales

Aberystwyth, Ceredigion, Wales SY23 3BU
Tel: + 44 (0)1970 632 800
Website: www.llgc.org.uk

The National Library of Wales holds much information that is relevant to Welsh genealogy including material that has been transferred from TNA: PRO in London. The library contains original documents such as bishops' transcripts, probate records, legal and administrative records, estate records, historical newspapers, etc. It is open Monday to Saturday and has its catalogue available on line, along with leaflets and descriptions of the records it holds.

## Society of Genealogists (SoG)

14 Charterhouse Buildings, Goswell Road, London EC1M 7BA
Tel: + 44 (0)20 7251 8799; fax: + 44 (0)20 7250 1800
Website: www.sog.org.uk

Located about five minutes' walk from Barbican tube station, the Society of Genealogists has the largest collection of family-history-related material in the United Kingdom. As well as thousands of printed books, there is also a wealth of unpublished research in the form of indexes, family trees, biographies and other material. The library is split across three floors and is open 10.00–18.00 (Tuesday to Saturday) except Thursdays, when it is open until 20.00. Check the website for public holidays and periods of closure. Annual membership allows unlimited access to the library; otherwise a search fee is payable (see website for details).

The library catalogue is available on line and basic enquiries will be answered by phone/e-mail. Pencil only is permitted in the library and self-service photocopying is available.

## British Library

96 Euston Road, London NW1 2DB
Tel: + 44 (0)20 7412 7332
Website: www.bl.uk

Despite the controversy surrounding its cost and design, the new home of the British Library (located minutes from King's Cross and Euston stations) provides an efficient service and comfortable environment in which to work. Aside from its unparalleled collection of published works, the British Library also holds a vast collection of original manuscripts.

A catalogue of its manuscripts is available on line, as is a catalogue of its printed works. Ordering books takes around half an hour, but if you already have a card then advanced reservations are possible. Many printed volumes relating to public records are on open access in the Humanities 1 reading room.

Access is free, but gaining a card can take a while, depending on queues. It can sometimes be necessary to prove that the book you are after is not available to you through other sources. Access to some manuscripts is restricted and some books have to be ordered from outside repositories, so it is best to check access and availability ahead of time. Photocopying and other methods of reproduction can be expensive.

## London Archives

The size and complex history of the City of London and Greater London means that its records are not stored centrally in a single CRO. Those seeking London ancestors will, however, probably end up using one of the three main archives described below. In addition, those seeking London ancestors should consult Boyd's Inhabitants of London index, housed at the Society of Genealogists' library (see above).

### *Corporation of London Record Office*

Corporation of London Record Office, Guildhall, London EC2P 2EJ
Tel: + 44 (0)20 7332 1251
Website: www.cityoflondon.gov.uk/Corporation/leisure_heritage

Located at London's Guildhall, the Corporation of London Record Office (CLRO) holds archives that pertain to the Corporation of London, the governing body of the

City of London. These include the records of schools, hospitals and businesses that come under their jurisdiction, as well as records relating to law and order, mayors, freemen and cemeteries. At the time of writing the CLRO is undergoing a refurbishment and its archives are temporarily housed at the London Metropolitan Archive (see below). Check the website to see what the situation is. The CLRO website holds various leaflets describing its records, and its archive is currently being catalogued as part of the Access to Archives database (www.a2a.org.uk). For information on the CLRO genealogical holding see the articles in *Genealogists' Magazine* (vol. 20, 1982, parts 10 and 11) or the now out-of-date but still useful Jones and Smith (1951).

*London Metropolitan Archives*

40 Northampton Road, London EC1R 0HB
Tel: + 44 (0)20 7332 3820
Website: www.cityoflondon.gov.uk/Corporation/leisure_heritage

Located in the City of London, the London Metropolitan Archives (LMA) are Britain's largest local record office and contain the vast majority of London's records, including those relating to associations, businesses, charities, courts, churches and local and health authorities. At the time of writing the LMA is temporarily housing the archives from the Corporation of London Record Office (see above). The LMA is free and is open Monday to Friday and on select Saturdays; see its website for details. Its 'London Generations' online archive is accessible through the website.

*Guildhall Library*

Aldermanbury, London EC2P 2EJ
Tel: + 44 (0)20 7332 1862
Website: www.cityoflondon.gov.uk/Corporation/leisure_heritage

Founded in 1420, the Guildhall Library is first and foremost a reference library of printed material concerning the history of London, but it also holds a number of other archives relating to livery companies, land taxes, insurance records and others (mostly on microfilm). It is open Monday to Saturday and access is free, but check the website for any closures. The records held by the Guildhall Library are described in a series of leaflets (available through the website) or in the old, but still useful, volume by Jones and Smith (1951). The Guildhall holds (and in some cases sells) a number of handlists relating to its holdings of parish registers, marine collection, business archives, livery companies, parish vestry minutes and rate assessments (see website for details).

## Institute of Historical Research

Senate House, Malet Street, London WC1E 7HU
Tel: + 44 (0)20 7862 8740; fax: + 44 (0)20 7862 8745
Website: www.history.ac.uk

Located within walking distance of Euston, Euston Square, Russell Square and Goodge Street tube stations, this often overlooked library can be an exceedingly useful resource for the genealogist.

This library holds published works that concern British history. Almost all its books are on open access, which makes researching quick and easy. The library is spread across four floors and has a considerable number of works of interest to the genealogist, including many volumes that are not in the SoG library. Its catalogue is available on line. Annual membership provides unlimited access to the library; otherwise a daily search fee is applicable.

## University Libraries

Some of the older English universities (and some American ones too) hold significant numbers of original manuscripts in their libraries. Some of these relate to property once owned or managed by the university (e.g. manorial rolls); others are private documents that have been deposited there by individuals or larger institutions (e.g. much of the Diocese of Ely's archive is in Cambridge University Library).

Of especial note are Cambridge University Library (West Road, Cambridge CB3 9DR; tel: + 44 (0)1223 333000; website: www.lib.cam.ac.uk) and Oxford University's Bodleian Library (Bodleian Library, Broad Street, Oxford OX1 3BG; tel: + 44 (0)1865 277180; website: www.bodley.ox.ac.uk), both of which have substantial holdings of original manuscripts.

Their holdings have not yet been electronically catalogued, but paper catalogues do exist within the libraries themselves. A useful guide to the Bodleian Library's manuscript holdings before the twentieth century can be found in Turner (1878).

The published holdings for over twenty British university libraries can be searched simultaneously using the COPAC catalogue, which is available on line at: copac.ac.uk. This can be useful when searching for rare books.

## Church of Jesus Christ of Latter-Day Saints (Mormons)

35 North West Temple Street, Salt Lake City, Utah, USA 84150–3400
Tel: + 1 801 240 2584; fax: + 1 801 240 3718
Website: www.familysearch.org.

The Mormon Church has made a significant (if somewhat surprising) contribution to genealogy. This has come about because the Mormon Church permits its members to baptise their ancestors into the faith; over the years the Church has ploughed a great deal of time and money into gathering together vast amounts of genealogical data and then making them available through a worldwide network of libraries and resource centres as well as through the Internet.

The Mormons are best known for their online FamilySearch facility (www.familysearch.org), which contains millions of baptism and marriage records (but few burials) taken from parish registers and other resources worldwide. This facility also contains many pedigrees that have been obtained from published family trees or from the unpublished research of individual genealogists. A search for one's ancestry using FamilySearch is worth a try, but it should be noted that many of the trees contain inaccuracies. If you do find anything of use, then check the information for yourself.

More fruitful can be the large collection of pedigrees that are held at the Mormons' central Family History Library in Salt Lake City, Utah. This collection contains copies (usually on microfilm) of hundreds of documents that are of genealogical interest. It is possible to search the library's holdings on line (by surname and place name) at the Mormons' website. If you find documents that may be relevant to your research, then for a small fee it is possible to get the microfilm sent to your nearest Mormon Family History Centre (there are hundreds of these; a searchable list is available on the website). Here you can consult them and/or make copies from the microfilm.

## Local, Family and Specialist History Societies

For a list of these societies (of which there are too many to list here) and their contact details, I suggest consulting the GENUKI website (www.genuki.org.uk) or making an enquiry at CROs (see above and Appendix One).

Local history and family history societies rarely hold any original documents themselves, but they are often responsible for the publication of local records and can be useful sources of information. The majority now have websites, which normally have a facility for listing their members' research interests and/or an online bookshop which will give you an idea as to whether the society's interests coincide with your own.

## 2.2. PUBLISHED VOLUMES

A surprising amount of genealogical material is available through libraries as published volumes. This opens up the world of genealogy to many people who are unable to consult with original manuscripts in places such as TNA: PRO. It can also greatly speed up the research process by providing indexes to records and English translations. The individual sections within this book list published sources that are available for each class and type of document. This section is merely intended to give an outline of the more useful types of publication and who has produced them.

## Local History and the Victoria County History (VCH)

If you have managed to trace your ancestor to a particular parish or region, then it can be useful to find out a bit about that area's history. Local libraries often contain historical guides to individual parishes, towns or villages, and there may even be larger, often multi-volume, guides that cover entire hundreds or counties (the SoG can be a good source for these). However, probably the best starting point when it comes to tracing an individual parish's history and seeing what documents may be available is the Victoria County History series.

The Victoria County History project (VCH) was formulated in 1899 with the intention of providing a detailed historical survey of every parish in England. The VCH is still ongoing, with new volumes being produced at the rate of two or three per year and, although incomplete, it provides one of the most useful local history resources available.

Currently, the coverage of the VCH is patchy, with only thirteen counties having completed all their volumes. The state of progress for individual counties can be found on the VCH website (www.englandpast.net). The level of detail provided by the VCH can be quite breathtaking, especially in the more recent volumes. The history of individual manor houses, families and other local institutions such as churches, schools and local government can be given in great detail. Even if your ancestors are not mentioned (which, unless they were sizeable landowners, is likely), the VCH should be able to provide you with new leads in your research or, if nothing else, give you some idea of the history of the region in which your ancestors lived. The VCH is widely available in many larger libraries, but if it does not cover your parish or town, then try looking for other local history volumes in CROs, local libraries or the British Library.

## Local History/Family History Societies

The following societies and organisations have produced journals and/or publications that could be of use to genealogists. (Some of these societies are now defunct.) These publications will commonly be found in university and large town libraries or in public libraries local to the society concerned. Individual volumes can usually be ordered on inter-library loan. The British Library, the Society of Genealogists and the Institute of Historical Research also hold many of these.

*General*

British Association for Local History (www.balh.co.uk)

*England*

Bedfordshire Historical Record Society (www.bedfordshirehrs.org.uk)
Buckinghamshire Archaeological Society and Record Society
Cambridgeshire Antiquarian Society (www.arch.cam.ac.uk/cas)
Cumberland and Westmorland Antiquarian and Archaeological Society
    (www.cwaas.org.uk)
Derbyshire Record Society (www.merton.dircon.co.uk/drshome.htm)
Devon and Cornwall Record Society (www.cs.ncl.ac.uk/genuki/DEV/DCRS)
Dorset Record Society
Dorset Natural History and Archaeological Society
    (home.clara.net/dorset.museum)
Surtees Society [Durham] (www.dur.ac.uk/surtees.society/surtees.htm)
Bristol & Gloucestershire Archaeological Society (home.freeuk.net/bgas)
Bristol Record Society (humanities.uwe.ac.uk/brs)
Hampshire Record Society
Southampton Record Society [Hampshire]
Portsmouth Record Society [Hampshire]
Hertfordshire Record Society (www.hrsociety.org.uk)
Kent Archaeological Society (www.kentarchaeology.org.uk)
Chetham Society [Lancashire and Chester] (www.chethams.org.uk)
Lancashire and Cheshire Record Society
    (www.gmcro.co.uk/guides/record_society/record_society.htm)
Lincoln Record Society
London Record Society (www.history.ac.uk/cmh/lrs/LRSpubs.html)
Norfolk Record Society (www.norfolkrecordsociety.org.uk)
Northampton Record Society
Thoroton Society [Nottinghamshire] (www.thorotonsociety.org.uk)
Oxford Historical Society (www.execulink.com/~ocbogs/hist/history.html)
Oxford Record Society
Banbury Historical Society [Oxfordshire]
    (www.baughen.demon.co.uk/Banhists.htm)
Shropshire Record Series (members.lycos.co.uk/srseries)
Somerset Record Society (westcountrygenealogy.com/somerset/somrecsoc.htm)
Staffordshire Historical Collection
Staffordshire Record Society (www.genuki.org.uk/big/eng/STS/SRS.html)
Suffolk Records Society (www.suffolkrecordssociety.com)
Surrey Record Society
Sussex Record Society (thesussexweald.org/SRS.asp)

Dugdale Society [Warwickshire] (www.shakespeare.org.uk/main/3/37)
Wiltshire Archaeological Society
   (www.genuki.org.uk/big/eng/WIL/WANS/society.htm)
Wiltshire Record Society
Yorkshire Archaeological Association
Yorkshire Archaeological Society
North Riding Records [Yorkshire]
Bradford Historical Society [Yorkshire]
Thoresby Society [Leeds, Yorkshire] (www.thoresby.org.uk)

*Wales*

University of Wales Historical and Law Series
Cymmrodorion Record Society [Pembrokeshire]
West Wales Historical Society (www.quintinpublications.com/wales.html)
Caernarvonshire Historical Society (www.chs.cymru.org)
Flintshire Historical Society
South Wales and Monmouthshire Record Society
South Wales Record Society

*Channel Islands*

Société Guernesiaise [Guernsey, Alderney and Sark] (www.societe.org.gg)
Société Jersiaise [Jersey] (www.societe-jersiaise.org)

## 2.3. THE INTERNET

Given that genealogical research relies on being able to search large amounts of data, the Internet has proved to be a useful means of giving family historians access to information that would otherwise be difficult or costly to obtain. It also gives people a cheap and quick means of publishing their family history research and allows access to the catalogues and archives of many important institutions such as TNA: PRO and the British Library (see Section 2.1). This in itself can save hours and in many cases allow copies of documents to be ordered for less than it would cost to take a train to look at them in person. Some institutions have begun wholesale programmes, the aim of which is to place entire collections of documents on line.

   Aside from access to institutional catalogues, much online information concerning genealogy comes from individuals or small societies that have, for whatever reason, created websites that detail their own research into specific family histories, regional areas or particular areas of genealogy. These can often be found using Internet search engines.

## Random Searching

Websites that may have a relevance to your family history research can often be found by performing a random search using an Internet search engine (e.g. www.google.com). Try using a combination of the name you are interested in (remember there may be variations in spelling) plus other details such as the parish/town/region from where they originated.

When dealing with common names, most search engines will allow you to look for specific phrases by placing the words inside double quotes. This can narrow down a search very effectively; e.g. a search for "Paul Chambers" will return only those websites that contain this exact phrase. Without quotes it would return every website that has the words Paul and Chambers in it regardless of their proximity to one another.

Of course, just because you find information of relevance on the Internet does not automatically mean that it is factually accurate. Being open access, any information placed on the Internet does not need to be vetted and consequently many errors may be found there. It is not unusual to see individual researchers linking their family trees back to various medieval monarchs or even to legendary figures such as Robin Hood. Other errors are more subtle and can include typos or misunderstandings. Any information obtained from the Internet should be checked and then double-checked, just to be sure.

It is also advised to be wary of commercial genealogical websites that offer to give you information in return for a fee. Be sure that the website holds information that is likely to be relevant to your research and is not just offering a search of a general database. Also make sure that the information is not available for free elsewhere (e.g. through published volumes in a public library).

CHAPTER THREE

# DOCUMENTS

## 3.1. LATIN

As you move further back in time with your research, you may find that an increasing number of government, church and other official records are written out in Latin. This is because before 1733 Latin was regarded as an official language of record, with English generally only being used in situations involving the common populace (e.g. local trials, wills, deeds, etc.). For those researching early modern documents Latin is not the obstacle that it might seem, as many Latin documents are official and important and so will have been transcribed, translated and published as 'calendars' (individual chapters have details of these publications). You may, however, still encounter Latin in some local documents, especially those associated with manorial and ecclesiastical courts (Chapter 7 and Section 4.4). If so, do not panic, as it is still perfectly possible to obtain the information you need from the documents without having to take a degree in Latin.

### Resources for Understanding Latin

Specialists often note that the Latin used in British documents contains many words that cannot be found in traditional Latin dictionaries. This is because over the centuries British Latin has evolved away from the classical language of the Romans, so that by the seventeenth century it contained many English words while other traditional Latin words and phrases took on different meanings.

I can attest that a classical Latin dictionary is of limited use when dealing with documents produced in England and Wales; instead more specialist dictionaries are needed. Particularly good are Latham (1980) and Martin (1982). Also useful are the smaller but targeted word-lists in Morris (1989) and McLaughlin (1999). A number of Latin vocabularies are available for free on the Internet. For an understanding of the grammar used in Latin I recommend Gooder (1978) or Stuart (2000). Those already familiar with Latin grammar (or that of Latin-based languages such as French and Spanish) will have an advantage here but, as will be explained, it is not necessary to have a knowledge of Latin grammar in order to make sense of a document (although it does help). Specialist books dealing with the transcription and translation of specific types of document (e.g. manorial records, title deeds, etc.) are listed in the relevant sections of this book.

## Coping with Latin

To the amateur genealogist with little or no knowledge of Latin, the language can look impenetrable and off-putting. However, things may not be as bad as they might seem.

When I first entered the world of genealogy my knowledge of Latin was practically zero. Now, after several years of handling historical documents, I am still not proficient in Latin but I have developed techniques that can allow me to recognise quickly those parts of a document that are of interest, and from there to transcribe and translate them well enough to understand what is being said.

When it comes to translating Latin, the first comment I would make is that many official documents have already been transcribed and published. If you can get hold of these transcriptions, this will automatically remove the very considerable problem presented by illegible handwriting on original documents (see Section 3.2). It is usually possible to obtain cheap photocopies of published works, which means that you can work on a document at your leisure rather than being forced to do it during library opening hours.

However, there will be occasions when transcriptions and translations are not available and you will be faced with a roll or parchment sheet that is filled with apparently illegible Latin scrawl. How does one even approach transcribing and translating such documents?

The first issue will doubtless be the unfamiliarity of the handwriting (Section 3.2) and the use of abbreviations. Both of these can initially be off-putting, but are not insurmountable problems. In my opinion probably the most useful skill to acquire when reading original documents is the ability to recognise your ancestors' names while scanning down a page. The ability to scan-read a document, just picking out the pieces that are relevant to your ancestors, can save hours of work. After all, there is no point in painstakingly trying to translate an entire manorial court roll (which may be a metre or more in length) when your ancestor is mentioned only once in a short paragraph in the middle.

Most genealogists learn the art of picking out a name while scan-reading printed documents quite quickly (it is one of the survival skills of genealogy). Similarly, learning to recognise a person's name in a variety of old handwritings and spellings while scanning at speed through a Latin document is something that comes with practice, but it is a skill that does not take long to acquire. However, I do not recommend scan-reading for long periods at a time as the mind quickly becomes tired (and often bored), leading to mistakes.

Scan-reading will allow you to isolate those parts of the document that are of particular interest. The next step is to understand what the document has to say about your ancestor. Even at this stage, a knowledge of the Latin language is not necessary.

The real key to understanding Latin documents is knowing what type of document you are looking at. Is it, for example, a manorial terrier? Or is it a title deed or a feet of fine, assize record, etc.?

This question is relevant, as most documents are highly structured, laid out in a formulaic manner and use the same set phrases and expressions. This can be used to great advantage. Find out the type of document that you are dealing with (e.g. ask a librarian), then turn to the relevant section in this book; this will (it is hoped) tell you what to expect from the document and how it should be laid out. It should also give you a clue as to what keywords to look for and where to find similar published examples.

It is useful to have published examples of similar documents to hand (of transcribed Latin and, if possible, their English translation) when you are trying to make sense of a document. Many of the phrases or keywords from the published versions will be the same as those in the document you are looking at. You can use these set phrases to identify what process is being recorded (e.g. a piece of land being passed from one person to another).

Sometimes documents are so structured that it is not necessary to translate the Latin word for word, as the position of the names within the document will tell you what the role of the person is (e.g. the buyer, defendant, juror, etc.) and what they are doing (e.g. selling a piece of land, being fined for non-attendance, sitting on a jury, etc.).

Some documents, such as the subsidy rolls and manorial rentals, are simply lists of names with the occasional comment placed beside them (such as 'widow'). In these cases it is merely a matter of recognising what information the document is recording (e.g. an assessment of an individual's wealth) and being able to understand the handwriting.

I would add that when it comes to difficult or lengthy documents, I prefer to work from copies rather than from the original manuscripts. This means that I can take my time at home rather than trying to make rushed decisions at a library. However, this is not always possible (usually because of expense or conservational reasons). There are, of course, professional genealogists who will be able to transcribe and translate your problem documents, but they will charge for it. See advertisements in family history magazines for details.

## Latin Contractions and Abbreviations

As if the language barrier and handwriting were not bad enough, Latin was also commonly written in a highly abbreviated form, with special symbols being used to truncate long words into just a few letters. The abbreviation process used by scribes bears a similarity to the truncated text messages that people currently send one another on mobile phones. The problem is that in the same way that a non-English speaker would find it difficult to read an abbreviated mobile phone text message, it is just as difficult for a non-Latin speaker to try to make sense of abbreviated Latin, adding another hurdle to the problem of understanding a historical document.

Abbreviated Latin can be difficult to read and it has caused me problems in the past. I also witnessed one document defeat a trained Latin scholar. Despite this, it is not impossible to decipher a page of abbreviated Latin, but it does take some getting used to.

The good news is that the abbreviations follow a set convention and are, for the most part, used consistently. Thus, provided that you have a good guide to hand, it is possible to untangle the mass of abbreviations into sensible Latin once more. I recommend Johnson and Jenkinson (1915) or Stuart (2000), which contain lists of the commonly used abbreviation symbols, while Martin (1982) has a list of commonly abbreviated Latin words.

In some volumes you may encounter an old font known as 'record type'. Many historians wanted to be able to reflect the Latin abbreviations used by scribes in published transcriptions; the result was 'record type', a font that mimics the common abbreviations seen in Latin handwriting and thus has the effect of producing a more faithful representation of the original Latin document in print. It also has the effect of making it more difficult for non-Latin specialists to make sense of those records reproduced.

Latin records published in record type make the task of translating them more complex, but not impossible. Although it may not seem so at first, record type follows a set of rules that, when you know what they are, can turn the abbreviated words back into plain Latin again. See Chambers (2005) for further details.

## English Used in Records

Before the eighteenth century there was no consensus on English spelling, so many words, especially nouns, could be spelt in any way that the scribe saw fit. Take the following example from the 1612 will of my ancestor Robert Chambers:

> In the name of God Amen, I Robert Chambers the elder of Swaffham Prior in the county of Cambridge yeoman being sicke in body yet in perfect memorye (God I give hym thankes for yt) do make this my last will and testament viz. Ffirst I bequeath my soul unto almightie god my master and redeemer and my bodye to be buryed in Saint Maryes Church in Swaffham Prior aforesayd.

Although there are differences, the English used in the early modern era is for the most part still recognisable to twenty-first-century eyes. Once the problems of handwriting and spelling have been overcome, it is perfectly possible to make complete or near-complete transcriptions of such documents.

As with all manuscripts, knowing what function the document serves will give you major clues as to the structure and phraseology of the document. Problematic words can often be worked out by looking at the context of the sentence in which they occur. Work through the document in a steady and logical manner; it may take several passes before it is possible to fill in all the gaps. Try pronouncing problematic words or, if you are really stuck, look them up in a dictionary.

## 3.2. HANDWRITING AND SPELLING

Often handwriting presents more of a problem than Latin or English in that, in order to be able to deal with the language, one must first be able to discern what was written in the first place. Of course, the handwriting problem can be circumvented by using printed transcriptions of documents. These are especially common for national records, and their availability is outlined in the relevant sections in this book. However, when it comes to multiple, local or specialist records, it is unlikely that anybody will have had the time or inclination to transcribe and/or translate the records that you are after (although do check with local history societies and CROs). At this point you will have to deal with actual handwriting, but it is not just the literacy of the scribe that will determine whether or not a document is legible; there may also be problems with a document's state of preservation.

### Issues Concerning Document Quality

Water staining, fading, insect damage, and wear and tear may serve to render all or part of a document illegible. In some cases the use of an ultraviolet lamp can help (you will have to enquire about this in the library/repository that you are using). I have also had some success in using document images that have been scanned into a computer. Such digital scans can sometimes be obtained by ordering them from the institution concerned (e.g. TNA: PRO will make digital scans of any of their documents), but I have also had good results by digitally scanning photographs of documents. However, because of copyright issues, check with the person and/or organisation that made the photograph to make sure that they are happy for you to do this, especially if you want to publish it on the Internet or elsewhere.

The advantage of digital images is that they can be manipulated using photo-imaging software (such as Photoshop or Paint Shop Pro). It is often possible to adjust the contrast/brightness so that words that are hidden by staining or fading can become legible once more. You can also use the magnification function to enlarge individual words in order to make them easier to read (to do this effectively make sure that you have first scanned the document in at a high enough resolution).

In general terms, the documents that are easiest to read are those that were written for a formal purpose; this includes many public records. The trickiest to read are those that are either written in haste (such as the transcription of the proceedings in manorial or other courts) or those produced for a limited or local use only (e.g. manorial surveys, wills, personal letters, etc.). It is often local documents such as these that are the most useful to the genealogist and the least likely to have been transcribed. This can mean that amateur genealogists must sometimes confront some of the most illegible and badly preserved documents of all. None the less, the art of reading unfamiliar handwriting from damaged documents can soon be acquired with practice.

## Learning to Read Old Handwriting

There are few shortcuts when it comes to deciphering other people's handwriting. It comes down to a matter of experience and persistence. Like language and spelling, the writing style used in documents has evolved through time and, in addition to this, varies in legibility depending on the skill of the scribe and the intended use of the document. This means that it is sometimes possible to find older documents that, because they were well written, are relatively easy to read while more recent ones may be almost illegible.

In addition to the handwriting, there is also the problem of variable spelling, particularly acute for older English documents, and the use of abbreviations, a particular problem with Latin (see Section 3.1). When it comes to reading old handwriting, it is a case of practice makes perfect. However, to get started you will need to have a good reference book to hand, especially when it comes to abbreviation marks and/or unusual means of writing letters. I particularly recommend Wright et al. (1879) and Munby (2002); the former has a large number of plates displaying handwriting styles through the ages. Other guides worth consulting include Hector (1966) and Grieve (1978). When used in conjunction with some of the language dictionaries recommended earlier, these guides should be able to help you identify most problem words or tricky abbreviations.

Keep practising, and if a document defeats you on one day, put it to one side and try another time.

## Spelling of Personal and Place Names

As has been outlined earlier, variations in spelling are a common feature of older documents, but less of an issue after the eighteenth century. An especial hazard for the genealogist is the wide variation in the spelling of people's surnames. When you look through a document (whether original or a published transcription), you will need to be able to recognise such variations.

*An example of 'old law hand', which was commonly used on sixteenth- and seventeenth-century documents but which faded in popularity afterwards.* (From Wright *et al.* 1879)

A surname such as Vail may be spelt phonetically in any number of ways – for example, Vayle, Vale, Veil and Vill. Such variation is remarkably common, and the further back in time you go, the wider the variation will be. You may even find the surname written in its Latin equivalent (Martin, 1982, contains a lengthy list of Latinised first names and surnames).

You will need to be familiar with these variations in spelling because some indexes and computer databases (including the TNA: PRO online Catalogue) routinely use the older spellings and not their modern equivalents. The same holds true for the spelling of place-names. These may be subject to huge variations in spelling. I have seen the modern town of Swaffham spelt as Swafham, Swafam, Sopham, Soffham, Soffam and Suafham (among others). Parishes and towns that contain English words in their title, such as Little Drayton, Great Hatfield, Henstridge Marsh, etc., should also be searched for using the Latinised forms of the English words concerned (e.g. Magna Hatfield for Great Hatfield).

Also bear in mind that some place-names have changed over time. The modern town of King's Lynn was Lynn before the time of Henry VIII. Consulting local historical guides, such as the VCH, should give you any name changes.

## Numerals

After the seventeenth century most numerals are expressed either in their Arabic form (1, 2, 3, 4, etc.) or written out (e.g. sixty-two). In older documents many numbers will be expressed as Roman numerals (e.g. LXII), which are the same as those we see today with a couple of exceptions.

Roman numbers may be written in lower case, with the last 'i' in a number often written as a 'j', while the number four is commonly written as 'iiij' rather than the 'iv' used now. Confusingly, some scribes did not put the dots above the 'i's, making it problematic to discern some numerals. The following displays how numbers are commonly expressed in historical documents:

| | |
|---|---|
| 1 | i, j or I |
| 2 | ij or II |
| 3 | iij or III |
| 4 | iiij or IIII |
| 5 | v or V |
| 6 | vj or VI |
| 7 | vij or VII |
| 8 | viij or VIII |
| 9 | ix or IX |
| 10 | x or X |
| 11 | xi or XI |

| 20 | xx or XX |
|---|---|
| 30 | xxx or XXX |
| 40 | xl or XL |
| 50 | l or L |
| 60 | lx or LX |
| 100 | c or C |
| 500 | d or D |
| 1,000 | m or M |

Examples of Arabic numerals through the ages, together with more specialised (and rarely encountered) numeral expressions, such as those used by auditors and merchants, can be found in Johnson and Jenkinson (1915).

## 3.3. DATING DOCUMENTS, MEASUREMENTS AND MONEY

Most documents will have an exact date recorded on them somewhere. However, the manner in which these dates were recorded may differ from those that are used today. Further guides to reading Latin dates can be found in Stuart (1992, 2000).

### Regnal Year

Before the nineteenth century you may find documents that have been dated using a regnal year. This means that the year, instead of being expressed as a number, as we do today (e.g. 2004), will be described as the year within the reign of the then monarch. For example, 13 James I means the thirteenth year in the reign of King James I. However, whereas our year begins on 1 January and ends on 31 December, the beginning of the regnal year starts on the date that the monarch succeeded to the throne. So the date 11 James I, when translated into modern terms, actually runs from 24 March 1615 to 23 March 1616. In other words, it cuts across two of our years. This means that to be sure in which year a document was written, you must also look at the day and month. Be especially aware that the last year of a monarch's reign is invariably much shorter than a calendar year, as death will usually occur before the final year could run its course. Appendix Two provides a list of the correct regnal dates for all the monarchs in the early modern era.

### The AD System

The practice of dating the year from the birth of Christ (expressed as *anno domini* or AD) has its origins in sixth-century Rome and is the same as the one we use today. The year is expressed as a number usually written out using words, but sometimes in

Arabic numerals or Roman numerals (e.g. one thousand six hundred and sixty-six, 1666 or MDCLXVI). These may be encountered on documents at any point in the early modern era, although the use of Roman numerals becomes less common after about 1660.

Before 1752 England and Wales used the Julian calendar, in which the historical year began on 25 March. After 1752 the Gregorian calendar was adopted, and afterwards the New Year began on 1 January. This means that before 1752 you will have to bear in mind that any documents or events dated between 1 January and 24 March will have taken place, by our calendar, in the following year. This can have a significant bearing on certain genealogical events. For example, the baptism of an ancestor on 20 February 1740 would, by our calendar, have taken place in 1741, something that needs to be borne in mind when searching for the marriage of the parents. It is common for modern historians and genealogists to express dates that fall into this cross-over period in the following manner: 20 February 1740/41.

## Measurements

Before the introduction of the metric system in the late twentieth century, England and Wales used the imperial system; weights and measures were commonly expressed in pounds, ounces, feet, yards, acres, etc. By the seventeenth century these were pretty much standardised across the whole of England and Wales. A brief list of commonly used land measures is given below, but it is still possible to encounter specialist measures used by some trades (e.g. horses' heights are measured in 'hands') or in certain circumstances. If you come across a term that is unknown to you, I recommend consulting Zupko (1968).

| | |
|---|---|
| acre | 4,840 square yards |
| foot | twelve inches or a third of a yard |
| furlong | the length of a furrow; 16.5 feet long or 40 perches |
| inch | twelfth of a foot |
| perch | generally 16.5 feet |
| pole | see perch |
| rod | see perch |
| rood | eighth of a mile |
| yard | three feet |

## Money

Across the whole early modern period the currency system used was pounds, shillings and pence, a system that continued to operate in England and Wales until

1971. A shilling was worth 12 pence and a pound worth 20 shillings, or 240 pence. In documents the names of these coins are normally abbreviated thus:

pence     usually abbreviated to 'd' for *denarius* or *denarii* (a Roman coin); e.g. $x^d$

shilling    usually abbreviated to 's' for *solidus* (a Roman coin); e.g. $vi^s$

pound    usually abbreviated to 'l' for *libra* (a pound weight); e.g. $iii^l$

mark     usually abbreviated to 'm' for *marca* or *Marcus*; e.g. $ix^m$

Thus, using these abbreviations, three pounds, six shillings and ten pence would be written as: $iii^l$ $vi^s$ $x^d$.

Trying to compare modern prices with those in the past is notoriously problematic and usually relies on the comparison of the cost of living and of certain objects and services. The Economic History Services website (www.eh.net) has a function for comparing modern currency values with those as far back as 1264.

# CHAPTER FOUR

# CHURCH AND PARISH RECORDS

This chapter deals with those documents and papers that were generated by the church or parish authorities, as these are the two institutions that were most closely connected to the lives of ordinary people. Whereas national records, such as those related to taxation (see Chapter 5), are often able to confirm whether an individual was living in a particular place at a particular time, they usually give little detail about people's lives. Local records, on the other hand, concern issues and events that are closely connected with parishioners' lives, including their work, behaviour (good and bad), financial circumstances and, most fundamentally, records of major events such as their birth, marriage and death. If you have managed to trace an ancestor to an individual town or parish, then it can be very worthwhile seeing what local records are available, most of which are held at CROs.

## 4.1. PARISH REGISTERS

Those researching their family history in Victorian and modern times will almost certainly have had to use the civil registration records of births, marriages and deaths, the indexes to which are held in the Family Records Centre, London. The civil registration records are a reliable (if somewhat tedious and expensive) means of tracing a person's birth, marriage and death records, but they go back only to 1837. If you want to find records of your ancestors' births, marriages and deaths before the Victorian era, then you will need to start using the registers belonging to parish or other local churches.

The information held in parish registers forms the backbone of pre-Victorian genealogical research, and it is perfectly possible to reconstruct an entire family tree back to the sixteenth century using only these records. Parish registers are a necessity when trying to trace your ancestors from the pre-Victorian era. (Note: they can also be a cheaper and quicker means of tracing ancestors than the civil registration records in Victorian and modern times.)

The origin of the parish register system dates to 1538, when Henry VIII ordered that the clergy should keep a record of the baptisms, marriages and burials taking place in their church. Such records were to be kept in a special book, and the records stored at the church, where they could be consulted by the members of the public or officials. Although in theory all parish registers should date from 1538, many of the earliest records were lost, damaged or were never created in the first place. Only a handful of parishes actually have registers that date back to the 1530s; most start somewhere between 1550 and the early 1600s. At various points in time coverage may be patchy (sometimes because of a lackadaisical priest or church warden) or the records lost or destroyed. In general all parish registers are patchy or non-existent between 1653 and 1660 (the Commonwealth period), when an elected local official was required to register births, marriages and deaths (but not baptisms and burials), usually in separate books, few of which have survived. If you encounter incomplete or spoiled parish register entries, then sometimes the missing information can be found in the bishops' transcripts (see below).

## The Location of Original Parish Registers

In 1978 the Parochial Registers and Records Measure demanded that all church records over 100 years old should be stored at a local records office unless the church itself could be proved to have suitable facilities. In practice this means that the vast majority of original parish registers are to be found in the CRO pertaining to the parish itself.

If you know the county in which your ancestors' parish is located, then you will probably be able to trace the whereabouts of the parish registers by looking on the websites of the CROs, most of which now display their parish register holdings (see Appendix One). Alternatively, you could consult the *National Index of Parish Registers*, a series of publications by the Society of Genealogists that shows the coverage and whereabouts of all the parish registers (including Nonconformist churches) for each county before at least 1837. The *National Index of Parish Registers* is particularly useful when it comes to finding the parish registers for churches located in large cities (especially London), as these may sometimes be held in unexpected places. Most counties and towns also have local guides to their historical or genealogical resources, which will provide a detailed breakdown of the coverage and whereabouts of parish registers, including published transcripts (e.g. Farrar, 1994 does this for all Cambridgeshire parishes). For Nonconformist and foreign parish registers see Section 4.5.

## Bishops' Transcripts

By 1598 the alarming rate at which parish registers were being lost or destroyed prompted Elizabeth I to pass a law requiring that a copy of the church's registers should be made annually and sent to the bishop (or other higher church official) in whose jurisdiction the parish fell. This practice remained standard until the start of civil registration in 1837, after which it ceased to become common.

In theory the bishops' transcripts should act as a useful back-up to the parish registers and could potentially fill in any gaps caused by missing records. However, the survival rate of the bishops' transcripts (most of which were written on loose parchment) can also be patchy, especially in the seventeenth century, with none at all surviving from the Commonwealth period (1649–60).

Bishops' transcripts are usually to be found with other diocese records, which, in most cases, are housed in CROs, although some are housed in other archives such as university or church libraries. The *National Index of Parish Registers* (see above) lists the coverage and whereabouts of the bishops' transcripts for each parish, as does Gibson (2001). It is common practice for bishops' transcripts to be included in the transcriptions of parish registers made by local history societies (see below).

## Microfilm, Microfiche and Transcripts

The popularity of genealogy means that most record offices will not allow access to the original registers without a good reason. Instead you are most likely to find them available on microfilm or microfiche, which can be consulted using machines on site. In addition, CROs may hold typed, written or printed transcripts of some parish registers, which often incorporate, or have been checked against, the bishops' transcripts. The task of making such transcriptions was (and still is) often undertaken by volunteers in local history or family history societies, with the resulting volumes being much easier and quicker to consult than the original registers, especially as most are indexed. However, personal experience shows that these transcriptions are not necessarily entirely accurate, and mistakes or omissions are sometimes made. If you suspect an error, you will need to consult the original parish register (or a microfilm of it) to make sure.

Microfilms, microfiche and transcripts of parish registers are usually to be found in CROs, but institutions such as the SoG library also hold many copies (a list of their holdings is given on its website), as do some local libraries. Some parish registers, especially those from London churches, have been published by the Harleian Society and Phillimore Ltd, and may be found in larger libraries; a full list can be found on these two publishers' websites.

It is often possible to buy microfilm or microfiche copies of either the original registers or their transcripts from CROs or from local history or family history societies. Some are also now available on searchable CD-ROM. These are usually inexpensive, and, if your family was based in a particular region, it can be more cost effective to buy copies of the parish registers than to travel a long way to consult them. Second-hand microfiche and microfilm readers can be found in most local libraries or bought cheaply (try www.ebay.co.uk). I possess microfiche copies of many parish registers relating to the regions of Cambridgeshire, south Wales and other places where many of my ancestors lived. This has allowed me to chase up loose ends immediately rather than having to travel many miles to CROs.

## Information Held in the Parish Registers

Before the 1730s some parish registers Latinised the first names of their parishioners, but their layout and simple language make them straightforward to interpret. The oldest registers may combine baptisms, marriages and burials on the same page, whereas later registers usually separate them out.

In theory, the parish register should contain a record of every baptism, marriage and burial performed at that church. The priest should record the person's name, the full date, the parents' names (in the case of baptism and child burials), the spouse's name (in the case of marriages and burials) and information such as the person's sex, marriage status (bachelor, spinster, widow, widower), any wedding witnesses and other relevant matters.

In practice, the information contained within parish registers can be very patchy indeed. Some priests were more conscientious than others, which means that even within the same register you may find that, while one priest might have recorded bountiful information on the individuals concerned, his predecessor or successor might have made only minimal notes and, in some cases, may have made no notes at all or have neglected to include entries. As with much genealogy research, it is the luck of the draw.

*Baptisms*

The baptisms should record the date, the name of the child, the sex and the name of both parents. Earlier parish registers may record only the father's name, while later ones may also include other details such as the parents' names, address and occupation (this was actually required by law from 1813). Other details, such as a child's illegitimacy or the wife's maiden name, can also be recorded.

The following is a typical entry from the baptism register in Wicken, Cambridgeshire. It shows that even in the same year the degree of information recorded can vary wildly:

Baptisms for 1693
Apl   2      Owrs   Edward son Robert and Mary
        9      Barrow Maray dau. Easter and Maray
       16      Bannam-Halet  Bannam base born son of Thomas Bannam and
                   Maray his concubine.
Jun          Folks   Dannall son Dannall and Margrat
Jly    3      [BLANK]       Miles son John and Susann
        6      Gray    William son of the late Mr Edward and Gene

*A page from the baptism register for 1733 for St John the Baptist Church, Clerkenwell. The handwritten entries (and rough corrections) are typical of older registers. (London Metropolitan Archives)*

*Marriages*

The information given on marriages varies with time. The oldest entries tend to give just the date and the names of the husband and wife. Again, the following example comes from Wicken:

| | |
|---|---|
| 10 Jun 1565 | Thomas Duffielde and Annes Tybolde |
| 23 Jun 1565 | John Patricke and Ellen Hancocke |

As time progresses you may find more information given, such as a person's marriage status (bachelor, spinster, widow or widower), parish of origin (if outside the parish where the marriage is taking place), whether by licence, and the groom's occupation. This example is from Fen Ditton, Cambridgeshire:

1763

Nov 27        Chamberlaine John s.m. [single man] OTP [of this parish] –
                Grace Bunten, s.w. [single woman] of Exing parish.

Dec 11         Burton Hall s.m. OTP – Mary Johnson widow of Hornsey

Lord Hardwicke's marriage reform of 1754 (which was designed to stop shotgun weddings) required couples to announce their intention to marry in their respective parish churches for three consecutive Sundays. This was to make sure that anyone who might object to their marriage was aware of the couple's intentions. Details of these announcements, which are called banns, may sometimes be preserved in the parish register. They normally record the parish of origin and marriage status of each person.

Between 1653 and 1660 Parliament decreed that all marriages were civil and thus could not take place in a church. This has led to many being omitted from the registers, although some do survive. In some cases the parish register will contain the entire civil marriage contract. Such is the case for my direct ancestor Richard Chambers, whose marriage to Ann Riply at St Cyriac's Church, Swaffham Prior, Cambridgeshire, provides a great deal of useful genealogical information concerning who their parents were and where they lived:

Jun 19 1654  Chambers Richard – Ann Riply

An agreement of marriage betweene Richard Chambers the son of Samuell and Ann Chambers of Swaffham Prior and Ann Riply the daughter of Alse Riply of Reach widow belongeinge to the parrish of Burwell was delivered unto me in writeinge May 18 1654: and published in the parrish Church of Swaffham prior three several Lords dayes next after the receipt of the saide agreement by me Thomas Barber

Richard Chambers and Ann Riply June ye 19 1654 haveinge expressed there consent unto marriage in the manner and by the wordes expressed in the act of Parliament were married before me in the presence of Robert Chambers Thomas Hindman and thereupon declared to be thence forth husband and wife by me Roger Rant.

*Burials*

The register of burials is a much more useful record of death in the parish than the handful of headstones preserved in a church's graveyard. Indeed, burial registers can be more complete than those of baptisms and marriages for the same period. As with all registers, the older entries tend to give less information than the newer ones, but aside from the date and the name of the deceased, the entry should reveal the name of the parents (if burying a child), spouse (if burying a husband or wife) or marital status (if a single adult or widowed). Later entries can include the person's age, occupation and other comments (such as 'a very old man'). From 1813 all burial entries had to include the age, and place of residence of the deceased.

The following examples are all taken from the parish registers of Fen Ditton, Cambridgeshire; they demonstrate the historical progression in burial entries:

1538
Nov 24      Harris Dorothie
Dec 30      Smith John
Jan 15      Cooper John

1664
May 19      Isatson Ann dau. widow Isatson
Dec 3       Hunt Martha wife of John
Feb 26      Seabrooke Edward son Edward

1769
Jan 2       Belton Elizabeth dau. John and Mary
Feb 16      Morley Elizabeth wife of Richard

1821
Jan 2       Tayler William 29
Nov 11      Wilkin William 88 pauper of Horningsea

## Fleet Marriage Registers

London's Fleet Prison had been used to hold debtors since medieval times (see Section 13.4) and had long claimed to be exempt from Church law. In the seventeenth century eloping couples began to visit the prison in order to get married by one of the handful of clergymen who were always incarcerated there or they might even bring along their own priest. The couple would pay a fee to the clergyman and be married in the prison chapel or in chapels set up in buildings in the surrounding streets. The cheap, no-nonsense, no-questions-asked service offered by the Fleet clergy was popular with all sectors of society, and by the mid-eighteenth century several thousand marriages a year took place there. The practice ended only in 1753 with the passing of Hardwicke's Marriage Act, which required couples to announce their intention to marry in the parish church for the three Sundays before the wedding day.

Like other churches, the Fleet chapels were required to keep registers of the people they married, and those that have survived may now be found in TNA: PRO RG 7, with one additional register in the Bodleian Library, Oxford.

The oldest registers date from the 1680s and are best accessed through Herber (1998–2001), who has transcribed and indexed the TNA: PRO registers.

It should be noted that couples wishing to marry in Fleet would often pay to have the date of the marriage altered (usually to cover up a pregnancy), or that one or other of the names might be forged. Given the numbers of marriages taking place in Fleet, it is worth checking the registers for those marriages that have escaped you elsewhere.

## Tracing Ancestors Using Parish Registers

Continuing the ancestral trail beyond the use of civil birth, marriage and death certificates is not as tricky as it might sound. You should be able to get your ancestor's parish of birth from a birth, marriage or death certificate. Next you need to find whereabouts in the country this parish is (or was, there have been many boundary changes). For this use either an Internet site such as GENUKI (www.genuki.org.uk) or a historic atlas such as Humphrey-Smith (1995). Then find where the relevant parish records (or copies of them) are located using the resources listed above. Then, when you actually start searching through parish registers, it is worth bearing the following in mind.

First, the registers do not usually record the exact birth or death date of an individual, merely the day on which they were baptised or buried at the local church. Burials were normally reasonably prompt (for obvious reasons), and for many years it was traditional to baptise a child before the Sunday following its birth. However, some parents were less fussed than others and there are sometimes delays of weeks, months or years. Some of my eighteenth-century ancestors were lax when it came to baptisms, and I have in a number of instances been faced with up to four children being baptised on the same date (probably because the local priest had pressurised them into doing so), the eldest of whom was assumedly several years old. In circumstances such as these it is difficult to work out even the approximate ages and order of the children, although other clues, such as the order in which they marry or their age at burial, can help resolve this.

Stillborn and children who survived only a few days were also baptised, so it is not unusual to find a baptism and burial record for the same name on the same day. Often parents would reuse the names given to deceased children, so it is worth checking the burial registers at the same time as baptisms so that you can exclude deceased children from being potential ancestors.

If you identify a baptism entry relating to an ancestor, this should give you the name of the child's parents. The next task is to try to track down the marriage of those parents, which, if you are lucky, will have taken place in the same church. If it is not there, then you will have to start searching the registers for neighbouring parishes. To help narrow down when the wedding could have occurred, try finding other baptism entries relating to the parents, as the eldest child was normally born within a year or so of the wedding (although many were born only a few months afterwards!).

Assuming you find it, the marriage entry should give you the maiden name of the mother. It is then a case of going back to the baptism entries and trying to find the entries relating to the groom and the bride. Most people got married in their early twenties, but I have found brides who were as young as fourteen, so it is worth beginning your search reasonably close to the marriage date.

Some family historians are more casual about tracking down burial dates than they are for the dates of marriages and baptisms. I would recommend tracing the burial entries for the people on a family tree, as they can sometimes identify mistakes or resolve issues by giving additional information about an individual, such as age or marital status at the time of death.

## If You Cannot Find an Entry

Even before the Industrial Revolution people would move from village to village, within towns, or marry people who came from different parishes. All these movements can lead to a marriage or baptism entry not being found in the register of the parish where an ancestor is known to have lived. Missing entries are normally because people moved parish or, in the case of marriages, because the marriage took place in the parish of the other spouse.

Fortunately, in most cases people did not move too far, so a search of the registers of adjoining parishes usually turns up the missing ancestor. If it does not then you will have to spread your search further afield. The Mormons' International Genealogical Index (IGI) holds thousands of baptism and marriage records (but few burials), while Boyd's Marriage Index contains entries (arranged chronologically and alphabetically) from dozens of parish registers from England (but not Wales) and is a useful shortcut when searching for missing marriage entries nationwide between 1538 and 1840. The original Boyd's Marriage Index volumes are available at the SoG library (beware of Boyd's phonetic spelling of surnames; e.g. Lynes becomes Lines in his volumes), but they are now also available through the Origins Network (www.originsnetwork.com). Less comprehensive is Boyd's London Burial Index, which covers 1538–1853; it is also available through the SoG or the Origins Network.

If you cannot find the bride's baptism, then check that she was not previously married: widows usually remarried with their first husband's surname, not their maiden name (e.g. my ancestor Eleanor Boutle turned out to have been previously married to Francis Boutle and was in fact born Eleanor Sizar). Some firstborn children were baptised in the parish of their mother's origin (assuming that it was different from the father's), while those whose job or circumstances (the most compelling of which was poverty; see Section 4.6) required them to move about the countryside may have had children baptised across a number of parishes. Wealthy people may have held property in more than one parish.

The parish register system is far from perfect, and there are occasions when a marriage, baptism or burial entry simply cannot be found. I have not been able to trace the marriage of George Chambers to his wife Sarah, which must have taken place around 1720, and, to confuse matters, the bishops' transcript record for the baptism of one of their children has her name as Frances. Having searched high and low, I now assume that the marriage entry was omitted by a priest. In such cases it is to be hoped that other sources of information, such as probate records (Section 4.2), can provide the missing information.

*Change of Name*

People who wanted to change their name could do so on a whim and without formality. Those who wanted to register their new name could do so by getting a solicitor to enrol a deed poll (this is a deed which names only one person) with the Chancery's close rolls (see Section 17.3). They could also apply for an Act of Parliament (see Section 18.1) or royal licence, the entries for which are in TNA: PRO SP 44 (1680–1782, arranged chronologically) and HO 38 (1782–1868, arranged chronologically).

Formal changes of name were also commonly carried in newspapers, most notably the *London Gazette*. Phillimore and Fry (1905) have compiled an index of name changes (chiefly by royal licence or Act of Parliament) mentioned in newspapers and other sources between 1760 and 1901. This is the best place to start your search.

## 4.2. WILLS AND PROBATE RECORDS

Wills and other probate records are highly prized by genealogists for the amount of detail that they can provide about the deceased and their immediate family. Much of this detail is often unobtainable elsewhere and can give a fascinating snapshot of the life of an ancestor, with information on occupation, property holdings, wealth, status and relationship to the local community.

The purpose of making a will was (and still is) to allow individuals to dispose of their money, land and other possessions as they saw fit. A will could also be used to make certain stipulations about the deceased's funeral arrangements, how any money or property should be utilised or any conditions regarding the remarriage of the spouse or the upbringing of children, etc.

The practice of willing possessions dates to Anglo-Saxon times, but the written will as we know it did not come into being until the late twelfth century. In time the making of a will became commonplace (at least it did among the wealthy), and it was realised that there needed to be an official means of legitimising any bequests

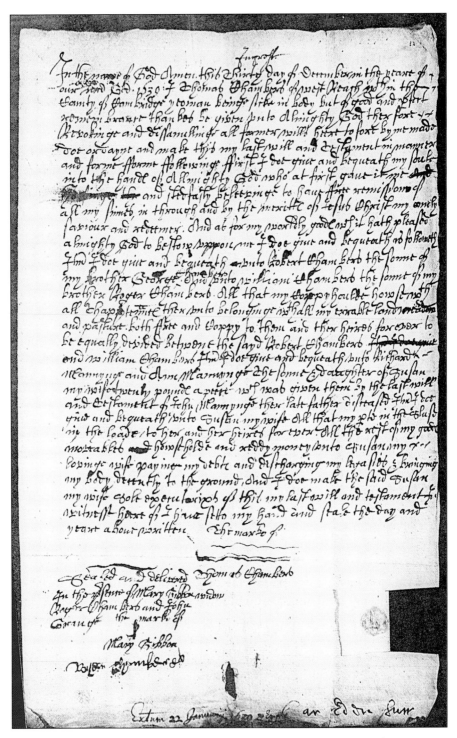

*A rare example of an original will made in 1639 by Thomas Chambers, a cousin to one of my ancestors. Being original (as opposed to a copy made in a probate book), it contains the original signatures of both Thomas and his brother Roger. (Cambridge University Library)*

and a legal means of settling any disputes that subsequently arose. Thus it was that the church ecclesiastical courts were given the power to legitimise (or 'prove') a will and to sit in judgment on any objections made about the will by relatives or creditors.

During the process of proving, the ecclesiastical courts would make a written copy of the will in their Probate Act Books, many of which survive and some of which date back to the fourteenth and fifteenth centuries. The interest in probate records by the genealogical community has ensured that the majority of records are easily accessible and that copies of most documents can be obtained quickly and cheaply. In addition to these, some original wills do exist and may be found in institutions such as TNA: PRO, CROs, the British Library and also private collections.

## Testamentary Procedure in the Ecclesiastical and Peculiar Courts

Up to the eighteenth century a will would often be made only when the individual was on a deathbed; this may be indicated in the will itself by the person recording that he or she is 'sick in body' and by the fact that the will is proved only a matter of days after it was made. If death came through sudden illness or an accident, then there would sometimes be no time for a will to be made. However, by the eighteenth century it was more common for a will to be made well in advance of death, especially among the wealthy.

The will would commonly be dictated by the testator (testatrix, if a woman) to a scribe or lawyer in front of two or more witnesses (usually trusted friends) and then afterwards kept in a safe (but accessible) location. After the death of the testator, the will would be retrieved and then the named executor or executrix (the man or woman given the task of carrying out the deceased's written instructions) would take it to an ecclesiastical court to be proved (i.e. legally validated). If there were no objections, the will would be authenticated by the court, an act of probate granted and the will proved. A copy of the will's text was then written into the court's Probate Act Book.

In rarer circumstances it was possible for an individual to make a verbal will to two or more reliable witnesses. It would be written down at a later date and then probated as above. These were known as nuncupative wills and were outlawed (except for the military) in 1838. If a will were nuncupative, this would usually be noted in the probatum (see below).

If someone raised an objection to the content of the will, then a caveat would be entered into the court's Act Book and the dispute would then have to go through an ecclesiastical court using the plenary court procedure (see Section 4.4). The court's judgment would then be entered into the Probate Act Book as a sentence (some courts charged for this service, which means that not all such disputes are recorded in the Act Books). Whereas most wills are written in English, many sentences are written in Latin. A caveat could be lodged with the court before the death of an individual so that the will could not be proved without the caveat's creator being notified.

Original wills were private property and so very few have survived through to the present day. However, copies of individual wills made in churches' Probate Act Books have survived in great numbers and are available to us as public records, although searching for them is not entirely straightforward.

Before the state centralisation of probate records in 1858, the proving of wills was handled by individual ecclesiastical (or church) courts (see Section 4.4 for more details). For any one parish or town there could be several levels of ecclesiastical court, and in order to locate an individual will it is first necessary to know which ecclesiastical courts served the area in which an ancestor lived.

In general, it was more usual for a will to be proved within the archdeaconry court for the parish where the deceased died. However, if the deceased owned property in more than one archdeaconry's jurisdiction, then the will would usually be taken to the more powerful diocese court belonging to the local bishop. If the deceased held property in the jurisdiction of more than one diocese, then the will went to the prerogative court of the provisional archbishop. Finally, if the will fell between two prerogative courts, then the last resort was the Prerogative Court of Canterbury (PCC), which held jurisdiction over all the other ecclesiastical courts.

In addition to the ecclesiastical courts there were the so-called peculiar courts, which held jurisdiction over particular parishes and were exempt from the archdeaconry and consistory courts. Often these peculiars were administered by a dean or by a dean and chapter, but they could also fall under the administration of other institutions such as colleges (e.g. Oxford and Cambridge Universities had their own peculiar courts), guildhalls or manor houses. There are dozens of peculiar courts in England and Wales; for a list of these see Gibson (1974).

Sometimes an individual would stipulate that their will should be proved by a higher church court than was strictly necessary, either for reasons of vanity (wills proved by the PCC were considered a sign of wealth) or because the higher courts had greater authority to settle any arising disputes.

## Finding a Will in the Ecclesiastical and Peculiar Courts

When searching for an ancestor's will it is first necessary to find out which ecclesiastical courts covered the parish(es) in which your ancestors lived. This is not straightforward, as the jurisdiction of the courts could be erratic, crossing county boundaries and including outlier parishes that are miles away from the court's central power base. It is also possible that an individual parish may be covered by two or more courts. For example, ancestors of mine who died in the same Cambridgeshire parish have wills that were proved in three separate courts (Consistory Court of Ely,

Court of the Chancellor of the University of Cambridge and the Prerogative Court of Canterbury). Thus, when looking for a will it may be necessary to search the records of several different ecclesiastical or peculiar courts.

There are a number of guides that list all the ecclesiastical and peculiar courts in England and Wales and the parishes that they cover. The most useful of these are Camp (1974) and Gibson (1974). It is also worth contacting the CRO that covers the region in which you are interested, as it will know where all the probate records are for a particular parish or town.

Most of the larger ecclesiastical courts have indexed their records, and many of these have been published by the British Record Society or by local history societies. An out-of-date list of these is in Gibson (1974), but the volumes themselves will be held by CROs, the British Library, SoG and larger local and university libraries. Most are indexed alphabetically by surname and make allowances for spelling variations. When looking for a will in a particular court you should consult these indexes first.

A few courts, especially the peculiar ones, have yet to have their probate records indexed. In these cases you will need to contact the institution that holds the original documents (usually a CRO) to see if it has a suitable finding aid.

## Finding a PCC Will

If you have had no joy with local ecclesiastical courts, try searching the wills proved under the PCC. As the highest church court in England, the PCC had power over all smaller courts and was thus sometimes used to settle disputed wills from lower courts or by the rich, who wanted to make sure that their bequests were officiated by the highest court in the land. The earliest PCC will preserved dates from 1384 and they are continuous from then until the present day. During the period of the Commonwealth (1649 to 1660) all English and Welsh wills had to be proved in the PCC.

The Probate Act Books for the PCC are held at TNA: PRO in class PROB 11, while any original wills are held under class PROB 10 (but cannot be examined without five working days' notice). Microfilm copies of all the wills in the PCC Probate Act Books are on open access at TNA: PRO, at the Family Records Centre in London and also at the SoG library. Published indexes to the wills are available at all these locations, as well as at other libraries, but the best finding aid is TNA: PRO's new 'documents online' Internet service.

In 2003 TNA: PRO made all one million plus of its PCC wills available through the 'documents online' facility on its website (www.nationalarchives.gov.uk). This facility is much more convenient and efficient than the older printed indexes, and the database is more complete too. The database can be searched by name, date, place, occupation and keyword. It is worth varying the spelling of the people and places that you are looking for as (in my experience) the search engine is not too good at finding variations on its own. Once you have located the will that you are after, you can then download it for a cost of £3.50 per will. It is delivered as a PDF file, whose resolution is just about sufficient to deal with the tricky handwriting on some of these documents. This online service is of great value to genealogists and the ability to search the PCC wills index is a genealogical tool on its own.

## Other Will Repositories

The records of other ecclesiastical courts are spread around the country, but the Probate Act Books (or microfilm copies of them) are generally to be found in the CRO that is local to the town in which the court was based (e.g. the Consistory Court of Ely wills are to be found in Cambridgeshire CRO). The location of the peculiar court records can be more random. A slightly out-of-date but useful guide to the location of all the court records in Britain can be found in Gibson (1974). If in doubt, try contacting the relevant local CRO or look at its website.

## Format of the Will

Most post-medieval wills are written in English (although some seventeenth-century ones may be in Latin), but sometimes the handwriting and use of English can be problematic (see Chapter 3). This can be especially true if one is working from a photocopy of the original document or a printout from microfilm. Fortunately most wills were written to a set format, making it easier to decipher what is said.

A will usually begins by stating the day and date, then the name of the testator (or testatrix) and where he or she lived, including the county and/or diocese. Next the testator will usually state that he or she is of healthy (or good/sound) mind (or remembrance) and then give thanks to God for this. The first bequest will normally be that the person's soul be given to God Almighty and that his or her body be buried in a named church. Older wills may bequest money to the poor of the parish, the parish church and other local causes. Then the business of disposing of personal land and property begins.

In many wills the testator's eldest son usually received the lion's share of the family wealth, although, if the testator's wife were still alive, then she would normally be given life enjoyment of the house and land, sometimes on condition that she did not marry again (see also Section 6.1 on restrictions associated with property ownership). The remainder of the land, money and possessions would then get parcelled out in ever smaller amounts to the other sons, with the daughters often being given sums of money or furniture rather than land. Underage children would usually be instructed to wait until either their marriage day or until they reached twenty-one years of age before receiving their legacy, but other than this it was traditional for most bequests to be paid out in the weeks or months following the death of the individual. By the nineteenth century this pattern was beginning to break down, with the division of property and money between wife and siblings becoming more even-handed.

After the immediate family had been dealt with, distant relations, servants, friends and others could be mentioned, as would any special clauses or requests. Sometimes this pattern varied, e.g. occasionally the land and other wealth would be split evenly between the children and in some northern counties it was traditional to give one-third of the property to the widow, one-third to the children and one-third to friends, relatives and good causes.

Finally, the testator would end the will by nominating one or more executors (or, if female, executrix), whose job it would be to ensure that the instructions in the will were carried out properly. The will would be validated by the testator placing his or her mark on it and by being delivered in front of two or more witnesses, most likely friends or noted local dignitaries.

After the testator's death, the will would be proved by an ecclesiastical court. It was then copied into the court's Probate Act Book, and the date and place where the will was proved would be written underneath as a 'probatum'. Before the 1730s the probatum is usually in Latin and normally states the date, the name of the court and its presiding official(s), the name of the deceased and where he or she came from, the name of the executors and the date by which the executors should have acted on the will's instructions. For information on translating a Latin probatum see Stuart (2000), while Raymond (2004) provides a list of words and phrases commonly associated with probate records. As wills were normally (but not always) proved within days or weeks of a person's death, the date in the probatum is a good guide as to when the individual died.

It should be noted that, while wills can be an indispensable source of information, they often do not tell the whole story. In many cases the testator will have already given away parcels of land, money or property to family members, which can mean that some sons and daughters do not get mentioned at all. Other wills only concern themselves with the spouse and eldest son, the rest of the family being left out of the picture. It must not be assumed that, because an individual is not mentioned in a will, he or she was dead or did not exist at all.

The following is the last will and testament of Robert Chambers, a cousin to one of my direct ancestors, who was buried on 29 March 1732. His will is laid out in a typical way and is particularly useful because it lists the married names of his daughters, which allowed me to identify their marriages in the registers from surrounding parishes.

In the name of God Amen I Robert Chambers of Reach in the county of Cambridge and diocese of Ely being weak in body but of sound and perfect mind do make and appoint this my last will and testament in manner and form following Ffirst I commend my soul into the hands of God my creator hoping this please to Jesus Christ to devise pardon for my sins and my body I commend to the earth to be buried in a decent manner according to the custome of the parish and as to my worldly estate and goods which it hath pleased God to bestow me with all I give and dispose of in manner following IMPRIMIS I give and bequeath unto my son Robert Chambers all my real estate whatsoever to have and to hold to him and his heirs for ever the particulars whereof are as follows namely one house standing in Reach in the parish of Swaffham Prior together with two orchards yard barns stable outhouses and all their appertenances whatsoever tweleve acres of arable land lyeing in the open fields of the parish aforesaid one dolver parcel of land of ffour acres and a half in the Higher Ffenn and a like parcel in the Little Ffenn both lyeing and being in the grounds of Swaffham Prior aforesaid which said house orchards barns stable and land abovementioned I give and bequeath unto my said son Robert Chambers and his heirs for ever which said Robert Chambers my son and appoint my sole executor of this my last will and testament to pay or cause to be paid out of the estate abovementioned all my debts ffurnerall charges and legacies hereafter mentioned ITEM I give and bequeath unto Elizabeth Shereman my daughter the sum of twenty pounds of good and lawfull money of Great Britain to be paid her by the said Robert Chambers my son and executor at within the space of one year from the time of my decease and likewise my will and mind is that the said Elizabeth Shereman my daughter shall have and enjoy immediately upon my decease one cow which she her self shall chose out of what stock as shall be left at my decease and also the ? chamber bed bedstead bedclothes and hangings as it now stands ITEM I give and bequeath unto Mary Steel my daughter the sum of three pounds of good and lawful money of Great Britain to be paid for by my above named executor at or within the space of one year after my decease and also my will and mind is that she the said Mary Steel my daughter shall have and enjoy immediately upon my decease one cow which she shall chose next after her sister All the rest of my stock debts money and chattells whatsoever I give and bequeath unto Robert Chambers my said son and executor In Witness whereof I have hereunto sett my hand and seal the twenty sixth day of March in the year of our lord one thousand seventeen and thirty two Robert Chambers his X mark sealed signed and acknowledged in the presence of Jervis Carer Ffrancis Wakelin Samuell Golding Hannah Wakelinge Proved 25 May 1732

*Probatum coram domino apud Ely die 25 Maii 1732*
This will was proved before the Lord at Ely on the 25 May 1732

## Administrations (Admons)

If a person with property died without a will, he or she was deemed to be intestate. In order to divide up the estate, one or more of the relatives or acquaintances would have to apply to the probate court for a grant of Letters of Administration. These would give the named individual(s) the power to distribute the deceased's estate in an honest fashion. This action was usually recorded in the court's Administration Act Book and an administration bond (admon. bond) filed. These bonds could be filed in a number of places, either loosely or sometimes as copies in the Act Books. In many cases the published indexes of individual courts' probate records will record the whereabouts of administration bonds. If not, then you should consult the CRO or archive that holds the probate records of the ecclesiastical courts covering the region where your ancestor lived. Before 1733 such records are likely to be in Latin.

Several of my family died intestate, leading to the creation of administration bonds. This was the case with George Chambers, who was buried in 1658 but whose wife Alice was not granted a Letter of Administration by the Consistory Court of Ely until 1662 (I have wondered whether this may have been due to the Commonwealth regulations).

Letters of Administration would also be granted to third parties in circumstances where a named executor was unwilling or unable to undertake his or her duty. In such cases this will usually be noted at the end of the will. This was the case with Christopher Chambers, a relation of mine who died in 1785 but whose chosen executrix died before the will could be proved. The court therefore granted Letters of Administration to his principal creditor; the original administration bond is located in the administrations register with a note placed beneath the will in the Probate Act Book:

> Letters of Admon. of all and singular the goods chattels and credits of the deceased with his will annexed were granted to Joseph Butcher a principal creditor of the said deceased (Sarah Chambers the sole executrix herein named dying without proving the same) the said Joseph Butcher being first sworn in due form of law and before the Revd. John Shepard Surrogate.

## Inventories

Associated with administration bonds are inventories, which are detailed surveys of the deceased's estate made by either a trusted acquaintance or a professional valuer. As well as being performed for intestates, inventories could also be carried out by those who did leave a will at the request of the testator. Inventories were most commonly used in the seventeenth and eighteenth centuries.

Generally, inventories were carried out on a room-by-room basis and they are highly useful documents for judging the wealth and status of an individual, but do bear in mind that much of the estate may have been divided up before the individual's death. Inventories are generally not copied into the Probate Act Books but may instead have been filed with the administration bonds (see above) or as separate documents. Fortunately, most of the published indexes to the probate courts also list the whereabouts of inventories. If not, then consult the CRO or archive that holds the probate records of the ecclesiastical courts that covered the region where your ancestor lived.

The following example is an inventory made after the death of my direct ancestor George Chambers of Reach in Cambridgeshire. It was filed in the Consistory Court of Ely's Administrations Register:

Feb 15 1710 apprizal inventory of the goods and chattels of George Chambers late of Reach in the parish of Swaffham Prior deceased January 18th 1710.

| | |
|---|---|
| Item His prize and wearing clothes | 01–00–00 |
| In the parlor | |
| One bed and bedstead pillows and bolster | 01–10–00 |
| Item for six chairs | 00–04–00 |
| Item for one chest of draws and a little table | 00–10–00 |
| Item for one looking glass | 00–04–00 |
| Item for brass and pewter | 01–00–00 |
| In the Hall | |
| One pewter case, one oval table and a little table | 00–18–00 |
| Item for eight chairs and a booke case | 00–02–06 |
| Item a pistll and moiter, spits, tonge, fire pann and other pans | 00–03–00 |
| In the Parlour chamber | |
| ffor sheets and linen | 00–15–00 |
| Item one bed and bedding and bedstead | 00–10–00 |
| Item for ?, a little table and four chairs | 00–05–00 |
| Item for one set of curtains and one quilt | 01–00–00 |
| Item for one boal | 00–15–00 |
| Item for four tubs and two kilderkuis | 00–03–00 |
| Item for turf | 00–01–06 |
| Item for lumber things seen and unseen and forgotten | 00–03–00 |
| The Summ is | 09–15–00 |

## 4.3. FUNERAL AND CHURCH MONUMENTS

Some churches may contain physical traces of your ancestors' lives in the form of grave headstones or more elaborate funeral monuments such as inscribed slabs laid into the church floor. At the very least these may be photogenic features to add to your family tree, but some may also provide valuable information about your ancestors' lives.

## Graveyards and Headstones

Visiting an ancestor's grave can be a poignant moment; they are one of the few three-dimensional and photogenic relics that can be traced by family historians. In addition, grave monuments such as headstones can also provide small pieces of information that are not necessarily obtainable from the parish registers, such as an occupation, cause of death, birth date or connections to other people.

The erection of headstones to mark the death and burial of one or more persons is a relatively recent tradition. Almost all graveyard headstones and other grave monuments will date from the late eighteenth century or later. There will inevitably be some older ones, but these tend to belong to wealthier individuals.

Tracing an ancestor's grave can be tricky. If you know the place of burial from the parish register (see Section 4.1), then obviously the first place to check is that church. However, you should be aware that not all burials had a headstone erected for them (this is especially true for poorer people) and that even if they did, there is no guarantee that the headstone will still be standing or that any inscriptions on it will still be legible after decades of exposure to the British climate.

To avoid disappointment it is worth checking with the church's local CRO or the SoG library to see whether or not they have a record of the monumental inscriptions from the churchyard where your ancestor may have been buried. In addition, Gibson and Hampson (1998) contains details of some county indexes to gravestones.

Many local history societies have braved the British climate in order to transcribe headstone inscriptions. These written records can be invaluable as they preserve information that has been or will eventually be lost through erosion, vandalism or development. Inscriptions from churchyards that were purposefully demolished between 1922 and 1993 have been recorded and lodged in TNA: PRO RG 37 (use the 'browse' option in The Catalogue to see the churches covered); the majority were in urban locations.

The Chambers family has a long association with the Cambridgeshire parish of Swaffham Prior, and on my first actual visit there I managed to find several headstones in Saint Mary's churchyard relating to my family history. However, to my frustration some of the headstones had inscriptions that were partially or completely illegible. Later, on a visit to Cambridgeshire CRO, I found a typed transcription of the church's monumental inscriptions that had been prepared by the Cambridgeshire Family History Society some decades earlier. From this I was able to obtain the full inscriptions:

To the memory of/ George Chambers/ who died June 10 1828/ aged 84 years/ Elea Chambers/ who died May 4 1810/ aged 67.

Sacred to the memory of/ Mary the beloved wife of William Rayment/ son of George and Eleanor/ Chambers of Swaffham Prior who died June 11 1837/ aged 52 years.

George and Eleanor Chambers were my great-great-great-great-great-grandparents, but I had hitherto been unable to find Eleanor Chambers's (née Sizar) baptism record. Knowing her age when buried enabled me to narrow down my search when looking in the registers from surrounding parishes.

## Cemeteries

From 1819 onwards cemeteries began to be used in large urban areas in order to cope with the increased population density. They quickly became popular with the poor and working classes. However, as cemeteries received burials from a wide range of parishes, it can be tricky tracing an ancestor's burial, especially before 1837, when you will not even have a death certificate to help narrow down the person's place and date of death. If you suspect that an ancestor may have been buried in a pre-Victorian cemetery (of which there are very few), then the most practicable, but time-consuming, route is to discover where the nearest cemetery was to where your ancestor lived (a local history book or CRO should be able to tell you this) and then to find where that cemetery's burial registers are located (again they are usually in CROs or other similar large archives). It is then a case of searching for your ancestor's name. If discovered, this should give you the name, address, age and parish of residence. Those searching for adult male London burials could try using Boyd's London Burial Index, which covers the years 1538–1853 and is available at the SoG or on line through the Origins Network (www.originsnetwork.com).

## Monuments inside the Church

In addition to the headstones and monuments placed outside in the churchyard, there may also be a number of dedications and funeral monuments to be found inside the church. Unlike churchyard monuments, those inside the church can date back centuries and were by and large erected by the parish's wealthier individuals, often in return for a donation to church funds.

The commonest surviving funeral monuments inside churches are inscriptions carved into stone slabs or the more solid brasses. These may have been inlaid into the floor or walls of the church and may be hidden in unlikely places (do not forget to look behind curtains and under rugs and pews – but do get permission beforehand). Other monuments can include carvings in wood, stained-glass windows or chest tombs. Larger churches and cathedrals may contain dozens of funeral monuments.

Because they are protected from the elements, monuments inside a church are more durable than headstones, and so are often not recorded by family history societies. Instead they are more likely to be recorded in books on local history or guidebooks to individual parishes and their churches. To see what is available try checking with CROs, the VCH series or the closest museum and/or public library to the church. You could also try contacting the local vicar. There are many older descriptions of church interiors that may include monuments that have been lost or damaged over the years (see below).

One type of funeral monument that is particularly well catered for is the brass, a large metal plate that usually contains a picture of the deceased (often with his or her spouse), with an inscription (sometimes in Latin) that gives name, location and date of death. Because brasses contain pictures, they have long held a fascination with people and at one time making brass rubbings (see below) was a popular hobby.

The oldest brasses date from the late thirteenth century; it is rare to find them after the end of the seventeenth century. The majority of brasses in Britain have at one time or another been included in publications. A good starting point is Stephenson (1926) and its supplement volume, Guiseppi and Griffin (1938).

Many volumes give pictures and details of local brasses. A county-by-county list of local publications is available on the website of the Monumental Brass Society (www.mbs-brasses.co.uk). In addition, William Lack, H. Martin Stuchfield and Philip Whittemore are updating Stephenson's 1926 list in a series of volumes that are being published on a county-by-county basis. This series, published by the Monumental Brass Society, is being produced alphabetically beginning with Bedfordshire, with the volume covering Essex having just been published (see the Monumental Brass Society's website for further details). Funeral monuments may also display a coat of arms which can itself be a major source of genealogical information (see Chapter 20).

Robert Chambers, the brother to one of my ancestors, has a magnificent and often-commented-on brass in Saint Mary's Church, Swaffham Prior, Cambridgeshire. Not only does Robert's brass give us a glimpse into his opulent life, but the death date, 1638, allowed me to trace not only his PCC will, but also a later sentence that details a legal battle that took place between his wife Elizabeth (his executrix) and my ancestor (his brother) Samuel over the non-payment of part of the will.

## Missing Monuments

The ravages of time, building work, accidents, theft and vandalism have all served to ensure that many of the brasses, plaques and other funeral monuments that once existed inside our churches have long since vanished. Other monuments have been moved (often several times), causing inscriptions to become separated or mixed up.

*This rubbing was taken from the brass of Robert Chambers, the brother to my ancestor Samuel, of Swaffham Prior parish, Cambridgeshire. He died childless and was buried on 20 August 1638, leaving a large part of his estate to my ancestor Samuel. (Author's collection)*

Fortunately it is sometimes possible to undo some of the more recent damage inflicted on funeral monuments by consulting historical descriptions of the churches in which they lie.

From the seventeenth century onwards written descriptions of the monuments inside a church were often included in books devoted to local or regional history and/or architecture. Finding such volumes is not always easy, but a good starting point is to get in touch with the local CRO to see what it holds or to consult the VCH volume for the parish (assuming one exists). Other good resources for local history volumes can be the Institute of Historical Research, SoG and the British Library.

For example, those searching for monuments inside London churches should consult one of the many updates of John Stow's original 1605 *Survey of London*, which contains transcriptions of many church monuments. For example, Stow (1734) lists dozens of inscriptions from St Sepulchre's Church, including:

Upon a grave-stone at the south side of the Communion table rails:
Here lyeth interred the body of the truly virtuous *Elizabeth*, late the wife of *Sam. Blackerby*, of Stow market, in the county of Suffolk, Esq; daughter of *Nathaniel Barnardiston*, Esq., second son of *Sir Nathaniel Barnardiston*, of Ketton, in the said county, Knt. and dyed Nov. 8, 1691, in the 33rd year of her age.

Here also lyeth the body of *Barnardiston*, the youngest daughter, and last child, of the said Samuel and Elizabeth, dyed March the 18th 1689.

Also, *Lettice*, grand-daughter to the said *Samuel* and *Elizabeth*, Oct. 31 1714.

## Recording Monuments

Photography is an obvious means of recording a headstone or funeral monument. Outdoors this is straightforward (although seeing the inscription on older headstones can be tricky), but inside a church photography can be problematic as shiny surfaces may cause bright reflections from a camera's flash. To avoid this, try turning the flash off and instead use a tripod and/or a high ASA/ISO film (or set your digital camera to a higher ISO setting). Or try standing at a slight angle to the object you are photographing so that the flash is reflected away from the camera. If photographing stained-glass windows, simply use the light coming through the window.

If deciphering a faded or corroded inscription, then do so without damaging it further. It is generally acceptable to brush away loose dirt or accumulated debris, but unacceptable to rip off any attached plants (such as ivy and moss), as this might cause further damage. If in doubt, consult the vicar or other local official.

Aside from photography, most churches will permit people to make rubbings of brasses, graves or other monuments. The necessary materials (thick paper, wax crayons and masking tape) can be obtained from larger art stores. It is then a case of taping the paper over the monument and rubbing over the top of it using the wax crayons. The trick is not to move the paper and to rub over the brass thoroughly, leaving as few gaps as possible.

Making rubbings, especially of brasses, was at one time a very popular hobby in Britain, and some churches have since banned the practice to prevent their monuments from being damaged. Others have had copies made of their most popular monuments to stop the erosion of the originals. In all circumstances phone or write to the vicar before your arrival, as you will need his or her permission before making a rubbing and in any case may need to obtain a key. Most churches make a charge for rubbing.

## 4.4. ECCLESIASTICAL (CHURCH) COURT RECORDS

One of the objectives of the Church was to uphold (and improve) the moral character of its citizens. From this arose a complex set of ecclesiastical laws that were meant to deal with criminal and civil cases involving either church property, the clergy or the social and moral fibre of the nation. Such cases would be brought before one of several ecclesiastical courts and heard by a judge (usually a senior church official). In addition, the ecclesiastical courts had jurisdiction over probate matters (see Section 4.2). Like those of the common law courts, the ecclesiastical court records can be of genealogical value, producing information about people's spouses and other relatives, their occupation, place of residence, financial and other matters. For a more detailed guide to church court records and examples of their documents see Tarver (1995).

### The Court System

In the late eleventh century the ecclesiastical courts had their legal powers curtailed so that they could act only where the moral code of the Church had been broken, such as in cases of heresy or witchcraft, or where a criminal or civil act had been committed against or on church property (including money owed to or by the church) or a member of the clergy. In general terms the business of the court was divided into two main categories: that of 'office' and 'instance' business.

#### Office Business

Office business concerned criminal matters relating to the church, the spiritual welfare of members of the clergy and their parishioners, and also matters relating to the administration of the church. This included the general moral behaviour of the vicar and parishioners, ensuring that parish and church officials had the correct licences and were following prescribed procedures, any matters relating to the financing of the church and to the physical fabric of church buildings. Under this heading came charges of immorality (including adultery, incest, clandestine marriage, etc.), assault against church officials, unlicensed preaching, perjury, non-attendance of church, etc.

## Instance Business

Instance business concerned civil cases that would be brought by an individual or group of individuals (the plaintiffs) against another individual or group of individuals (the defendants) with whom they were in dispute. Such cases could relate only to church matters and most commonly concerned probate disputes (unpaid legacies, etc.), matrimonial matters or debts (e.g. unpaid tithes).

Other than probate records (which are dealt with separately in Section 4.2), some of the instance business more interesting to family historians is that concerning the courts' power of marriage. The church courts were empowered to deal with issues related to marriage, which included the issuing of premarital contracts and the restitution of conjugal rights. The courts' ability to dissolve marriage contracts (i.e. divorce) is discussed separately below.

It was not just the clergy who could bring cases before the ecclesiastical courts, but also parishioners. There are many instances of members of the laity successfully suing errant vicars.

Within England and Wales there were four levels of ecclesiastical court, each attached to a particular rank of church official. The lowest was the court of the arch-deacon (archidiaconal court, also known as the court of first appeal), then that of the bishop (diocese court), then that of the archbishop (provincial court) and, finally, that of one of the king's courts. In most cases an action would be heard by the archidiaconal court, with any appeals being heard by the diocese court. The final resort was the king's court, which had replaced the pope's papal court in Henry VIII's Reformation.

Cases would usually be drawn to the attention of the courts via members of the clergy or the laity, or during the periodic visitations made by church officials to each parish when the local clergy would be invited to make presentations about the behaviour of their parishioners.

## Court Procedure

When a case (known as a cause) was brought before a court, it would be heard by the judge, and a summary of the proceedings recorded in the court's Act Book (also known as a Muniment Book). Causes were generally dealt with in one of two ways.

Those causes that did not involve a dispute or appeal, such as the proving of a will or the granting of a marriage licence, would be dealt with straightforwardly and the result recorded in the Act Book.

Causes that involved criminal or civil suits were more complex and usually involved both the plaintiff and the defendant engaging the services of an advocate or another legal professional to act on their behalf. After this the cause could continue using either 'plenary procedure' or 'summary procedure'.

## Plenary Procedure

Plenary court procedure was conducted almost entirely using written pleas and statements that, if they have survived, can be of great genealogical value. The first stage in a plenary procedure was for the advocate to issue a libel (in an instance or civil case) or a *querela* or *informatio* (in an office or criminal case) for examination by the judge. If the judge agreed that the cause was one that could be dealt with by his court, he would issue a citation, which would then be delivered on behalf of the plaintiff (who was technically known as the *pars actrix*) to the defendant (the *pars rea*). If the defendant could not be located or refused to acknowledge the citation, he or she could be excommunicated by the court. Assuming that the citation was accepted, the plaintiff's advocate would issue a written statement containing the charges against the defendant. The judge would summarise these into a number of salient points that he felt needed answering. These would be submitted to the defendant, who would then be expected to give his reply (his *responsa personalia*) in writing. If the defendant rejected the charges against him, written witness statements, based on written questions (*interrogatories*) asked by the court, and any further documentary evidence could be submitted. Finally the judge would reach a point where he felt that there was enough evidence to resolve the case and would issue a definite sentence, which outlined his judgment and any further actions or punishments that needed to be handed out. A bill of any costs incurred would also be issued, together with instructions as to how they were to be paid.

## Summary Procedure

Summary court procedure was used only in criminal (office) cases and relied chiefly on oral testimony. The accused person (defendant) would be brought before the court and made to hear the charges being levelled against him. This stage is sometimes referred to as 'articles'. If the defendant denied the charges, he would be forced to swear his innocence on oath (an *ex officio* oath). He would then have either to plead his case to the court and hope that the judge would believe him and find him innocent or, alternatively, to be able to produce six people (who did not need to be witnesses to the crime) who were prepared to swear on oath the defendant's innocence. This latter situation was known as a 'wager of law', and, if the required number of people could be found, an intimation of purgation would be filed and the case dismissed. Those found guilty would be subjected to the judge's sentence and be liable for any costs.

The punishments meted out by ecclesiastical courts varied from penance (for minor offences of immorality such as fornication) to excommunication to more physical punishments such as branding or even death by hanging or burning (although these were rarely handed out). For a full history and in-depth explanation of the ecclesiastical courts and their procedures see C.R. Chapman (1992).

## The Courts' Records

The official written records of the ecclesiastical courts were the Act Book in which the details of charges, citations and sentences would be recorded plus summaries of any day-to-day proceedings from within the case itself. Most pre-1733 books are in Latin and, because of the speed at which the clerk would write, can be difficult to read. Other records relating to the courts may also survive, including a variety of other court books and individual documents used during trials (although these are more rarely preserved). These will normally be found in the same archive as the Act Books.

From the Act Books it is possible to get the names of the plaintiffs and defendants, plus an outline of the case in which they were involved. Interpreting original Act Books can be problematic because of the legal terms and different court procedures used. Tarver (1995) provides a practical guide to the use and interpretation of the Act Books.

An Act of Parliament in 1962 decreed that all records relating to the ecclesiastical courts should be housed in diocesan record offices. In most cases this means that the records have been placed in the CRO belonging to the county in which the diocese's cathedral is to be found. When looking for the original ecclesiastical court records (or any published or unpublished transcriptions of them), the CROs are the first place to check. The records of some of the many courts associated with the provinces of Canterbury and York are held in other institutions, such as university libraries or within Lambeth Palace. C.R. Chapman (1992) provides the location of some of the records relating to the provinces of Canterbury and York.

I have found a number of church court records relating to my family history, including the judgment on a 1639 dispute between my ancestor Samuel Chambers and Elizabeth, the widow of his brother Robert. It is in Latin and highly illegible, although it is possible to get the gist of what is happening.

The example below is of an enrolled deed from the Consistory Court of Ely made at the instigation of William Manning, the father of Philippa, who was due to marry Robert Chambers, a relation of my family. The deed, which becomes illegible towards the end, appears to act as a type of prenuptial contract so as to prevent Robert Chambers exercising a claim over one of William's properties, which has instead been given to a Martin Hill. This document was useful to me as it confirmed the names of Philippa's and Robert's fathers.

This indenture made the thirteenth day of November in the seventh year of the reign of our sovereign lord William the Third by the grace of God of England Scotland France Ireland King defender of the faith – Anno Domini 1695 Between William Manning the older of West Reach in the county of Cambridge yeoman on the part of Martin Hill of Swaffham Prior in the county of Cambridge aforesaid clerk on the other part witnesseth that the said William Manning of a marriage agreed between to be had between Robert Chambers the younger son of Robert Chambers the elder of Swaffham Prior aforesaid yeoman and Philippa Manning the daughter of William Manning aforesaid – and for diverse other good causes and considerations him the said William Manning hath given . . . unto the said Martin Hill and his heirs all that my messuage with the appurtances wch was was [*sic.*] lately on Hockley estate and being in or nigh to West Reach and now in the occupation of Widow Spalding the younger together with those orchards ajoining to the said messuage . . .

## Divorce Records

The ecclesiastical courts offered one of the few means of obtaining a legal divorce from one's partner, usually on the grounds of adultery, cruelty or impotence. In practice divorce was very rare (some courts handled fewer than a dozen cases a year), as the court cases were often scandalous affairs with witnesses on both sides brought in to assassinate the other person's character.

Those seeking divorce through the church courts could apply for one of three types of separation. A declaration of nullity was the most extreme of these as it had the effect of rendering the marriage void from the date of the wedding, which would mean that any children born in wedlock would be declared illegal and the wife would lose her right to inherit her husband's estate.

An annulment would grant a separation from the date of the court case, thus preserving the children's legitimacy and the wife's rights. However, the annulment was not a full divorce and prevented the wife and husband from remarrying.

The divorce *a mensa et thoro* ('from bed and board') would permit the separated couple to remarry, but it could be applied for only on grounds of cruelty or adultery, which produced some spectacular court cases. Tarver (1995) describes a number of such cases where various servants, innkeepers and relatives were dragged into court to testify to one party or another's drunkenness/violent temper/adulterous behaviour, etc.

### Other Means of Divorce

There were ways other than the church courts by which a couple could legally acknowledge their desire to separate.

Legal deeds of separation could be agreed between husband and wife and then filed through the Chancery courts. These deeds were enrolled in the close rolls (see

Section 17.3). From 1670 it was possible to obtain a divorce by an Act of Parliament, but the number of instances when this occurred is very small indeed. Such Acts are preserved among the parliamentary records, but they were so rare (and often so scandalous) that references to them were usually made in newspapers (see Chapter 19).

Other references to broken (but not necessarily divorced) marriages can be found among the records of the assizes, quarter sessions and central courts, where the deserted partner would sometimes apply for reparation against his or her errant spouse or even, in some cases, against a lover (see Chapters 12 and 14).

The following rather extreme example of a court case comes from Howell (1816–28) and concerns the then Countess of Essex, who was suing for divorce on the grounds of non-consummation of her marriage to Robert, Earl of Essex. To help prove her claim necessitated her undergoing a rather personal examination:

> Whereupon it was decreed by the Court, that six midwives of the best note, and ten other noble matrons, out of which they themselves would chuse two midwives, and four matrons, should inspect the Countess [to find] . . . 1. Whether the lady Frances were a woman fit and apt for carnal copulation without any defect, which might disable her for that purpose. 2. Whether she were a virgin carnally unknown by any man. Whereupon they went from the presence of the Commissioners into the next room where the Countess was left alone with the said ladies.

## 4.5. NONCONFORMIST RELIGIONS

### Nonconformist and Foreign Parish Registers

The establishment of the Anglican Church (the Church of England) in the sixteenth century saw Catholicism and other minor religions demoted to a second-class status, with their followers often being distrusted or even persecuted by the state. Even so, over the centuries there have been a great many minority and Nonconformist religions operating within England and Wales to which our ancestors may have subscribed. This chapter lists genealogical resources relating to some of the better-known Nonconformist religions operating in the early modern era, but there are others.

A good general starting place is to look in TNA: PRO RG 4, where, in 1837, the baptismal, marriage and burial registers for many Nonconformist churches were gathered and deposited. To see which churches and religions are held in RG 4 (and the later ones in RG 8) use the 'go to reference' function in the TNA: PRO Catalogue.

For published inventories of Nonconformist registers and other records see the List and Index Society (vols 265 and 266), Steel (1973) or the Society of

Genealogists' multi-volume *National Index of Parish Registers*, arranged geographically (see Section 4.1). In addition, Graham (1980) provides a guide to Nonconformist and foreign parish registers in the London region, while HMSO (1986) and Stell (1991, 1994) provide a list of Nonconformist chapels and meeting-houses in south-west, north and central England.

## The Catholic Church

The split of England and Wales from Rome in 1534 led to many decades of turbulence as Catholic supporters were at first persecuted by the Anglicans and then, during the reign of Queen Mary, became themselves the persecutors of the Protestants. The reign of Elizabeth I (1558–1603) saw Protestantism return and become the established faith of England; Catholicism was outlawed, with those caught hearing Mass being liable to a possible death sentence under the new offence of 'recusancy' (a refusal to submit to established authority). During the seventeenth century the practice remained illegal and was accompanied by a general paranoia among the public (and many authority figures) about the presence of Catholics within Great Britain. In the event of a crisis, whether political, accidental or natural in origin (e.g. the Great Fire of London), many would try to find a way of pinning the blame on the Catholics. The enthronement of the pro-Catholic James II caused such public discontent that in 1688 he was forced to step aside in favour of the Protestant William of Orange. With so much prejudice around and with many legal bars against them, it is perhaps little surprising that Catholics did not begin openly to practise their faith until the eighteenth century (even then they were subject to periodic attacks: the infamous Gordon Riots of 1780 were sparked by anti-Catholic sentiment). Only with the Catholic Relief Act of 1829 did the religion gain any degree of freedom.

Before the nineteenth century Catholics formed only a small minority of the population (less than 1 per cent, by some estimates) and in general terms there were more Catholics to be found among the gentry and also in the north of England than anywhere else. Before the eighteenth century there were few records kept by Catholic priests themselves (it was too dangerous), but the government was always keen to keep tabs on Catholics and their movements (especially after Guy Fawkes's attempt at blowing up the Houses of Parliament), which means that there are some records to be found.

Good general guides to tracing Catholic ancestry in England and Wales include Gandy (2001, 2002). The Catholic Record Society (12 Melbourne Place, Wolsingham, Durham DL13 3EH; tel: + 44 (0)1388 527747; www.catholic-history.org.uk) claims to have no interest in genealogy but has none the less collated and published many records (especially from TNA: PRO) that are of great use to family historians. Its website contains a list of publications and a list of articles from the journal

*Recusant History*. For a list of other active Catholic historical and family history societies see www.catholic-history.org.uk.

## Early Catholic Records

Before the eighteenth century, practising Catholicism in England and Wales was a risky business, especially during Cromwell's puritanical reign. Consequently much effort was devoted to gathering the names of those who openly or surreptitiously did so.

During the late sixteenth and early seventeenth centuries many Catholics were tried and convicted for non-attendance at Anglican services at local courts such as the quarter sessions, assizes and ecclesiastical courts (see Chapter 12 and Section 4.4). However, between 1592 and 1691 those Catholics who were caught and charged (most were fined or had land seized, but were not executed) had their names entered on to the recusant rolls, the originals of which may be found in TNA: PRO E 376 and E 377, arranged by county. The recusant rolls were drawn up by each county's sheriff and list the names of Catholics being prosecuted and then the land, goods or money seized by the sheriff. Published editions of the recusant rolls may be found in the Catholic Record Society's 'Record Series', vols 18 (1592–3); 57 (1593–4); 61 (1594–6) and 76 (1603–25). Related to the recusant rolls are documents in TNA: PRO E 379 (Sheriffs' Accounts of Seizures) and E 368 (Memoranda Rolls). Recusants are also noted in the Proceedings of the Committee for Compounding with Delinquents (1643–60) in TNA: PRO SP 23, calendared in Green (1889–93). Other early records include references to Catholics in the lay subsidy of 1641 (see Section 5.1).

The following example is taken from the Buckinghamshire Recusant Roll of 1593–4 (Catholic Record Society, vol. 57) and concerns the leasing of land that had been seized from the Catholic John Gardiner:

> *Farm.* A: Henry Eveside, one of the chaplains to the Queen [lessee] C: £63–16–10. D: The whole capital messuage with an estimated 50 acres of meadow land, in the tenure of Thomas Tasburgh, esq., together with various other manors, messuages, lands and tenements . . . being a parcel of the lands and possessions of B: John Gardiner of Fulmer, Bucks., recusant.

## Later Catholic Records

After 1700 the climate was marginally less oppressive for practising Catholics, and it is from this time that Catholic priests began to keep their own registers, which included details of baptisms, marriages and burials. Gandy (1993a) provides an atlas of Catholic parishes in Great Britain, while Gandy (1993b) gives a list of Catholic missions and registers between 1700 and 1880. Copies of some of these registers are held by the Catholic Family History Society (www.catholic-history.org.uk).

Following the Jacobite rebellion of 1715, all Catholics were required to swear an oath of allegiance to the King. The resulting 'Return of Papists', which lists Catholics' names and their estates, can be found in TNA: PRO E 174; some of these have been published by local record societies. Records of further Returns of Papists undertaken in 1705 and 1767 are to be found at the House of Lords Record Office. Other oaths made by Catholics are to be found among the Privy Council's papers in PC 1, but they are not indexed. Jacobites, many of whom were Catholic, were also subject to examination by the Forfeited Estates Commission, which, from 1716, looked into the holdings of traitors, Catholics and other people involved in the uprising of 1715. The records of the Forfeited Estates Commission are to be found in TNA: PRO FEC 1, with details of the Commission's activities and its records in Barlow (1968).

Before 1831 Catholics were, for tax purposes, classed as foreigners and thus liable to pay double land taxes (see Section 5.1). TNA: PRO IR 23/122–126 contains volumes relating to appeals to a Select Committee of the House of Commons against being charged double for the post-1828 land tax. These are divided into appeals that were successful and unsuccessful and then arranged by county.

Published biographies of English Catholics include lists of martyrs (Newdigate, 1935; Miller, 1970), and general historical accounts (Gillow, 1885–1902; Kirk, 1968; Bevan, 1985).

The following example comes from the 1705 Return of Papists made for the parish of Standish, Chester. It lists the head of each household, occupation, ages of children (and servants) and the years of residence.

|  | Occupation | Age | Resident |
| --- | --- | --- | --- |
| Mary Holden – widow | spinster | 34 | 1 |
| Alice Holden – child |  | 16 | 1 |
| Fanny Holden – child |  | 14 | 1 |
| Margret Holden – child |  | 8 | 1 |
| Eliz Brown widow | spinster | 85 | 9 |
| Law Turner | weaver | 17 | 9 |
| Ann Turner | spinster | 18 | 9 |
| Eliz Turner |  | infant | – |
| John Whittle | husbandman | 50 | 15 |

## Catholics and the Oath Rolls

Fear of Catholicism was a main inspiration behind the oath rolls (see Section 17.1). Some rolls contain the names of Catholics, especially the Protestation Return of 1641 and the 'sacrament certificates'. In addition to the general sources listed in Section 17.1, a list of Catholics refusing to swear to the 1714 Security of the Sovereign Act can be found in TNA: PRO C 203, while a list of Catholics taking oaths from 1778 to 1829 can be found in CP 37.

## Methodists

*Documents and Archives*

The Methodist movement was founded in the 1740s by the brothers John and Charles Wesley, and was immediately popular, especially among the poor and working classes. For many years Methodism remained broadly within the umbrella of the Church of England, which means that before the nineteenth century there are very few separate Methodist registers of baptisms, marriages and burials, but the numbers increase from 1800 onwards. Information relating to earlier Methodists may be obtained from the minutes taken at the many local and national meetings. Especially useful are the minutes from circuits (Methodist geographical districts), quarterly meetings and local church meetings, many of which are in CROs. It is also worth checking with CROs to see if they hold any material relating to the many Wesleyan schools that once existed.

Leary (1993) provides a detailed guide to Methodist archives and a list of the whereabouts of the church registers at TNA: PRO and SoG. In addition, Rose (1981) gives a list of historical Methodist magazines and newspapers (check also the British Newspaper Library).

The Methodist Archives and Research Centre (John Rylands University Library of Manchester, Oxford Road, Manchester M13 9PP; rylibweb.man.ac.uk/data1/dg/text/method.html) holds many documents and papers relating to Methodist family history, especially concerning those people who were ministers or preachers (lay and itinerant). The website gives a list of their collections and guides to using them.

*Publications*

A number of publications based on the Methodist archives may be of use to family historians. Rogal (1997) provides detailed biographies of eighteenth-century Methodists, as does Atmore (1801), while Hall (1897) and Beckerlegge (1968) provide a list of Methodist ministers and their circuits between 1765 and 1932. In addition, the Reverend William Leary has produced a number of useful documents based on the Methodist archives, including lists of obituaries and biographies; these are held by The Methodist Archives and Research Centre (see above) and details can be found on its website.

The following example is taken from volume two of Rogal (1997) and concerns Nathaniel Gilbert, an ancestor of my wife's family whose ancestry had proved problematic until, by chance, I discovered that one of his sons had been an active Methodist. Nathaniel turned out to have been a Methodist as well, and appears in a number of works on early Methodism. Most of these refer to his background in the West Indies, which explains why I had previously had problems finding him in the British records. Knowing this, I was able to trace further documents relating to Nathaniel's training as a lawyer and to the family plantation on Antigua.

GILBERT, NATHANIEL (? – 1774). Brother of Francis Gilbert and father of Mary Gilbert (see above for both). A lawyer, planter and slave owner, and a person of property who spent most of his life on Antigua, in the West Indies. Gilbert served, for a time, as the speaker of the House of Assembly there. After his brother Francis had been converted to Methodism by Vincent Perronet, John Fletcher, and JW – and after Nathaniel had read the *Appeals* and heard JW himself preach – Nathaniel became influenced in that direction (c.1759–1760), and for the next fourteen years, both of the brothers became Methodist itinerants throughout the West Indies. At Nathaniel Gilbert's death, the Methodist society on Antigua numbered two hundred persons. JW baptized two of Gilbert's black servants (slaves, actually) at Wandsworth on 29 November 1758. 'One of these is deeply convinced of sin; the other rejoices in God her saviour and is the first African Christian I have ever known.'

## Quakers

The Quaker movement was founded in the 1640s in the English Midlands. The central archive is in the Library of the Society of Friends (Friends House, 173 Euston Road, London NW1 2BJ; www.quaker.org.uk); its website has an outline of its collections, an online catalogue and guides to its genealogical resources. Especially useful are its 'digests' of births, marriages and burials from the mid-seventeenth century onwards (copied from the registers before they were handed over to TNA: PRO).

The best published guide to finding Quaker ancestors is Milligan and Thomas (1999); this details the movement's organisational structure and the whereabouts of registers, minute books and more obscure material.

In addition, Quakers were often listed as part of the oath rolls (see Section 17.1). There is also an 1833 roll in TNA: PRO CP 10 listing the declarations of Quakers who wished to become attorneys. Other similar rolls are alleged to be found in C 214 and C 217.

## Jews

The expulsion of the Jews from England in 1290 left the British Isles devoid of a sizeable Jewish population until Tudor times, when European Jews (especially Portuguese and Spanish) began to settle. It was not until the late seventeenth century that the first official synagogue was founded in London, after which time Jewish immigration from Europe increased, especially from Germany (for sources on Jewish immigration see Section 15.3).

Before the mid-nineteenth century Jews were barred from holding positions within many spheres of life, including the civil service, army and navy and the law, as barristers. Also, before 1837 no system of registration of births, marriages or burials was enforced, all of which can make tracing Jewish ancestors problematic. For general guides to tracing Jewish ancestry see Mordy (1995) and Wenzerul (2000).

When you are looking for Jewish ancestors in the early modern era, a good place to start is the SoG, which holds a number of special collections relating to British Jews. These include the Colyer–Fergusson Collection (containing pedigrees, wills, newspaper cuttings, etc.) and the Hyamson Collection (containing mostly pedigrees), both of which are indexed in Zubatsky and Berent (1984), and the additional collections of Jewish genealogical material made by D'Arcy, Hart and Mordy. The last of these is indexed and the whole collection is available on microfilm through the Mormon Church's Family History Centres.

Births, marriages and deaths of Jews were sometimes announced in newspapers and magazines; try using the indexes associated with *The Gentleman's Magazine* (see Section 19.1) or the index to Jewish obituaries, 1731–1868, in *Miscellanies* (vol. 4, 1948, pp. 30–60). A list of burial registers associated with Spanish and Portuguese Jews in London, 1657–1735, is in *Miscellanies* (vol. 6, 1962). Jews were entitled to make and prove wills in the same manner as everybody else (see Section 4.2).

The Jewish Genealogical Society of Great Britain (www.jgsgb.org.uk) has a number of relevant publications, including transcripts of marriage records from the Great Synagogue, London, 1791–1850. At the time of writing the Society is trying to obtain access to the extensive burial and marriage records held by the United Synagogue.

The following example is taken from the 1834 minute book of Portsmouth synagogue in which a number of members have signed a measure concerning people's behaviour (taken from *Jewish Historical Society of England*, vol. 6).

At a meeting convened this 28th day of September 5594 (1834) of the elders and congregation, we, the undersigned, have, in order to secure due and proper decorum in our Synagogue, upon all and every occasion, and not to allow any talking or irregularity of behaviour . . .
Signed M. Solomon, Philip Batnard, L. Joseph, Sam. Joseph, I. Myers, Geo. Levy, Joseph Moses, D. Lazarus, S. Simpson, Michael Emanuel, S. Moses, Y. Yoell, Isaac Moses

## Other Religions and Ethnic Groups

The little-known Inghamite denomination is an eighteenth-century offshoot from the Anglican Church, most of whose followers lived in Lancashire, Yorkshire, Nottinghamshire and Westmorland. Oates (2003) details the scope and whereabouts of records relating to this religion and also provides indexes to a number of its registers of baptisms and deaths.

The Congregationalist Church can trace its roots back to the sixteenth century. A detailed list of the archives for each county in England and Wales is given in Clifford (1997).

The Freemasons are a controversial and obscure society that is sometimes thought of (incorrectly) as being semi-religious. The Freemasons' archives are held at the Freemasons' Hall (60 Great Queen Street, London WC2B 5AZ; freemasonry.london.museum) and are open to the general public. A description of and guide to their collections is available through their website. Membership registers are not available for general consultation, but searches will be made for individual names for a fee (see their website). For a guide to these and other Masonic archives see Lewis (1999).

The Baptist Union has a complex history and organisational structure. The best guide to finding Baptist ancestors is Breed (1995), who outlines some of the issues connected with tracking down baptism, marriage and burial records and provides a list of individual Baptist church registers held at TNA: PRO. Also useful are White (1983) and Brown (1986), who provide information on English seventeenth- and eighteenth-century Baptists.

Ruston (1993) provides a guide to tracing Presbyterian and Unitarian ancestors. Floate (1999) provides a guide to tracing gypsy ancestors, and Rickard (1995) and McGowan (1996) give examples of documents relating to travellers, vagrants and gypsies.

## 4.6. PARISH AND LOCAL RECORDS

Aside from the church registers, the parish authorities would make, and sometimes preserve, a wide variety of other records, which could concern anything from the election of churchwardens and other officials through to censuses. Such records were kept locally, often in a large chest, and so preservation tends to be patchy before the nineteenth century. Almost all local parish records may now be found in CROs. This section will list some of the more commonly encountered records; a fuller list (and discussion) of parish records may be found in Tate (1969).

Before 1834 the parishes of England and Wales were administered by their vestry, a council of local people usually chaired by the parish priest. In addition a parish would normally have two churchwardens (elected men who would take care of the church and its associated bodies such as charities), a constable (the local law officer), overseers of the poor (members of the vestry in charge of administering care to the parish poor) and haywards and waywardens, who took care of the parish hedges and roads. All these officials generated their own minutes, accounts and other records in which may be found references to local people. The following may be of especial interest to genealogists.

## Parish Rate Books

From the sixteenth century onwards the parish vestry was given an increasing amount of political power that compelled the members to undertake the maintenance of highways, bridges, prisons and other infrastructure, as well as oversee the administration of money and alms to the parish poor. Many of these functions had previously been undertaken by the manors or had been performed using charitable donations, and so, to help the parish fund its new duties, they were given the power to raise money through local taxes, called rates, levied on all parishioners except the chronically poor.

Most parishes made annual assessments for rating purposes, the resultant documents from which are usually referred to as rate books. They may contain a list of most of the parish's adult population and include those who were exempted from rates. Almost all rate books are now held by CROs, although only a few date back as far as the sixteenth century.

## The Parish Poor, and Settlement and Removal Records

The problem of what to do with those who were poverty-stricken and/or incapable of earning a living through illness, disability or bereavement has been an eternal one. In medieval times the poor were largely dealt with and supported by the Church, but in the sixteenth century an increasing number of vagrants presented a problem for law and order. Initial attempts at solving the problem of 'vagabonds' did not work, and so, in 1601, a national poor law was passed by Parliament. In it the churchwardens and at least two local freeholders were required to become overseers of the poor, a duty that entailed distributing money to the poor and, where necessary, finding work for them to do. This law, which was initially intended to be temporary, was emended and extended in coming years to include a compulsion for parish constables to round up rogues, vagrants and 'lewd women' (which included those with illegitimate children) and place them in correctional houses.

The biggest change to the poor law system came with the Settlement Act of 1662, which was aimed squarely at solving the problem of vagrancy. The Act declared that only those who had lived in a parish for a month could claim poor relief, while those newly arriving in the parish could remain only if they either rented a tenement of £10 in value or provided a certificate from their home parish confirming their residency and their right to return there. This had the effect of limiting the movement of labour and it restricted many poor people to working in the parish where they lived. Others were more cunning and presented forged certificates or tenancy agreements; further Poor Acts following in 1691, 1696 and 1723 tried to close off these and other loopholes. The laws of settlement and removal (as these Acts were collectively known) had little effect on rural poverty, and, in the opinion of many, the provision of parish relief seemed only to encourage the poor into idleness, drunkenness and the reckless production of children. The result was the 1834 Poor Law Act, under which the poor could get relief only if they agreed to undertake work (which was usually unpleasant) assigned to them by a Board of Guardians. This led to the creation of the brutal and poorly managed workhouse system that features in so many Victorian novels. The records of the 1834 Act are beyond the range of this book; for these see Gibson *et al.* (2005), who list the whereabouts of post-1834 records for every county in England and Wales.

The Settlement and Removal Act created a number of local records that may be found in CROs. Some of these are the settlement certificates, or copies of them, that people needed in order to gain temporary residence in a foreign parish. These usually state the name of the person, the parish of residence and an agreement by officials in that parish that the person is free to return there to live. Other records may include the proceedings of settlement examinations, interviews conducted by the parish vestry and any new arrivals, the objective being to ascertain that strangers would not ask for parish money should they fall ill. Finally, those who were deemed undesirables could be forcibly removed from the parish by the issuing of a removal order from the local Justice of the Peace. Sometimes individual parishes would bill the stranger's parish of residence for the costs incurred in obtaining the removal order. Pregnant women were especially liable to be the subject of removal orders, as local parishes did not want to be responsible for the upkeep of them and their children for several years. This was solved in 1744 when it was declared that the baby's parish of residence was the same as that of the mother, and therefore not necessarily the parish in which it was born.

Rickard (1995) and McGowan (1996) provide examples of records relating to travellers and vagrants. Tate (1969) gives examples of settlement and removal orders, including the following example of an examination undertaken on Humphrey Foulds in 1809.

County of Nottingham (To Wit).
The Examination of Humphrey Foulds taken upon Oath before me, one of His the said County, this seventh Day of April 1809 touching the Place of his Settlement. This Examinant, upon Oath, saith, That he is about the age of Thirty-Eight Years, and that he was born, as he hath been informed, and verily believes, in the Parish of Old Daulbey in the County of Leicester of Parents legally settled at Shelford in the County of Nottingham, That when about seventeen years of age he was hired to Mr. Simpson of Saxelby in the County of Leicester aforesaid for one year and served him Two years, That at Martinmas following he was hired to Henry Ellis of Shelford . . . That in the year 1800 he went to Great Grimsby in Lincolnshire and Married Fanny his now wife which gave him a Vote for Great Grimsby aforesaid, and there rented a House, at one pound ten shillings a year and paid rates and assessments about

five shillings a year . . . and was then Removed by a Warrant of Removal to the Parish of Shelford aforesaid . . .

## Parish Apprentices

Part of the 1601 national Poor Law Act allowed the parish authorities to turn orphans or pauper children aged over seven into parish apprentices. Unlike the apprenticeships associated with guilds and livery companies (see Chapter 8), the parish apprentices rarely learned a trade but were instead used as cheap labour in houses or on farms. Before 1757 the apprentices had to be bound to their master for a period of years (usually seven) by the use of an indenture (a type of deed; see Section 6.1). These indentures would outline the apprentice's circumstances, the master's details and would be signed by the master, overseers of the poor and a Clerk of the Peace. Indentures provide evidence of a person's age and status and, if their apprenticeship was in a neighbouring parish, may give a clue as to where to look for further records. The following example comes from Somerset and concerns George Turker, a seven-year-old boy who was bound to a master in a neighbouring estate where he would be taught 'husbandry' until the age of twenty-four.

This Indenture, made this Eighth Day of January in the twenty ninth Year of the Reign of our Sovereign Lord George the Second by the Grace of God, of Great-Britain, France and Ireland, King, Defender of the Faith, and so forth; and in the Year of our Lord One thousand seven hundred and fifty six, Witnesseth That Thomas Harvard and William Thomas Church-Wardens of the Parish of Muchelney in the County of Somerset And John Stuckey and Phillip Lork Overseers of the Poor of the said Parish, by and with the Consent of his Majesty's Justices of the Peace for the said County whose names are hereunto subscribed, have put and placed, and by these Present do put and place George Turker aged seven Years a poor Child of the said Parish, Apprentice to Thomas Emmory Occupier of the Estate of Walter Long Esquire with him to dwell and serve from the Day of the Date of these presents, until the said Apprentice shall accomplish his full Age of twenty four Years according to the Statute in that Case made and provided. During all which Term the said Apprentice his said Master faithfully shall in all lawful Business, according to his Power, Wit, and Ability; and honestly, orderly and obediently, in all Things demean and behave himself towards his said Master and all his during the said Term. And the said Thomas Emmory for himself, his Executors and Administrators doth Covenant and Grant to and with the said Church-Wardens and Overseers, and every of them, their and every of their Executors and Administrators, and their every of their Successors, for the Time being, by these Presents, That the said Thomas Emmory the said Apprentice in the Art of

Husbandry shall and will teach and instruct or cause to be taught and instructed And shall and will, during the Term aforesaid, find, provide, and allow unto the said Apprentice, meet, competent and sufficient meat, Drink and Apparel, Lodging, Washing, and other Things necessary and fit for an Apprentice. And also shall and will so provide for the said Apprentice, that he be not any way a Charge to the said Parish, or Parishioners of the same; but of and from all Charge shall and will save the said Parish and Parishioners harmless and indemnified during the said Term.

In witness whereof, the Parties abovesaid to these present Indentures interchangeably have put their Hands and Seals the Day and Year above-written. Francis Gaylard. J. Hows J. Strangways Thos. Emery.

## Ecclesiastical Censuses

The church was responsible for carrying out a number of local censuses, including Incumbents' Visiting Books (made by priests as they visited parishioners), Easter Books (which list those parishioners liable to pay the Easter tithe) and Communicant Lists (records of church membership). The survival of such censuses is sporadic, especially before 1837, but Gibson and Medlycott (2001) provide a detailed list of the surviving ecclesiastical censuses and their whereabouts, along with other national censuses (such as the few returns with names for the 1801 to 1831 civil censuses).

The following example comes from Stoke-on-Trent, where, on 2 June 1701, the rector Thomas Allen undertook a census of all his parishioners.

2nd June 1701

A collection of the names of every particular and individual person in the parish of Stoke-upon-Trent, in the County of Stafford, as they are now residing within their respective Liberties and Families within the said parish; together with the age of every such person, as near as can conveniently be known, as also the number of families and souls qualified (as to their ages) for communicating, in each family.

| | | |
|---|---|---|
| Elizabeth Hatton | Widow | 64 |
| Jane Hatton | Children | 31 |
| Elizabeth Hatton | | 20 |
| Abigail Hatton | Spurious | 5 |
| William Hatton | Jane's children | 2 Wks |

# CHAPTER FIVE

# TAXATION

## 5.1. EARLY STUART AND COMMONWEALTH TAXATION, 1603–60

For as long as there have been taxes, people have tried to avoid paying them, and so when monarchs and Parliament sought to raise some money it was often necessary to make long lists of those who had paid and those who, for whatever reason, had not. The resultant tax returns (which are normally carried out geographically by parish or hundred) can contain long lists of names, together with other information about people's financial or social status and their relationship to other people on the same list. Some tax records, such as those of the hearth tax, can be so complete that they act as a type of local census. Others, such as those associated with the reign of Charles I, record only the names of the rich. Tax records are a useful genealogical resource and can, for example, be used to confirm the presence of an ancestor in a particular place. There are several excellent guides to the various taxations imposed during the early modern era; these are listed in the relevant sections.

### The E 179 Database

In the mid-1990s, TNA: PRO decided that a complete re-evaluation of class E 179 (the one that contains the majority of the taxation records, including the nominal returns) was needed, and so initiated the 'E 179 (lay taxation) project', which looked not only at the documents stored in The National Archives, but also the whole area of national taxation. The first visible product was the publication of Jurkowski *et al.* (1998), which provides a comprehensive list of all the lay taxes imposed between 1188 and 1688 and is thus an invaluable guide to the subject.

The years that followed saw researchers examine every one of the thousands of taxation documents held at the TNA: PRO archive, checking that they had been correctly identified and catalogued. The work on documents filed under county headings was completed by 2002, and by 2006 the project was working its way through the large number of unsorted documents that exist under various headings, such as 'unidentified' and 'county unknown'. This re-examination has already produced some remarkable finds, including entire suites of documents that had long been thought missing or destroyed.

In the autumn of 2002 the project launched the E 179 database, an online computer catalogue based on the revised findings. The E 179 database is available at TNA: PRO and through its website, and is searchable using a number of different criteria, such as town, village, parish, individual taxations, etc. It is by far the most up-to-date and convenient means of checking the availability of taxation records for a particular place and should be the first port of call when looking for tax records before 1688. Once located, taxation records can be ordered through the usual channels at TNA: PRO. For further information on the E 179 project see *Genealogists' Magazine* (vol. 28, 2004, pp. 3–15).

## Lay Subsidies, 1603–42

During the reigns of James I and Charles I, Parliament continued to grant the monarch the right to raise money through a number of straightforward subsidies that covered the whole nation. Each Act of Parliament would grant the king the right to raise money over a specified number of years via a number of instalments. For example, on 17 May 1606, Parliament granted James I the right to raise three subsidies over the coming three years with the money being paid in six instalments (i.e. every six months). In addition, these Acts of Parliament would also set other conditions such as the rate of taxation, what was to be taxed (usually movable goods and/or land) and any thresholds or circumstances that could render people exempt from paying it. The aforementioned three subsidies of 1606 were, for example, payable on movable goods worth £3 at a rate of 1s 8d per pound at the first instalment of each subsidy and 1s per pound at the second instalment. On land worth 20s or more the payment was 2s 8d per pound for the first instalment and 2s for the second. Aliens (i.e. foreigners) had to pay double this, with those falling below the tax threshold forced to pay a poll tax of 4d per head instead. Details of the conditions laid out for each subsidy can be found in Jurkowski *et al.* (1998) or on the E 179 database (see above).

Parliament granted lay subsidies on the following dates:

    1606 (three subsidies)
    1610 (single subsidy)
    1621 (two subsidies)
    1624 (three subsidies)
    1625 (two subsidies)
    1628 (five subsidies)
    1640 (four subsidies)
    1641 (two subsidies)

For each payment relating to each subsidy, appointed commissioners would travel the towns and countryside drawing up a list of taxable individuals and the amount they needed to pay. These 'assessments' would be returned to the Exchequer and filed together with 'certificates of assessment'.

The assessments relating to these subsidies can be very useful genealogical documents, as they will contain the names of many parishioners and give a rough idea of their wealth and local status. However, the high tax thresholds mean that often only the names of the wealthier people are listed.

The online E 179 database will tell you which assessments containing the names of individuals survive for individual parishes; the original documents are all filed in class E 179 at TNA: PRO.

The following example is the assessment for Swaffham Prior, Cambridgeshire, of the single payment made for the two subsidies of 1641. My ancestor Samuel Chambers (and his brothers Roger and Robert) were obviously among the better-off in the parish, although their wealth is insignificant in comparison to Roger Rant, the owner of Swaffham Prior Manor:

*Swaffham Prior cum Reach*

| | | |
|---|---|---|
| Roger Rant gent. | lands | £8 |
| Ann Waters vidua. | goods | £3 |
| Robert Chambers | goods | £2 |
| Nicholas Clarke | lands | £1 |
| Lawrence Oatley | lands | £1 |
| Thomas Rolphe | lands | £1 |
| Henry Parsley | lands | £1 |
| William Cooke | lands | £1 |
| Richard Parkin | lands | £1 |
| Joane Baker vidua | lands | £1 |
| Roger Chambers | lands | £1 |
| Thomas Wiseman | lands | £1 |
| John Drury | lands | £1 |
| Richard Manning | lands | £5 |
| Richard Norridge | lands | £2 |
| Thomas Nicholas | lands | £2 |
| Samuel Chambers | lands | £1 |
| Richard Waters | lands | £1 |
| Total | | £14.8 |

## Fifteenths and Tenths, 1290–1625

The system of lay subsidies dates back to the late thirteenth century when the king began to tax people based on their *movable* wealth (i.e. their cattle, crops, etc.). These were referred to as lay taxations, as they affected only the laity (laymen) and not the church. Between 1290 and 1332 there are several lay subsidies that are important and useful documents to genealogists, as the name of each taxpayer was recorded (see Chambers, 2005). However, after 1334 towns and parishes were instructed to gather the money from their inhabitants on the Exchequer's behalf, so few or no names were recorded. These later lay subsidies are often referred to as being fifteenths and tenths because of the proportion of a person's movable wealth that was required to be paid as a tax. The fifteenths and tenths carry through into Stuart times, with the last one being levied by Charles I in 1625. They are of little use, but information about each individual taxation may be found in Jurkowski *et al.* (1998), while a list of surviving documents for an individual town or parish may be obtained from the E 179 database (see above) and the original documents viewed at The National Archives.

## Prerogative Taxes

The Stuart monarchs (and especially Charles I) were continually locked in a battle of wills with Parliament over the issue of taxation. Faced with Parliament's frequent refusal to grant them money, some monarchs resorted to other means of raising cash from their subjects. In medieval times monarchs had the right to raise money during times of emergency (such as war) without Parliament's permission. In Tudor and early Stuart times the monarchs abused these ancient powers and used them to levy taxes on the populace. Some of these prerogative taxes have produced documents that are of use to the genealogist. A full list of all these taxes can be found in Jurkowski *et al.* (1998), with further information about their background obtainable from Dietz (1964).

### Privy Seal Loans

The most favoured means of raising money was via a 'forced' loan, which, by Stuart times, was more commonly referred to as a privy seal loan.

Forced loans were, as the name implies, a crude stealth tax in which the king would ask his wealthiest subjects to loan him a sum of money that (in theory) would be paid back in a couple of years' time, after the emergency had finished. Predictably, many forced loans were never fully repaid and they were generally viewed by the populace as a form of taxation.

Those lending money would in return receive a privy seal, a parchment that acknowledged the amount of the loan and a promise to repay it at the appropriate time. Many of these privy seals, or copies of them, still survive at TNA: PRO, although they are often unsorted.

A more useful resource is the nominal returns that were produced with many of these forced loans; they record the names of individual taxpayers on a parish-by-parish basis. Like most other taxations, the forced loans had minimum income thresholds, which meant that the poorest people were not liable to pay. These thresholds were particularly high in Stuart times, so that these taxes often record only the names of the better-off.

Privy seal loans were implemented in 1604, 1611, 1625, 1626 and 1628, while forced loans were implemented in 1626 and 1639. Of these the loan of 1626 is generally regarded as the most useful (having been collected under the threat of military action by Charles I) and that of 1628 the least useful (having been widely flouted by the populace). It was Charles I's readiness to implement such taxes against the wishes of Parliament and the people that helped lay the foundations for the English Civil War.

Details of the surviving records from the privy seal and forced loans can be found by using the E 179 database (see above) and the original documents viewed at The National Archives. For further information consult the guides given at the start of this section or read Hoyle's guide (1994) to Tudor taxation, much of which can be applied to early Stuart records as well.

The following example is a return that lists the names of those who refused to pay the forced loan of 1626 in the Cambridgeshire parish of Litlington, together with the amount they owed. Those who continued to refuse were initially threatened with military service but were later arrested and imprisoned with a sentence of execution. Most, however, were released a year later.

*Litlington*

| | |
|---|---|
| Henry Adams | 1–00–00 |
| Daniel Russell | 1–00–00 |
| John Bowman | 1–00–00 |
| Nathaniel Bolnest | 2–00–00 |
| Charles Shereman | 0–13–04 |

*Ship Money*

In times of war the king had the right to demand money or fully rigged ships from the Cinque Ports (these were ports of strategic value) and some coastal counties. However, in 1628 Charles I abused his power and decided to extend the ship money demand to all England's counties. The attempt failed, but a few years later, in 1634, ship money was successfully demanded from the coastal counties and, the year afterwards, applied to the whole country. Thereafter the tax was levied yearly until it was declared illegal by Parliament in 1640. Ship money returns are arranged geographically and usually give the person's name, occupation and the amount paid.

Below is an example of a ship money return for the Suffolk parish of Wickhambrook, which is famous for having eleven village greens. The return is subdivided into the eleven greens, allowing us to see whereabouts in the parish those who paid the tax were living in 1635.

**Wickhambrook**

38li    13s    0d

*Badmondisfield End*

| | |
|---|---|
| North, Hen., Esq. | 1–06–02½ |
| North, Dudley, Esq. | 0–01–03½ |
| Smith, Jn. | 0–17–08½ |

. . .

*Ashfield Greene*

| | |
|---|---|
| Sheenes, Jn. | 0–08–06 |
| Flack, Jeffrey | 0–14–06 |

. . .

*Free Gifts, Benevolences and Aids*

Free gifts, benevolences and aids were not strictly speaking taxes (at least not in the eyes of the monarch), but were instead meant to be a voluntary contribution from his subjects as tokens of their good will. In medieval times such contributions were often required for specific events such as a royal marriage or, in the case of benevolences, the threat of war. However, from Tudor times onwards these taxes were often levied for spurious reasons. Again, the practice ceased after the end of the reign of Charles I. The taxes levied were as follows:

| | |
|---|---|
| 1609 | Aid to the knighthood of Prince Henry |
| 1612 | Aid to marry Princess Elizabeth |
| 1614 | Benevolence to defend Count Frederick |
| 1620 | Voluntary contribution to defend Count Frederick |
| 1621 | Free gift to defend Count Frederick |
| 1626 | Benevolence against the threat of war from Spain |
| 1639 | Contributions toward the defence of the kingdom |

## Clerical Taxes

The clergy were traditionally exempt from the lay taxations levied on the general populace, but they did not get away with it entirely and from the late thirteenth century onwards were required to pay separate clerical taxes. These taxations were generally annual and set at a tenth of the clergy's annual income as based on a papal assessment (called the *Taxatio*) made in 1291. The money would be gathered by each diocese and paid by the bishop to the Exchequer.

After the Reformation many changes were made to the clerical taxes, so that, after 1540, what had once been an automatic taxation could be levied only with the approval of Parliament. Generally a regional convocation (gathering) of clergymen would propose a rate of taxation and method of payment that would cover several years and Parliament would approve it. Thus each annual taxation was just one payment of a wider amount of agreed taxation. Each period of clerical taxation had its own peculiar rules, which often meant that different levels of clergy were exempt from payment in certain years and the overall payment of the tax could be unevenly split over the period of payment, with certain years being more heavily taxed than others. For example, the 1606 clerical taxation is described as being 'four subsidies' because a convocation of the southern clergy agreed to undertake four subsidies of 4s in the pound to be paid in eleven instalments across five and half years. Various clerical offices and benefices would be exempt from some of the subsidies, etc. These rules are often complex and rambling, but full details of each clerical tax are given in the E 179 database (see above).

The diocese authorities were in charge of collecting the money and passing it on to the Exchequer. They were also responsible for drawing up a list of those clergymen who had paid tax as well as those who were exempt or who had defaulted. These lists, together with certificates of assessment, lists of clergymen newly promoted to benefices or offices and other related material, are stored at TNA: PRO under class E 179. The E 179 database (see above) provides a detailed list of the records available for each parish.

Clerical taxation was suspended between 1641 and 1660 and, after a brief period of resumption, was abandoned altogether in 1664, when the clergy agreed to take part in all future taxations granted by Parliament.

## The Civil War and Commonwealth, 1641–60

In 1642 the outbreak of the English Civil War put an end to Charles I's tax-raising spree. However, if the populace thought that their wallets were now free from the attentions of the taxman, they were to be sorely disappointed, for Oliver Cromwell also had an urgent need to raise money to fund not only the Civil War but also conflicts and rebellions abroad and in Ireland.

Between the outbreak of war in 1641 and the restoration of Charles II in 1660, a myriad of taxes were levied upon the English people. Parliament approved over 100 different subsidies, loans, contributions, subscriptions and assessments. Many of these were targeted at individual counties (or other regional administrative units) or at specific sectors of the population, and thus their scope was limited. The money was almost always required for the defence of individual towns, counties or the country at large, or for the maintenance of the army. Some taxes were collected weekly or monthly. A full list of this bewildering array of taxations and loans is given in Jurkowski et al. (1998), while Gibson and Dell (1995) provide details and locations of taxation records between 1641 and 1642.

Assessments containing the names of individual taxpayers survive from some of these taxations, but the majority of records held at TNA: PRO contain only the total sum collected from each region. However, in the case of the county assessments, some lists of individual taxpayers may be found in CROs, where they were deposited by the county commissioners. Other loans and subsidies do contain names, but their targeted nature means that they often contain information only about a select group of people (usually the wealthiest members of society).

Again, a list of those records containing individual names for each parish or town can be found using the E 179 database, with the original documents being found at TNA: PRO.

The following example relates to the loan for the payment of the Scottish army in 1645 for the parish of Swaffham Prior, Cambridgeshire. The list of names is small, as only the wealthiest residents were subject to the 'loan', to be repaid at 8 per cent interest. The Roger Chambers listed was the brother of my ancestor Samuel, but it was the reference to Edward Drury that proved most useful to me, as it later led to his will, and, with additional research, I was able to connect his family to Johanna Drury, who married my ancestor Robert Chambers in 1577.

*Swaffham Prior*

| | |
|---|---|
| Mr Rant | £10.0.0 |
| Richard Norridge | £2.10.0 |
| Roger Chambers | £3.0.0 |
| Mr Edward Drurye | £4.0.0 |
| Thomas Nicholas | £4.0.0 |
| Anne Waters | £1.10.0 |

## 5.2. LATE STUART TAXATION (INCLUDING HEARTH TAX), 1660–89

### Hearth Tax, 1662–88

The hearth tax is an excellent and well-known resource for genealogists, and many of its most useful records have been transcribed and published by local history societies.

The tax itself was implemented in 1662 by Charles II, who, like his Stuart predecessors, was facing a dire financial crisis. Parliament granted the King permission to levy a tax of one shilling on each 'chimney hearth' (fireplace) within an individual's place of residence. The theory was that, the wealthier a person was, the bigger house he would have and therefore the greater number of hearths, although in practice those living alone in large properties did pay disproportionately more. The tax was levied twice per year (29 September and 25 March) and the tax itself survived until its abolition in 1689.

The successful gathering of the hearth tax required a detailed knowledge of a person's place of residence and the number of hearths in his property. Thus assessors were dispatched across the country to draw up written lists of the names of the head of each household, the number of hearths he possessed and any other relevant or interesting information such as title or marriage status. These assessments were made on a parish-by-parish (or town-by-town) basis and are the most useful of the hearth tax documents as they can contain the names of dozens of individuals.

That said, TNA: PRO generally hold assessments only from the years 1662–6 and 1669–74. The assessments for 25 March 1664 are usually considered to be the most comprehensive and complete. In other years collecting was undertaken by private firms, which did not need to return the assessments to the Exchequer. Some of these private assessments survive at TNA: PRO or at CROs, but they are rare.

The hearth tax was payable by those whose house was worth 20*s* or more and who were also local ratepayers. Those with houses worth less than this, who did not contribute to local rates or whose income was less than £100 per year were exempt from payment. Commercial and industrial hearths (such as those belonging to bakeries) were also exempt, as were those belonging to charitable institutions. In order to be exempt, a person would need to obtain a certificate of exemption from a church official and/or a Justice of the Peace. Fortunately, after 1663 a list of people exempt from the tax was generally included with the main assessment.

*Finding Hearth Tax Returns*

As stated above, the most useful part of the hearth tax returns is the assessments, with their long lists of local residents. Details of surviving assessments for individual towns and parishes held at TNA: PRO can be found on the E 179 database (see Section 5.1). Alternatively, Gibson (1996) provides a comprehensive list of surviving documents relating to individual counties.

The usefulness of the hearth tax returns has led many of the assessments to be transcribed and published by local history societies. A list of current publications is available in Gibson (1996) and on the E 179 database. At the time of writing The British Record Society is engaged in a project that aims to publish at least one complete hearth tax assessment for each county in England. Many of these volumes are already in existence and may be found at the SoG, the Institute for Historical Research and university and other larger libraries.

The following extract comes from the hearth tax assessment of Swaffham Prior, Cambridgeshire, for Michaelmas (29 September) 1664; it also lists the assessment made in 1662. The 1664 assessment contains 135 individual names of people who, between them, owned 296 hearths. Many parishioners were exempted from the tax, including some of my ancestors, and it is interesting to note that several chimneys seem to have fallen down since 1662 (was this a form of tax avoidance?). Records such as this are useful for keeping track of the whereabouts of ancestors or for finding ancestors who have moved about the countryside after their baptism or marriage. It also gives clues to the status of individual people. Roger Chambers, the

*This return for the 1664 hearth tax for Bottisham Parish, Cambridgeshire, notes that John Chambers, the owner of a house with two hearths, actually lives in nearby Wicken parish.* (TNA: PRO)

brother to one of my ancestors, is listed as owning two houses. From manorial and probate records, it is possible to determine that one of these was Shadworth Manor (rented from Queens' College, Cambridge); the other was a farm in the parish.

| 1664 | Name | 1662 | Notes |
|---|---|---|---|
| 18 | Roger Rant, esq. | 18 | |
| 1 | Edmund Gibson | 2 | one fallen downe since the return |
| 2 | William Dullingham | 3 | one fallen downe |
| 3 | Nicholas Clarke | 3 | now William Cooke junior |
| 3 | Robert Chambers | 3 | exempt |
| 1 | William Waters | 2 | enter'd and paid one short since the returne |
| – | John Edwards | 1 | poore and not rated to any rate |
| – | South, widd. | 2 | the house burnt down |
| 4 | Roger Chambers | 6 | for two houses entered and paid two short since the return |
| – | William Oswell | 1 | he hath three empty William Cooe is owner [he] liveth att Newmarket enter'd two short. |

Many exemption certificates associated with the hearth tax survive in class E 179/324–351 at TNA: PRO, where they are arranged by county. These simply contain the name of the parish and then a list of those people who were exempted from paying the tax. Some collections of exemption certificates have been printed by local record societies or by The British Record Society, e.g. Seaman (2001). For more detailed and background information on the hearth tax consult Meekings (1979, 1980), Schurer and Arkell (1992), Gibson (1996) and Jurkowski *et al.* (1998).

## Other Late Stuart Tax Records

The precarious state of the country's finances meant that other taxes, aside from the hearth tax, needed to be levied, especially during the early part of Charles II's reign. Among these were various poll and prerogative taxes as well as some subsidies, grants, aids and gifts. Some of these taxes are restrictive in their scope, aiming to include only the rich or better-off; others (especially the poll taxes) were widely ignored by the populace. Records of these are thus of limited use to family historians, especially in comparison to the fuller records provided by the hearth tax returns.

Among those taxation records that I have found more useful are those relating to the 1660 poll tax for disbanding the armed forces and the 1661 free and voluntary present to Charles II, both of which have assessments that include the names of individuals (at least they have for the parishes I have studied). The best method for determining which assessments have survived for the parishes in which your ancestors lived is to use the E 179 database or to check Gibson (1996), who gives the location of those few surviving returns relating to the poll taxes of 1660, 1667, 1678, 1689, 1691, 1694 and 1697. The original records are all held at TNA: PRO. A full and detailed list of the taxations between 1660 and 1679 can be found in Schurer and Arkell (1992), Gibson (1996) and Jurkowski *et al.* (1998).

The reign of James II (1685–8) saw no taxes levied upon personal wealth; instead money was raised via duties imposed upon alcohol and imported goods.

The following example is of a return for the 1660 poll tax from the Cheshire parish of Wimboldsley, which lists the head of each household, any other adults under their roof and their relationship, their occupation, annual income and the amount of tax they paid.

### Wymbaldsley

| | £ s d |
|---|---|
| John Wygglesworth in the Countie of Yorke | |
| Gent £30 pa | 00 12 00 |
|    Richard Shaw living in the said house | |
|    in stocke £100 | 00 02 04 |
|    Richard Shaw younger | 00 01 00 |

| | |
|---|---|
| John Acton servant | 00 01 00 |
| Samuell Dewce sevannt | 00 01 00 |
| Wm Stanwey servant | 00 01 00 |
| | |
| Charles Whishall £12 10 00 pa | 00 05 00 |
| Ann Whishall widow marryed | 00 00 06 |

## 5.3. HANOVERIAN TAXATION, 1689–1837

### The Land Tax, 1692–1963

The land tax has its origins in the seventeenth-century subsidies that assessed people on their personal wealth. The regular need to raise cash resulted in a 1692 Act of Parliament that used an individual's property holdings as a means of assessing their wealth. In the next decade this tax was refined further, until, by 1702, each county or borough was told the amount of money that it had to raise for the Exchequer and it was then up to them how they divided this between their various hundreds and parishes. In practice, this meant that individuals would be taxed based on the amount of land they owned; this process became known as the land tax.

Before 1772 the rate was variable locally, and anyone was liable to pay. After 1772 the rate was fixed at 4s in the pound with, after 1798, those owning property rated at less than 20s being exempt. Until 1831 Catholics were charged double.

It is the documents used to assess the land tax that are of value to family historians, as these can contain lists of names together with the amount of tax they were due to pay plus other information such as the name(s) of their property, their occupation and relationship to other taxpayers. As such, land tax assessments not only confirm the presence of a person within a parish or borough, but also give an idea of their general wealth (although the tax was not linked to inflation and so reflected older property values) and the location of any property. However, while the land tax is generally reliable in recording the names of property owners and long-term tenants, those (generally poorer) people renting smaller houses may not have their names recorded. The tax was also slow to be updated, so that deceased people sometimes have their names recorded by mistake.

*Finding Land Tax Assessments*

The land tax was levied continuously from 1692 until 1963, when it was abolished, but the preservation of the assessments before the nineteenth century is patchy. Before 1780 survival of land tax records is very poor indeed, with the exception of the City of London, whose records are on open access at the Guildhall Library. Between 1780 and 1832 preservation is better, as a duplicate set of assessments would be made and given to the Clerk of the Peace and other local officials in order

*A return for the hamlet of Reach, Cambridgeshire, from the land tax of 1758. From this it is possible to gauge the relative wealth of some of the villagers, including several members of the Chambers family.* (Cambridgeshire County Record Office) to prepare a list of eligible voters (see Section 18.2). Beyond 1832 the preservation rate increases substantially.

A detailed list of surviving returns and their location is given in Gibson *et al.* (2004), with most being held at CROs. Between 1780 and 1832 copies of land tax assessments may have been included in the quarter sessions records (see Section 12.2) by the Clerk of the Peace.

The big exception to this is the assessments for the 1798 land tax, copies of which were retained for the Exchequer and are now in TNA: PRO IR 23, with microfilm copies being available at many CROs. The assessments survive for almost all of England and Wales and are arranged by county, hundred and parish in 121 volumes.

The 1798 assessments were preserved by the Exchequer because from that year property owners were offered the option of commuting their land tax for life by paying the equivalent of fifteen years' tax in a lump sum. Those who took up the offer of this 'land tax redemption' will have their names recorded in the parish books of redemptions located in TNA: PRO IR 22 (arranged by county and then parish). Certificates relating to the properties of redemptioners may be found in TNA: PRO IR 24 arranged by certificate number; indexes exist in IR 22/206–207.

The following 1758 land tax assessment comes from the hamlet of Reach, Cambridgeshire, and concerns several members of the Chambers family, including the wealthy Robert Chambers and his son Christopher. The two George Chambers, who are father and son, are both my direct ancestors and, while not poor, seem to have fared less well than their distant cousin Robert.

Reach

| | | |
|---|---|---|
| £38 | Robt. Chambers £37/ Taylors Dolver £1 | 1 18 0 |
| £3 | George Chambers – fen | 0 3 0 |
| £3 | George Chambers – jun., house and close | 0 3 0 |
| £26 | Mr Richard Peachey | 1 6 0 |
| £1 | John Mansfield | 0 1 0 |
| £2 | Widow Gilson | 0 2 0 |
| £2 | Jn Leggett | 0 2 0 |
| £8 | Christopher Chambers | 0 8 0 |
| £6 | Robt. Hills and Jn Hills jun | 0 6 0 |
| £12 | Fred Boutle | 0 12 0 |

## Window Tax, 1696–1851

The window tax was one of the more unusual and unpopular taxes to be levied. First introduced in 1696, it assessed the occupiers of a property and not its owners, and levied on them a flat-rate house tax plus an additional tax that depended on the number of windows a house possessed. Before 1766 the window tax component was only levied on those houses with ten or more windows, but afterwards this dropped to seven windows and then, after 1825, increased to eight windows. The house tax component was abandoned in 1834 but the window tax continued to be levied until 1851. Those who were exempt from paying church or poor rates were also exempt from the window tax.

This tax was controversial and caused many people to brick up their windows, the scars from which can still be seen in some old buildings. A complicated list of commercial windows that could be exempted only added to the chaos. There was widespread evasion and fraud associated with the tax.

The window tax returns list the name of the house's occupier, the number of windows and the tax due. The returns are generally found in CROs and are even scarcer than those for the land tax. Gibson *et al.* (2004) offer a list of the whereabouts of surviving returns for each county.

The example below comes from the window tax return of 1777 and concerns the Preston area of the Westmorland town of Whitehaven (Cumbria Family History Society, 2002). The houseowners are listed on a street-by-street basis, making this a useful means of locating exactly where people were living at this time.

**Addison Alley**

| | |
|---|---|
| Samuel Norman | 0. 2 ½ |
| Elizabeth Cowman | 0. 2 ½ |
| Jane uxr [wife] Robert Clarke | 0. 3 ½ |

. . .

**Brackanthwaite**

| | |
|---|---|
| Alexander McDonald | 0. 1 |
| Henry Littledale Sr. | 0. 1 ½ |
| Henry Littledale Jr | 0. 1 ½ |

## Marriage Duty Act, 1695–1706

From 1695 until 1706 a tax was levied on every birth, marriage and burial, as well as annually on bachelors over twenty-five and childless widowers. To do so the assessors made use of the parish registers (see Section 4.1) and produced returns that contained the names of many members of the community.

Surviving returns are usually held in CROs; a list of their whereabouts can be found in Gibson (1996). Some urban centres have a significant coverage, including London (the returns are in the Corporation of London Record Office and those for people living within the walls are indexed in London Record Society (vol. 2, 1966)) and Bristol, which have been published by the Bristol Record Society (vol. 25, 1968).

No returns survive for any areas in which my known ancestor lived, and so the following example has been taken from the Bristol Record Society (vol. 25, 1968). It concerns the inhabitants of St Mary Redcliffe parish:

### St. Mary Redcliffe

An assessment made on the Parish of St. Mary Redcliffe within the City of Bristoll pursueant to an Act of Parliament Entituled an Act for granting to his Majestie certain Duties upon Marriages Births and Burialls and upon Batchellers and Widowers for the term of Five years for carrying on the Warr against France with Vigour to the Second years payment by that Act approved of this [blank] day of June one thousand six hundred and ninety six.

| Inhabitants' Names | Burials | Births | Marriages | Batchelors & Widowers |
|---|---|---|---|---|
| John Yeamans and Tomasine wf. | | | | |
| John Tomasine and Elizabeth ch. | | | | |
| Mary Pool sr. | | | | |
| Richard Parsons and Jane wf. | | | | |
| Charles Francis Jane and Ann ch. | | | | |
| Thomas Hearn sr. | | | | |
| | 4 0 | 2 0 | 2 6 | |
| Henry Flower and Elizabeth wf. | | | | |
| William Flower and Margarett wf. | | | | |
| John William James and Mary ch. | | | | |
| John Harris and George Champan sr. | | | | |
| Ursley Rich wd. | | | | |
| Mary Shepton sr. | | | | |
| | 4 0 | 2 0 | 2 6 | |

### Death Duty, 1796 onwards

In 1796 the government imposed a death duty on the estates of middle- and higher-income families. Initially the duty was only payable on legacies valued over £20 (and this excluded the value of any freehold and leasehold property), and then only when the money went to a person who was not a direct relative (i.e. not children, parents, grandparents or spouses). Inevitably the scope of the tax was widened so that, as well as legacies, it included real estate and other personal wealth, although bequests to spouses remained exempt. Before 1805 it is estimated that only 25 per cent of estates were liable; in the years afterwards around 75 per cent were paying death duty; by the mid-Victorian era only those whose estates were worth less than £20 and those who died fighting for their country were excluded.

Before 1903 records of those whose estate was liable to death duty were kept in registers. The information held here can give you different information from that in the original will (e.g. it can show where the money actually went rather than where the testator hoped it would go), and it can give much more information in the case of administrations. A typical death duty entry will record the deceased person's name, address and occupation, together with the date of his or her will or administration, where and when probate was granted, and the names, addresses and occupation of the executors. It then gives details of the deceased's estates, legacies, trustees, legatees, annuities and, finally, the duty paid. Some entries also include an exact date of death and additional information about beneficiaries and family relationships.

All the death duty registers are held in TNA: PRO IR 26, but those before 1857 have been microfilmed and are available at both TNA: PRO and the Family Records Centre in London. Searching the registers on their own is not really a viable option, as their arrangement is complicated and the entries are organised by the date that probate was granted or administration issued and not by the individual's date of death.

To find an ancestor's death duty entry it is therefore necessary to use the indexes to the registers, which reside in IR 27. These have also been microfilmed and are available at TNA: PRO, the Family Record Centre and also on the commercial National Archivist website (www.nationalarchivist.com). Before 1857 there are several different indexes to the registers, depending on whether your ancestor was a testator (i.e. he or she had made a will) or died intestate and, in both cases, whether the will or administration was proved at the PCC or in a local court (see Section 4.2 for more details of probate courts). The table below shows how the indexes are arranged within IR 27. Once you have worked out which series of indexes you need, you should start searching for the year and then alphabetically by the deceased's surname.

PCC Wills (1796–1811) and Administrations (1796–1857)

| | |
|---|---|
| IR 27/1–16 | Covers PCC wills between 1796 and 1811, and registers IR 26/1–178. Arranged chronologically. |
| IR 27/17–66 | Covers PCC administrations between 1796 and 1857, and registers IR 26/179–286. Arranged chronologically. |

Local and Peculiar Court Wills (1796–1811) and Administrations (1796–1857)

| | |
|---|---|
| IR 27/67–93 | Covers local court wills (testators) between 1796 and 1811, and registers IR 26/287–437. Each court has its own index arranged chronologically. |
| IR 27/67–139 | Covers local court administrations (intestates) between 1796 and 1857, and registers IR 26/287–534. Arranged by individual court |

until 1811 and then chronologically. Note that before 1811 the administration indexes are filed with those relating to the individual court's wills.

## PCC and Local and Peculiar Court Wills (1812–81)

IR 27/140–419   Covers wills (testators) from PCC and local courts between 1812 and 1881, and registers IR 26/535–3292. Arranged chronologically with each year having an alphabetical index.

The indexes should give you the name of the testator and that of the executor(s), the probate court and a volume and folio number. The register and folio number will allow you to trace the actual death duty entry in the main registers in IR 26. For example, my ancestor George Chambers's entry in the 1828 index appears as follows:

| TESTATOR | EXECUTORS | COURT | REGISTER | FOLIO |
|---|---|---|---|---|
| Chambers George | Isaac Chambers Swaffham Prior Cambs. | Ely | 3 | 607 |

This arrangement of indexes means that searching for an entry before 1812 is more complicated than searching for one after that date. It helps if you know in which court and roughly when your ancestor's will or administration was proved (see Section 4.2 for details of how to find this), as this will reveal which set of indexes to check. If you do not know this but know where and when your ancestor lived and died, then you should first check the registers belonging to the local probate court starting in the year of death. After 1812 the process is simplified as some of the indexes are amalgamated, but you will still need to search on a year-by-year basis.

The index entries generally contain a year, the deceased's name, the court where the will or administration was proved and a page (folio) reference to the death duty register where the main entry will be found. Those with no page reference were exempt from the duty. For further information on death duties see Barbara English's article in the *Bulletin of the Institute of Historical Research* (vol. 60, 1987, pp. 246–9).

## Other Eighteenth-Century Taxes

As well as a tax on windows, the eighteenth century saw a host of other arcane and specialist taxations, the records of which survive at TNA: PRO. After 1784 these taxes were gathered on the same return as the window tax.

Other duties were at various times levied on game (1784–1807), horses (1784–1874), female servants (1785–92) and hair powder (1795–1861), few returns for which survive.

## Carriage Duties, 1747–82

Held in T 47/2–4 (years 1753–66) and organised chronologically, this taxation was levied on the number of four-wheeled carriages owned by a person.

## Gold and Silver Plate Duties, 1756–77

Held in T 47/5 (years 1756–62) and organised chronologically. A list of suspected and actual defaulters is held in T 47/6–7 (years 1757–68 and 1776).

## Male Servants Tax, 1777–1852

Held in T 47/8 (year 1780 only) and arranged by county. An index to this exists in the SoG Library. Servants working in farming or trade were exempted.

# CHAPTER SIX

# PROPERTY RECORDS

Before the Industrial Revolution the ownership of property was synonymous with wealth. Those who owned large amounts of land or buildings were generally richer than those who owned or rented smaller estates or who held nothing at all. Given the link between land, wealth and social status, most people were very careful when it came to the buying, selling, bequeathing or leasing of land, and as a result there were a number of ways in which land ownership and the transfer of land from one person to another (conveyance) could be legally registered. Equally well, those who owned land would sometimes undertake surveys or take out insurance policies. All these actions could generate paperwork that is of use to the genealogist. Land, houses and other property would sometimes remain in the same family for generations or could be given as part of a dowry, etc. If you suspect or know that your ancestors owned or leased property, then it is worthwhile searching for any associated records.

## 6.1. DEEDS AND LAND CONVEYANCE

A deed (sometimes called a charter) is a document that conveys a privilege, including the right to a property, from one person, group or organisation to another. In this section we shall be dealing with those deeds that were made in order to record the transfer (or conveyance) of land from one person or institution to another. Such deeds (sometimes referred to as feoffments or indentures) were used by the buyer and vendor (seller) as a permanent record of the transaction so that: (*a*) the buyer had proof of his or her purchase and (*b*) in the event of a dispute over rights of ownership or boundaries the deed could be consulted and if necessary produced in court.

### Conditions of Property Ownership

Since the Norman Conquest in 1066 all the land in England and Wales has been owned by the Crown, which means that anyone who holds land is ultimately a tenant of the incumbent monarch. However, the Crown is able to grant 'estates in land' to individuals or organisations, which gives them the right to occupy or sublet properties. Under this system of 'estate in land' (usually abbreviated to estate), a person (or organisation) could hold property under one of several different conditions. You may see the terms below referred to in the property deeds themselves or in your ancestors' wills.

## Fee Simple or Fee Simple Absolute

The fee simple estate (also known as 'estate in fee simple' and 'fee simple title') is the condition under which most modern property in England and Wales is held and is the equivalent of freehold. A person holding a fee simple estate is effectively its owner and is free to do what he or she wants with it and can lease it, sell it, give it away or will it to heirs without restriction. Naturally, this is the most desirable condition under which to hold land, although it was less common in the past than today.

Fee simple can be distinguished in a deed by the use of the phrase 'to X and his heirs', which means that A is free to give his property to whomsoever he chooses (unlike fee tail; see below).

## Fee Tail

Created in 1285, a fee tail estate is a restricted version of the fee simple and prevents the landowner from being able to sell, give away or in any other way alienate his or her land. Instead, the land can only be passed to one of the landowner's legitimate heirs, thus ensuring that the land cannot leave the family's possession.

Fee tails can be identified in a deed by the phrase 'to X and the heirs of his body', which restricts the owner to handing on his land to his legally recognised children. It was also possible to restrict the inheritance to male heirs (fee tail male), female heirs (fee tail female) or other relations (fee tail special). Land subject to these conditions was said to be entailed or in tail, with the restrictions themselves called entailments.

Should the owner die without heirs, the land would pass to the living descendants of the previous owner(s), but such situations would commonly result in civil law suits (see Chapter 14). Fee tail was widely unpopular, and it was possible to break the conditions through a complicated legal process known as 'common recovery'. Records of common recovery in England are found in the recovery rolls held in TNA: PRO CP 43 (indexes are available at TNA: PRO). Those for Wales were recently moved to the National Library of Wales. Fee tail was abolished in England and Wales in 1925.

## Life Estate

Life estate is property that is sold or given to a person only for the duration of their lifetime. This means that, once that person dies, the land reverts to its original owners or his or her heirs. This is quite complicated, but essentially it means that the person holding property under conditions of life estate cannot will it to heirs or anybody else. It was also commonly used to give a wife life enjoyment of a house or land while at the same time ensuring that after her death it would stay within the family. For example, a husband might will or give his property to his second wife as life estate on condition that when she died the land would revert to the children from his first marriage.

A person holding a life estate could sell or rent it out but the new buyer or tenant could use the land only so long as the person who sold/rented it to him or her was alive. As soon as the new buyer or tenant died, the land would revert to the original landholder or his or her heirs. Life estate was abolished in England and Wales in 1925.

Many of my ancestors were farmers who were concerned to keep the land they had accumulated within the family and consequently commonly took advantage of the life estate tenure laws. For example, in 1638 George Chambers decreed in his will that a portion of his estate be given to his wife 'to hold to her own proper use from the time of my deathe duringe her natural life and after her deathe to Robert Chambers my sonne and his heirs forever'.

### Leaseholds, Estates at Will and Terms of Years

A leasehold (usually abbreviated to lease) describes a property where a person (the tenant) has bought the right to occupy land or a building from the owner (the landlord) for a given length of time, usually measured in years or decades (99-year leaseholds are common today). Leasehold estates can be freely bought and sold on the open market but at the end of the lease period the property reverts to the landlord, although, in practice, the lease is often renewed before this. Many modern blocks of flats operate on a leasehold basis whereby the building is owned by a landlord who leases the individual flats to people (this usually means that the flat-owners have to pay a small annual rent to the landlord). The various terms of agreement will be set out in the written lease and will include details such as the length of leasehold, annual rent and any restrictions.

Leaseholds differ from the more informal rental situations whereby a short-term tenant will rent a piece of land, room or building from a landlord on a more casual basis, paying a weekly, monthly or annual rent. The main factor is that such short-term rentals (sometimes referred to as tenancy at will) can be terminated by either landlord or tenant at short notice.

Conditions associated with leaseholds varied widely, but there is one type of leasehold that may be of especial use to genealogists: the 'three-life lease'. Three-life leaseholds were in use between the sixteenth and nineteenth centuries, especially in the south-western counties of England. Under their terms the landlord would lease his land to three named tenants, with the term of tenancy expiring only after the death of all three people named (or ninety-nine years, whichever was sooner). Often the named people were related (e.g. father and sons), and most three-life leaseholds give the relationship and ages of the tenants. Such leaseholds could become complex affairs, as the original named tenants had the right to will their rights to the land to others. However, no matter how complicated the situation became, on the death of the third named tenant (or the arrival of the 99-year limit) the leasehold expired and the land reverted to the original owners.

*Copyhold*

Copyhold property is land that belongs to a manor but that can be held by individuals under the customs of the manor itself. Such customs could include the level of annual rent, any services that the individual would be required to perform for the manor (although this is rare in the early modern era) and any conditions associated with the inheritance or subletting of the property. It is called copyhold, because the individual could not have a separate deed but would instead hold the property by copy of an entry in the manor's court rolls (see Section 7.2 for more details). Copyhold was unpopular, and in the eighteenth and nineteenth centuries many copyhold properties were enfranchised (i.e. turned into freehold or leaseholds); the system was abolished altogether in 1922. If your ancestors held copyhold land, then there should be a record in the manor's court rolls, although separate documents might be found among the manor's other deeds.

The following is a documentary record of the transfer of some copyhold land to which my ancestor George Chambers acted as witness. I found this by chance in a box of title deeds relating to Hall Manor, Swaffham Prior, held at Cambridge University.

> Swaffham Prior, Hall Manor: Octob. the 8th 1705
> Be it remembered the day and year above written that Steven Hunk customary tenant of the manor above did out of court surrend. by the rod into the hand of the son of the said mannor by the hand of John Banyard in the presence of George Chambers teo customary tenants of the said manor according to the custom of the same All that his allotment with the appurtenancy lying and being in the fen called High Fen in Swaffham prior above said . . .

## Private and Title Deeds

Given the complexities associated with owning or leasing land, it is hardly surprising that, when it came to buying, selling or leasing land, both the seller (vendor) and buyer would desire to have a written and legally valid document that described the property concerned and outlined all the terms and conditions associated with it. The resultant documents registering the transfer (or conveyance) of land are referred to as deeds, although, to distinguish them from other types of deed, those concerning property are often called title deeds (as they record the transfer of a title to real estate from one person to another). They may also be referred to as an enfeoffment (a medieval term) or an indenture, consisting of two copies of a deed made on the same sheet and then separated by a wavy cut in order to prevent forgery. (If a dispute arose, the vendor and buyer could bring their two halves together and, if the wavy cuts fitted, be certain that neither was a later forgery.)

As well as deeds, which recorded details of individual property transactions, there could also be 'quitclaims', in which a former landowner would be required to renounce all his rights to a piece of land so as to avoid any repercussions later on.

Until the sixteenth century most land conveyance took place between individual manors and their tenants, with the transactions recorded during a sitting of the manor's court (see Section 7.2). However, as the importance of the manorial courts diminished and the number of independent landowners increased, so it became desirable officially to register the act of buying and selling of property. Thus by the early modern era the use of deeds had become widespread and would continue to increase until the present day.

Tracing deeds is notoriously tricky, but if your ancestors owned or rented property, then it may be worth making an effort to see if any deeds survive. The amount of useful genealogical information preserved in deeds is highly variable. Some will include details about the buyer and/or seller's marriage, parents, children, siblings or other relations as well as age, address, occupation, inheritance rights, etc. Most deeds also hold the names of other local people, including the witnesses to the documents. Conversely, some deeds may contain only individual names, with little additional information.

Before about 1550 almost all deeds were written in Latin, but from that time onwards they are more commonly (but not exclusively) in English. Latin deeds usually follow a set format and so can be understood even by those with limited experience of the language; see Stuart (2000) or Chambers (2005) for further information. In the early modern era the format of deeds became much more variable, but as most are in English this should not be a problem. For additional advice on how to read deeds, see Cornwall (1993) or, for a more detailed guide to deeds in general, see Alcock (2001).

The following deed from 1742 concerns property that had once been held by my ancestor Robert Chambers in Swaffham Prior parish, Cambridgeshire. The land concerned is sold as fee simple and the deed was later registered using the bargain and sale system (see below):

> This indenture made the second day of November in the sixteenth year of the Reign of our soveraign Lord George the second by the Grace of God of Great Britain Ffrance and Ireland. King defender of the faith and so forth and in the year of our Lord one thousand seven hundred and forty two Between Samuel

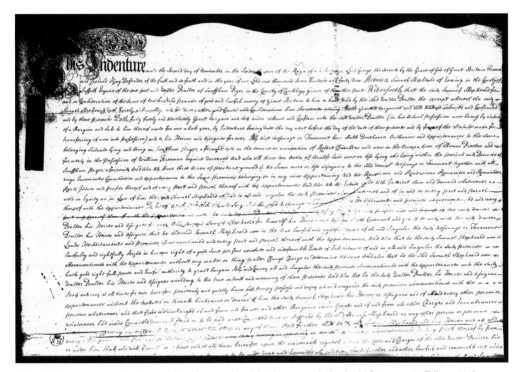

*This 1742 indenture details the sale of buildings and land held by Samuel Shepherd of Exning, Suffolk, to Walter Poulter of Swaffham Prior, Cambridgeshire. The deed mentions that the property being sold was once held by my ancestor Robert Chambers.* (Cambridge University Library)

Shephoard of Exning in the County of Suffolk Esquire of the one part and Walter Poulter of Swaffham Prior in the County of Cambridge Grocer of the other part Witnesseth that the said Samuel Shophorad for and in Consideration of the sume of two hundred pounds of good and lawful money of Great Britain to him in hand paid by the said Walter Poulter the receipt whereof the said Samuel Shophorad doth hereby acknowledge and for divers and other good causes and considerations him thereunto moving Hath granted bargained and sold aliened and confirmed and by those presents Doth fully freely and absolutely grant bargain and sell alien and confirm unto the said Walter Poulter (in his actual posession now being by virtue of a bargain and a sale to him thereof made for one whole year, by Indenture bearing date the day next before the date of those presents and by ? of the statute made for transferring of uses into possession) and to his heirs and assigns for ever All that messuage or tenement Barn Stable Dovehouse Outhouses and appurtences to the same belonging lying and being in Swaffham Prior a foresaid late in the tenure or occupation of Robert Chambers and now in the occupation of Thomas Preston . . . Signed Sam. Shepheard

## Locating Deeds

Most deeds were private documents and as such there was no compulsion to preserve them. Many have been lost, destroyed or sold to private collectors, but others have found their ways into CROs, TNA: PRO and other archives, while some remain in private hands.

Finding deeds (or copies of them) relating to property once owned by your ancestors is not easy. If your ancestor owned or leased land that belongs/belonged to an institution (e.g. a manor, church, university, charity, etc.), then you should find out where the archives of that institution are housed (usually the local CRO). If you know the parish in which your ancestor lived, then try the CRO, as many deeds were deposited there. Unfortunately, few have been catalogued and many deeds remain stored in individual bundles that relate to one individual property.

From various wills I am aware of several parishes in which my ancestors held property and also the names of several manors from which they leased land. I have traced some title deeds (all pre-1600) concerning my ancestors through the records of a manor that belonged to Cambridge University, and have found many references to copyhold land held by my ancestors in several manors whose records were deposited at Cambridge University Library and Cambridge CRO. However, I have not yet found any individual deeds that related to the other parcels of land and buildings held by my ancestors.

Aside from CROs, other good resources for deeds include TNA: PRO (especially exhibits used in court; see Section 14.7), the British Library, larger university libraries (especially the Bodleian Library) and some institutional archives (e.g. Lambeth Palace library). If searching for deeds relating to an individual manor, find out the whereabouts of the manor's court rolls using the Manorial Documents Register (see Section 7.3) and then look in the same place. You could also try searching the National Register of Archives (www.nra.nationalarchives.gov.uk) using the name of a place, property, institution or family surname, as this holds information about individual estates.

## Bargain and Sale and the Enrolment of Deeds

Before 1862 and the creation of the Land Registry there was no central means of registering titles to land. The courts could be used to register land titles in the form of fictitious disputes (see feet of fines, below), but from the sixteenth century it was possible to register the transfer of land in a central court or in the Court of Quarter Sessions (see Section 12.2) using a method known as 'bargain and sale'.

The bargain and sale in question were simply an acknowledgement that the buyer and vendor had discussed and agreed on the price and terms of the land conveyance. They would then register their agreement with the court, after which the buyer would become the legally recognised owner. Once the original deeds had been drawn up, the parties concerned had six months to register their deeds with the court or the conveyance became invalid.

Records of conveyance by bargain and sale may be found in the records of the central and palatine courts (see Chapter 12) and the Court of Quarter Sessions (see Section 12.2). The greatest number of deeds was enrolled with the Chancery courts, with many deeds enrolled with the close rolls; these are covered by the published calendars (see Section 17.3). Indexes to enrolled deeds held in other Chancery records may be found in TNA: PRO C 275/12–169, 205.

## 6.2. MAPS AND PLANS

For centuries mapmaking was largely the preserve of seafarers and not landowners, as the expense and inaccuracies incurred in drawing up a map were not deemed to be worth the effort. Instead many landowners preferred to make written surveys of their property, examples of which are described in Chapter 4. However, from the seventeenth century onwards changes in landownership patterns and advances in mapmaking led to an increased demand for estate plans, town maps and even regional-scale maps.

### General Sources for Maps

In general, most pre-Victorian maps are to be found either at TNA: PRO or at CROs, although local libraries and museums may also hold copies of important historical maps relating to their region.

Maps at TNA: PRO may be found in a wide variety of different departments, depending on the use for which they were drawn up (e.g. Admiralty charts are in ADM 1). Many of the TNA: PRO map holdings have been entered into The Catalogue and so can be searched for electronically, using the name of the parish or region you are looking for plus the word 'map' or 'maps' (hint: use AND to narrow down your search: e.g. 'cambridge AND map'). For a published list of the TNA: PRO's pre-Victorian map holdings for the British Isles see HMSO (1967). For general advice on maps at TNA: PRO see Beech and Mitchell (2004), which focuses more on Victorian maps, or its 'Domestic Records Information Leaflet 72' (available on line).

CROs also contain a substantial number of maps that, in most cases, have been catalogued (contact the CRO for details); some of these catalogues have been published. The catalogues should be able to tell you which maps are available for an area, what their scale is and for what purpose they were made.

In addition, the British Library also holds a substantial number of maps that are searchable using their online catalogue (see: www.bl.uk/collections/maps.html), as does the National Library of Wales (see: www.llgc.org.uk/dm/dm0067.htm).

## Enclosure Maps

These are two types of map that you may see referred to in relation to genealogy. Enclosure maps are large-scale maps that were made in order to record major local boundaries before or after Acts of Enclosure took place. Enclosure involved turning open fields or common pasture, which may have been shared by several different people, into a single field or piece of land that could be enclosed by a fence or hedge. By creating these larger coherent units, farmers could be more efficient and productive with their land, although, inevitably, some smaller tenant farmers lost out to their larger freeholder neighbours. Enclosure began in the seventeenth century and was initially a local affair, taking place by agreement between local landholders. However, during the late eighteenth century landowners began to use Acts of Parliament to initiate a local enclosure process that involved a commissioner coming to survey the land and the interests of those holding it, and then recommending how best to divide it up. The resultant document is known as an enclosure award, which would then be lodged either with the local Clerk of the Peace or one of the central courts (see Chapter 12). Enclosure awards will therefore be found either at CROs or at TNA: PRO. Parliamentary Enclosure Acts in 1801 and then in 1836 simplified the process, with the latter removing the need to apply for a private Act of Parliament in order to begin the enclosure award process.

Enclosure maps can be very useful documents for those whose ancestors held or rented land. Many can be extremely detailed, and, as well as providing a detailed map of the area in which your ancestors lived, they can also show you exactly where their landholdings were.

To trace any enclosure maps either consult Kain *et al.* (2004), which provides a full list of surviving enclosure maps between 1595 and 1918 in England and Wales, or use the associated online catalogue at: hds.essex.ac.uk/em/index.html. An older list of the whereabouts of enclosure maps and awards in England can be found in Tate (1978) or, for Wales, J. Chapman (1992). For detailed information on the nature and history of enclosure records see Hollowell (2000).

The following information was taken from the 1817 enclosure map for Swaffham Prior parish, Cambridgeshire, where my family were farmers. It reveals that by this time the majority of the parish had already been enclosed, and the map shows all the field (and other) boundaries, who owns or leases each field, the size of the field and who the freeholder is. My ancestor George Chambers held much land in the parish, all of it in the northern part. Some of this land was freehold, but other parts were held by copyhold from local manors. Knowing this permitted me to track down the court rolls relating to one of these manors (Swaffham Prior Manor), within which were many references to George and other members of the family. I have also used the map when visiting the parish to work out exactly where my ancestors held land.

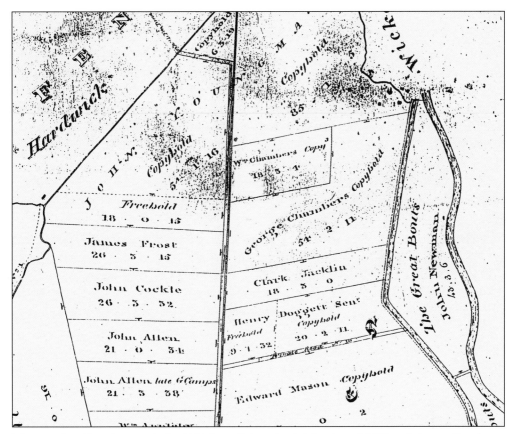

*This map of Swaffham Prior parish of c. 1817 shows all the main administrative and field boundaries as well as place and road names. Most importantly, it provides the names of the landowners and tenants, including my ancestor George Chambers and his son William.* (Cambridge University Library)

| George Chambers | 71:11:03 | Freehold |
| George Chambers | 23:01:07 | |
| George Chambers | 9:00:36 | Freehold |
| George Chambers | 4:01:05 | |
| George Chambers | 20:00:21 | Freehold |
| George Chambers | | Freehold |
| George Chambers | 4:01:07 | Copyhold Tothill Manor |
| George Chambers | 2:00:09 | |
| George Chambers | 7:02:30 | Freehold |
| George Chambers | 9:01:30 | Copyhold Swaffham Prior Manor |

## Tithe Maps and Surveys

The other main variety of map that you might see mentioned is tithe maps and surveys, which fall just outside the time range of this book. The tithe system dates back to the days when the Church was allowed to take a percentage of the produce and/or income derived from those who rented its lands. For complex reasons some of the Church's ability to raise tithes ended up in the hands of other landholders, who would use it to extract money from their tenants. Following growing hostility to tithes, Parliament passed the Tithe Communication Act of 1836, which commuted the tithes into an annual rent. To facilitate this, detailed local surveys were carried out and from them large-scale topographic maps were drawn up that listed all landholders and their tenants, while the surveys themselves carry notes about disputes between the landowner and his tenants.

Most tithe maps are held in CROs, with secondary copies available at TNA: PRO. Kain and Oliver (1995) provide a list of extant tithe survey maps of England and Wales, while Kain (1986) discusses the use of tithe surveys and provides a list of surviving tithe files for individual parishes in England and Wales held in TNA: PRO IR 18. For more information on the tithe survey process and its relevance to historians see Kain and Prince (2000).

## 6.3. MISCELLANEOUS PROPERTY RECORDS

In this chapter I have listed some other property records that are too specialised to be included in the above sections.

### Fire Insurance Records

Following the Great Fire of London in 1666, the first fire insurance companies were established in London with the aim of providing cover for businesses and individual homeowners. In the coming century the number of companies grew and their coverage spread outside London and into the countryside via a network of local agents and provincial offices. The majority of surviving records for fire insurance companies are located in the Guildhall Library, although Cambridge University Library houses those for the Phoenix Company. Hawkings (2003) describes the whereabouts and uses of fire insurance records, while Cockerell and Green (1994) discuss the history of insurance companies and also the records held at the Guildhall Library.

The Guildhall records include the policy registers for the following companies:

Hand-in-Hand    1696–1865; MSS 8674–8; registers are indexed by name
Sun             1710–1863; MSS 11936–7; indexes to 1714–31 and 1775–87
Royal Exchange  1753–9 and 1773–1883; MSS 7252–3; indexes 1775–87

An index that matches Sun policy numbers to their registers is also available at the Guildhall Library.

The registers of the Phoenix Insurance Company, founded in 1782, are in Cambridge University Library and include its subsidiaries Pelican Life and the London Guarantee and Accident Co. They are not indexed. Trebilcock (1985 and 1998) contains many examples from these records. For records relating to local fire insurance companies, try browsing under 'organisations' on the Access to Archives catalogue (www.a2a.org.uk).

Policy registers generally contain the policy number, name of agent and location of the agency; the policyholder's name, status, occupation and address; the names, occupations and addresses of any tenants; the location, type, nature of construction and value of the property insured; the premium; the renewal date; and any endorsements. The registers are arranged by policy number, which in most cases equates to a chronological order.

## Feet of Fines

In the late twelfth century a legal means of recording the outcome of property disputes was made available that permitted a court to acknowledge the agreement (or final concord) reached between the disputing parties and allowed the end result to be filed with the king's court and thus be open to inspection by the public.

Although originally designed to record the outcome of property disputes, the final concord system very quickly became subverted into a legal means of registering a transfer of land. To do this the buyer and seller would create a fictitious land dispute, the outcome of which would be recorded using a final concord. In reality the final concord recorded by the court was just the original deal reached by both parties. Almost all final concords were made before the common law courts (Chapter 12).

Typically a final concord would be written out three times on the same piece of parchment and then the three copies separated from one another by means of a serrated line. The purchaser (also known as the *querent*) would have one copy and the seller (or *deforciant*) another. The final part, which was usually the piece running across the foot of the page, would be kept by the court. It is these 'feet' of final concords (= feet of fines) that are most commonly preserved in the public records today. Any further disputes would require the three parties to come together, bringing their copy of the final concord with them. Because serrated cuts had been used to separate them, when brought together the three copies should fit like a jigsaw, proving that they were the original copy and not later forgeries. For further information on feet of fines, their uses and layout, see Chambers (2005).

### Information in a Feet of Fines

Final concords are in essence concerned with property conveyance and as such they normally list the buyer(s) and seller(s), a description of the property involved and the details of the final agreement itself. As such, a final concord will provide little detailed information on a named individual, but this is not to say that they are without value, as some basic family connections between named individuals may be given (wife, brother, sister, etc.), and the nature of the conveyance will, of course, provide a general insight into their lives.

*This 1705 tenancy agreement records the transfer of copyhold land between Stephen Hunt and John Banyard, both tenants of Hall Manor, Cambridgeshire. The document is witnessed by Thomas Chambers, a distant relation.*
(Cambridge University Library)

Final concords follow a set pattern. Before 1733 they were recorded in Latin and always began by stating their purpose, the court before which they were being held, the regnal year, the legal term (e.g. Michaelmas) and the names of the presiding judges. The names of the buyer (often abbreviated to 'q' for *querent*) and seller ('def' for *deforciant*) would then be listed, followed by a general description of the property involved and details of the agreement reached. The name of the county would be written at the bottom of the fine. By the fourteenth century the fictitious nature of many claims means that the price given on the final accord was nominal and did not reflect the true sums involved.

*Searching Feet of Fines*

All the feet of fines documents are preserved at TNA: PRO. The earliest final accords on record date back to 1182, although the feet of fines system as described above did not begin until 1185. Those made before 1509 are held in class CP 25/1, while those after this date are in CP 25/2. Indexes to the records CP 25/2 exist in IND 1/7233–7244 and IND 1/17217–17268 but see the note regarding their scope and use under the description of this class in the TNA: PRO online Catalogue.

Exceptions are for the palatine counties: Chester (1280–1831), which are held in CHES 31; Durham (1535–1834) in DURH 12; Lancaster (1377–1834) in PL 17 and the Welsh feet of fines, which have recently been transferred to the National Library of Wales.

## Inquisitions Post Mortem

Inquisitions post mortem (IPMs) are property surveys that were carried out on the death of one of the king's tenants-in-chief. They are thus concerned with the property of the wealthy but can contain much genealogical information such as death dates, spouses, heirs, etc., and the surveys themselves will often list the names of sub-tenants and the property that they held. The IPM also gives an idea of the wealth and status of an individual and size of the land they held. IPM documents for the years 1235–1660 are preserved at TNA: PRO, and for most of this time indexed English abstracts, in the form of calendars, have been made.

After the death of the tenant-in-chief a writ would be issued by the Chancery to the escheators (the people appointed to hold the inquest) in the county in which the lands were held. The escheators would then take nominal control of the lands and convene local juries to undertake a survey. This meant that, if the tenant owned land in many different places, several separate surveys would have to be undertaken and the results later assimilated.

In general the writs asked juries to look at the land held by the tenant-in-chief on his death (known as *diem clausit extremum*), but, if some time had passed between the death and the survey, another writ (known as *mandamus*) could also enquire as to who had taken profits from the land in the meantime. Other more rarely used writs included: *ad melius inquirendum*, which ordered a new survey over an old one; *plenius certiorari super vero valore*, which required a revised estimate of the value of a property; *de etate probanda* to determine whether an heir was of age, and a writ of *devenerunt*, when the land was already in the care of the monarch usually because the tenant's heir had not yet come of age. A more general writ of *melius certiorari* (to better verify) could enquire into any points or inconsistencies raised during the initial survey. Widows had life use of their husband's land, and a further writ (*de assignatione dotis*) could also be issued to establish this. The results of these writs would be included on the final IPM document.

Once gathered in, the various surveys would be written up in one document, a copy of which would be held by the Chancery, with a copy going to the Exchequer (under certain circumstances the Exchequer would receive the only copy). After 1540, copies would also be sent to the court of wards and liveries (see Chambers, 2005 for details of this).

After an IPM the legal heir to the land assessed could take ownership on payment of a sum of money, known as a relief, to the Crown (this could be as much as 100*s*). If the heir was or thought to be under age (usually twenty-one for a man, fourteen for a woman), then it would be held in wardship until proof of age was provided or until the heir came of age. Records of these, and other post-IPM transactions, can often be found in the fine rolls (see Chambers, 2005) and close rolls (Section 17.3). In 1660 the abolition of feudal tenures saw the end of the IPM.

*Finding Aids*

The majority of IPMs before 1509 have been published (in English but omitting the names of jurors) in *Calendars of Inquisitions Post Mortem* (HMSO, 22 vols, 1904–2002). Original documents after 1509 can be found at TNA: PRO:

| | |
|---|---|
| Chancery (1509–1640) | C 142 |
| Exchequer (1509–80) | E 150 |
| Ward and Liveries (1540–1640) | WARD 7 (see also Chambers, 2005) |

These records are searchable on line using the tenant-in-chief's surname, county and date. A combined index to all the IPM documents is held at TNA: PRO.

*Palatine Counties*

IPMs held in the palatine counties of Cheshire, Durham and Lancashire, and the Duchy of Lancaster are classified under separate classes at TNA: PRO. These are:

| | |
|---|---|
| Cheshire (*c.* 1277–*c.* 1640) | CHES 3 |
| Durham (*c.* 1311–*c.* 1640) | DURH 3 |
| Lancashire (1393–1538) | PL 4 |
| Duchy of Lancaster (1271–1643) | DL 7 |

# CHAPTER SEVEN

# MANORIAL RECORDS

## 7. 1. THE MANOR AND MANORIAL RECORDS

In modern-day Britain the word 'manor' conjures up an image of an opulent country house surrounded by manicured gardens, but in times past manors were central to most people's lives. Families could live and work on the same manor for generations, with many aspects of their lives subsequently recorded in the manor's written records. In medieval times the manor had a great deal of control over some of its tenants' lives; on some estates people were not allowed to marry, move house, bake bread or brew beer without the permission of their lord. Others could be tried in the manor's own courts, being fined for petty crimes such as trespass, drunkenness or short-changing. Although the importance of the manor and its associated feudal system decreases after the medieval period, their records continued to be made into the early twentieth century. Manorial records are still a valuable source of information, especially for the poorest members of society or in the absence of other parish records such as church registers. This chapter provides only a summary of manorial records; for a fuller treatment, including how to read and translate manorial documents, see Chambers (2005).

### The Manor and the Feudal System

For much of the medieval period the landscape of England and Wales was divided up into a patchwork of manorial estates. Some manors were small and consisted of only a farmhouse with a few acres; others were enormous and included entire villages and parishes within their boundaries.

Each manor was a miniature administrative unit, with the lord of the manor at its head, and several officials (such as the bailiff and reeve) underneath, who would oversee the running of the estate. Most manors had tenants, many of whom lived and worked their whole lives on the manor and were subject to its rules, regulations and customs. To help reinforce these rules and regulations, and to keep track of its tenants' movements and landholdings, each manor had its own system of courts, which, in addition to dealing with land conveyance, were also permitted to try their tenants for a range of mostly minor civil and criminal offences.

## The Manorial Hierarchy

In medieval times individual manorial estates could be leased and subleased several times, with the actual manorial lord who occupied the manor at the bottom of a chain of so-called mesne lords, a tenant-in-chief and, at the very top of the chain, the monarch, who ultimately owned all the land in England and Wales. Beneath the lord of the manor would be the manor's individual tenants, who could be either freemen (i.e. they did not owe any bond of allegiance to the manor and were free to do what they wanted with the land they leased from the estate) or bonded or unfree tenants (who owed a duty to the manor and could not leave it without permission). This complicated hierarchy of duty and allegiance is what is meant by the 'feudal system'.

By the sixteenth century this hierarchy of lords and tenants had broken down, with most manorial tenants leasing their land for money rather than having to perform tasks or duties on the manor itself. Freehold and leasehold land tenure started to replace the old system of copyhold, whereby a tenant could hold land only by the custom of the manor (see Section 6.1 for a definition of these terms). The manorial court system, once so important to keeping the peace, had authority to try civil and criminal cases whittled away by various royal courts (see Chapter 12). By the eighteenth century many manorial courts were dealing only with land tenure, but a ban on the creation of any new copyhold land meant that even this function dwindled in time. The enclosure of pastures and arable land, especially after the General Enclosures Act of 1836 (see Section 6.2), saw the end of many of the manor's everyday administrative duties; eventually many estates did not operate a court system at all. The abolition of copyhold tenure in 1922 effectively terminated the need for any manorial courts, although by then few remained in existence anyway.

Despite all this, many manors continued to generate records well into the nineteenth century, and, where they exist, these records can be of great use to the genealogist, providing a wealth of information about manorial tenants (and others associated with the estate) that can be difficult to find elsewhere. They are one of the few places where details of ordinary people's lives are recorded at any length.

## 7.2. TYPES OF MANORIAL RECORD

There are several types of manorial record that may be of use to the genealogist. These will be dealt with in summary here; for more detail consult either Harvey (1984) or Chambers (2005). Earlier records may be written on long parchment rolls, but as time progressed it became more common to write on individual sheets or in books. Before the mid-eighteenth century the records will commonly be written in Latin, but most records were written to a standard layout, and, with patience and practice, the language barrier need not be an obstacle. See Stuart (2000) or Chambers (2005) for advice on translating and transcribing manorial documents. The most commonly encountered manorial records are listed below.

## Manorial Surveys and Accounts

Manors were run as businesses and thus needed careful management. The bulk of the manor's turnover was reliant upon its tenants' rent and the sale of produce from the land; thus it was essential that the manorial managers knew what their land was being used for and what sort of return they could expect from it. To do this the manor's owner would periodically assemble a committee of trusted tenants to go around the estate making detailed notes about the size of the landholding, what it was being used for and how much income they could expect to derive from it. These manorial surveys would often include the names of all the manor's tenants, with notes about the size of their landholding and the rent or other obligations they owed. Other information, such as the names of spouses or notes about circumstance and status (e.g. freeman, widow, etc.), could also be included.

Surveys were time-consuming and costly processes, and so were carried out infrequently, with gaps of decades between surveys not uncommon. Often old surveys would simply be updated to reflect any change in ownership. In general, surveys become rarer during the eighteenth century, when the first manorial maps begin to appear.

The inclusive nature of most surveys means that they can act like a census, providing a snapshot of all the manor's tenants. They can be useful for those seeking to confirm the presence (or perhaps absence) of a family or individual from a particular area or for those seeking to gain an understanding of their ancestor's financial or social standing within the community. There are several types of survey, further details of which can be found in Chambers (2005).

### Custumals

A custumal is a list of the manor's tenants and the customary obligations that they owed to the estate in return for their house and land. By the sixteenth century most estates preferred to get cash from their tenants rather than a percentage of their produce or manual labour; hence custumal surveys are exceedingly rare outside the medieval era.

### Extents

An extent is a survey whose express aim is to estimate the value of the manorial estate. This structured document would provide a list of the manor's assets, usually beginning with the land exclusively used by the lord (demesne land), followed by a list of the manor's free and unfree tenants. Each tenant would have a description of the amount of land he or she owned and how much it was worth to the manor in terms of rent, etc. Extents were rarely made beyond the seventeenth century, but examples may still be found right into Victorian times.

*Terriers*

A terrier is a geographical survey of the manor's land that takes a metaphorical stroll around the manor's estate listing each smallholding, field, house, etc. in the order in which it is encountered (i.e. it is the written equivalent of a map). The terrier lists the size of each plot, where it is to be found, who owns it and how much it is worth. As many tenants owned more than one plot, the same person may be mentioned several times. It is often possible to relate the plots of land described in the terrier to modern field or road names or to topographical features. Terriers become rare beyond the eighteenth century, when they were replaced by proper maps.

*Rentals*

A rental is a straightforward list of the manor's tenants and the amount of rent they owe. They are usually in order of the tenants' status, beginning with the richest freemen. Only a minimal amount of information is usually given. The relative ease of making rentals means that they were undertaken more frequently than other types of survey. Rentals become common from the sixteenth century onwards.

*Accounts*

Accounts were the result of periodic audits undertaken by the manorial estate in order to give information on its income, assets, expenditure, liability and debts. Many accounts are just lists of the amount of land, cattle, rental income, etc. that the manor received, with little additional information supplied. Some do provide the names of tenants, but they are generally less useful than surveys.

The following example is of an extent survey carried out on the king's estates in the Island of Jersey in 1607. The extent makes notes of all the money, crops and other services due to the Crown, and also the names of those who owe it. The example below also mentions Quetivel Mill, a property that was once in the possession of my family.

**Wheats of the Kings property**

John Le Geyt fils [son] Thomas for Raulin Le Baylie for the discharge of Raulin Le Marquant in the right of his wiffe heire of Richard Founteine . . . 2 Cäb:

Mathie gallie in the right of his wife for Clement English in discharge of Jehannet Le Moigne . . . 2 Cäb:

**Milles**

Laurence Hampton or his assignes holdeth in fee simple to him and his heires for ever the Mill of Quettevill in this Parish, paying yearly for the same by even Portions (viz) Christmas, Easter, Midsomer, and Michaelmas . . . 21 Escus

## Manorial Title Deeds

Title deeds and charters were documents that record the rights of individual tenants to hold land on the estate. They were usually produced as written evidence of a land transaction having taken place, so that, should a dispute later arise, then either the vendor or the buyer could produce the deed in court to back up the claim. For further information on title deeds see Section 6.1.

## Manorial Court Records

The records of the manorial court are among the most eagerly sought after by genealogists, as they can often divulge information of great interest or use. Although they once had the power to try minor criminal cases and to settle civil disputes, in post-medieval times the manorial courts were largely concerned with the efficient management of the estate. In particular they would officiate and make a record of any buying or selling of land, as well as order tenants to mend fences or better to manage the land they held. They could also settle disputes over trespass, debt and other minor civil quarrels, but by the eighteenth century it was more common for such cases to be settled in the Chancery or other civil courts.

The manorial court would meet regularly (between two and six times a year), usually in the manor's great hall. It was customary for all tenants to be compelled to attend; those who were unable to offer a decent excuse were fined for their absence. The lord of the manor or one of his officials would preside over the court with a jury of a dozen or so tenants. The court would then hear of any infringements or disputes that had arisen since the last sitting, with the jury asked to judge each case. If found guilty, a person would often receive a small fine or be asked to right the wrong. Any land transactions would also be brought before the court, with the outcome being approved and recorded by the court.

The court's proceedings would be written down by the court recorder so that they formed a matter of record. It was common for court documents to be consulted several decades after they had been produced in connection with disputes over boundaries or rights of access. Early court records were written on long parchment rolls, but in time they were placed in paper books.

Manorial court records can provide very useful information. An October 1661 court roll from Swaffham Prior Manor (Cambridgeshire) records the death of George Chambers, gives details of his will and notes that the land he rents from the manor is to go to his wife Marian and daughter Anna. Other court rolls record dozens of other references to various members of the Chambers family, including a 1772 entry in which my ancestor George Chambers the younger was fined for 'uttering twelve profanities'. In addition to genealogical information about marriages, deaths and family relationships, manorial court records can provide glimpses into the lives, financials details and landholdings of our ancestors.

There were two main types of manorial court, the court baron and court leet, the roles of which are described below. However, by the seventeenth century the court leet was becoming increasingly rare, with the majority of court business instead focused on the property-oriented court baron.

### The Court Baron

The main concerns of the court baron were land tenures and disputes arising from them, the admission of new tenants and the departure of old ones (including by death and marriage) and matters concerning the upkeep of the estate or the use of estate's facilities (such as common ground). It should be noted that the manor's free tenants were not bound by some of the customary laws.

### The Court Leet

While the court baron dealt with local matters, the court leet would sit in judgment on cases of minor assault, burglary and other petty crimes, but as time went on the jurisdiction of the court leet became narrower, with criminal cases being referred to the king's courts. It is not unusual to see court leets referred to as 'the great court' or simply as the 'Court with view of frankpledge'.

The example below, from Waterbeach Manor (Cambridgeshire), provides a wealth of information about the late William Chambers and his family, including his death date, the names of his surviving sons (both under age) and his brother George, as well as the amount of land that he held from the manor.

**1824 24th April**
William Chambers, deceased.
Now at this court came William and Robert Chambers sons of William, deceased, by their attorney George Chambers brings in the last will of William deceased 12th Aug 1821 give and devise unto his two sons William and Robert their heirs land in Waterbeach. Thereupon the said William and Robert by their said attorney humbley pray for admittance 18 acres 3 rods and 4 perchs. At this court William and Robert infants under 21 appoints the said George Chambers their uncle their guardian during minority to receive and take rents and profits and course and account for.

## 7.3. HOW TO LOCATE MANORIAL RECORDS

Manorial records are private documents that were owned and stored by the manors themselves; consequently many have been lost, thrown away or destroyed. The best coverage of documents usually comes from those manors that were owned by religious houses, universities or other institutions that had central archives in which these documents could be properly stored. None the less, the records from

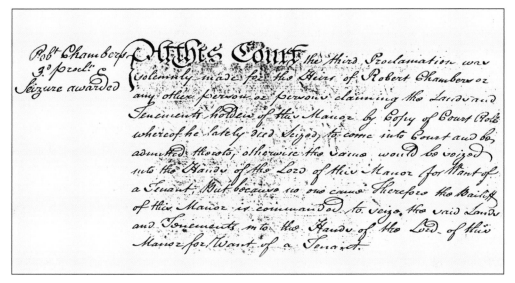

*This manorial court roll entry from 21 May 1787 makes a final plea for any heirs of Robert Chambers, deceased, to come forward to make a claim for the lands he held from Burgh Hall Manor, Cambridgeshire. No heirs came forward, so the land was reverted back to the manorial estate. (Cambridge County Record Office)*

independent manors do also survive and many now reside at TNA: PRO, CROs and a bewildering variety of institutions and private collections both in the UK and abroad.

## The Manorial Documents Register

Undoubtedly the best place to start when looking for information on a particular manor or the manors of a particular parish is the Manorial Documents Register (MDR), which covers all of England and Wales. The MDR is located at TNA: HMC at Kew, although it is in the process of being made available on line.

The MDR came into existence as a result of the 1922 Parliamentary Law of Property Act, which abolished the last remaining feudal functions of the manor, bringing an end to the production of any new manorial records. In order to preserve pre-existing manorial records, an amendment to the 1922 Act placed a duty on the owners of such documents to conserve them and to ensure that they were made available for public consultation. This Act, which was chiefly designed to make sure that information concerning ancient boundaries was not lost, applied only to court rolls, surveys, terriers and other information relating to the layout of the manor. Title deeds were purposefully excluded (see Section 6.1 for more information on these).

In 1924 the Master of the Rolls, in whose care the preservation of manorial documents was placed, decreed that there should be a register of the whereabouts of all the manorial documents in England and Wales. The result was a thorough and wide-ranging survey carried out by a government committee that produced the MDR, which until December 2003 was held at the Historical Manuscripts Commission in London but is now at TNA: PRO at Kew.

The MDR is a card index system with the entries arranged first by county and then in alphabetical order by parish. As a parish may hold more than one manor, there may be several cards for each parish. Some manors owned land in more than one parish, so it is worth checking the cards for neighbouring parishes.

There is an ongoing project to update and computerise the MDR's records. As the information for each county is placed on computer, so the cards for that county are removed from the MDR. By 2006 the records for all Wales and for the Riding counties of Yorkshire, for Hampshire, the Isle of Wight, Surrey, Middlesex and Norfolk had been computerised and can be searched on line at www.mdr.nationalarchives.gov.uk.

The following is an extract from the MDR entry for Fincham Manor, Norfolk, whose tenants included some of my ancestors.

Rental, with Boughton 1636–1637
NRA [Norfolk Record Office] 25130 Hare
Scope bailiff's accounts, with other manors 1637
NRA 25130 Hare
Bailiff's account, with other manors 1638
NRA 25130 Hare
Quit rental 1675
NRA 25130 Hare
Rental, with other manors 1690–1704
NRA 25130 Hare

The MDR is the first port of call when it comes to finding the whereabouts of manorial records. It should, however, be noted that the information held on the paper version of the MDR is mostly derived from the original 1920s survey and is not always accurate (I have encountered some minor problems with it). The online version, on the other hand, has been updated and does appear to be accurate.

### Other Places to Check

If the parish that you are interested in has been covered by the VCH series, then this can be an excellent source of information and will often give you an idea of the type of information that an individual manor's records contain. Hone (1906) has a survey of court rolls (down to parish level) held by various institutions, although this is now quite out of date.

Other than TNA: PRO (see below), the most likely repositories for manorial documents in the UK are: CROs; the British Library and large university libraries (e.g. the Bodleian Library and Cambridge University Library). It is worth checking with institutions such as these to see what they hold.

## Manorial Documents at TNA: PRO

TNA: PRO is the largest repository of English and Welsh manorial records, which have been placed in a wide variety of classes. Ellis (1994) is an excellent guide to the manorial documents held at TNA: PRO. No single index to all the manorial documents exists, but the following may be of general help.

### Court Rolls

Court rolls are mostly held under classes SC 2 and DL 30, but some have found their way into a multitude of other classes. There is an index produced by the List and Index Society (vol. 6, 1963), with additional manuscripts listed in *Union Place Name Index to Court Rolls*, which is available only in the TNA: PRO searchroom.

### Manorial Accounts

Manorial accounts are mostly held under classes SC 6 and DL 29. Check the list of documents in List and Index Society (vols 5, 8, 34).

### Surveys and Extents

Surveys and extents are held under a number of classes. Check the list of documents in List and Index Society (vol. 25, 1963, and Supplementary Series, vol. 4, 1968).

### Title Deeds

There is no central register for manorial title deeds, and they were specifically excluded from the MDR. It is, however, worth looking at the MDR (and the other sources listed above) to see where the court roll and survey records for a particular manor are to be found and then getting in contact with the institution concerned as the title deeds will often have been deposited in the same place. Individual title deeds may be catalogued in the TNA: PRO online Catalogue. For further information on charters and title deeds see Section 6.1.

# CHAPTER EIGHT

# OCCUPATIONS, TRADES AND RELATED RECORDS

In this section I have provided a list of professions, occupations and trades for which it is possible to get further information, either from archives or from published volumes available in the British Library, SoG library and the Institute of Historical Research. This list is far from exhaustive and mostly concerns those professions that I have had experience in researching. For a more comprehensive list of published occupational sources see Raymond (1997) and Culling (1999).

## Apothecaries

Apothecaries were once the equivalent of modern chemists and pharmacists, dispensing and prescribing herbal and other remedies to the ill or injured. Before 1841 apothecaries were not required to undergo any formal qualifications; they were merely required to be admitted to the Worshipful Society of Apothecaries of London. After 1841 the Royal Pharmaceutical Society regulated the profession.

Most apothecaries operated from a shop, and so it is common to see their businesses listed in trade directories (see Section 19.2). The only other sources of which I am aware are in the London Guildhall Library, which holds the membership lists, freedom admissions, apprentice bindings and other records of the Worshipful Society of Apothecaries of London, some of which date back to its founding in 1617 and continue to the mid-nineteenth century. The Guildhall also holds the Licentiateship of the Society of Apothecaries records, which date back to 1815. Those seeking apothecaries before 1617 will need to search the records of the Grocers' Company, also held at the Guildhall Library, which include freemen lists from 1345 to 1652.

The SoG library holds on microfilm a list of apothecaries operating between 1715 and 1840. A good general resource for tracing eighteenth-century medical ancestry is Bourne and Chicken (1994). Copeman (1983) provides a history of the Worshipful Society of Apothecaries.

Although he was not an ancestor, I once had cause to find some information on James Jones, an apothecary who operated in London during the 1750s and 1760s. I managed to find a number of references to him in trade directories, which gave me his address in Grafton Street, London and which then allowed me to trace his entry in Wallis *et al.* (1988), which told that he had been an army apothecary and that he was still practising in 1796.

## Apprenticeship Records

Between 1563 and 1814 those who wished to enter into a formal trade had first to undergo a period of apprenticeship. As part of the apprenticeship system a master craftsman would employ young men (but sometimes women) in exchange for providing them with formal training. Apprentices had to be young, single and had to live under the roof of their master.

Most apprenticeships were supervised by guilds and livery companies or by local authorities, and so any records of the apprentices' time with their masters will be found in the archives of these organisations. West (1983) provides a gazetteer of guilds and livery companies, while the London Guildhall Library holds the archives of many livery companies. Other apprenticeship records reside in CROs or are still with the organisations concerned (some of which are listed below).

In recent years Webb (1996–2002) has been transcribing the apprenticeship registers of the London livery companies and publishing them through the Society of Genealogists. This series at present runs to 41 volumes and covers the following companies (in order of publication):

Brewers' Company (1685–1800); Tylers' and Bricklayers' Company (1612–44, 1668–1800); Bowyers' Company (1680–1806); Fletchers' Company (1739–54, 1767–1808); Longbowstringmakers' Company (1604–68, 1709, 1714–17); Glovers' Company (1675–9, 1735–48, 1766–1804); Glass-sellers' Company (1664–1812); Woolmen's Company (1665–1828); Broderers' Company (1679–1713, 1763–1800); Combmakers' Company (1744–50); Fanmakers' Company (1775–1805); Frameworkknitters' Company (1727–30); Fruiterers' Company (1750–1815); Gardeners' Company (1764–1850); Horners' Company (1731–1800); Glaziers' Company (1694–1800); Gunmakers' Company (1656–1800); Needlemakers' Company (1664–1801); Pinmakers' Company (1691–1723); Basketmakers' Company (1639–1824); Distillers' Company (1659–1811); Makers of Playing Cards' Company (1675–1760); Musicians' Company (1765–1800); Saddlers' Company 1657–66, 1800); Tobaccopipemakers' Company (1800); Pattenmakers' Company (1673–1805); Spectaclemakers' Company (1666–1800); Loriners' Company (1722–31, 1759–1800); Gold and Silver Wyre Drawers' Company (1693–1837); Tinplateworkers' Company (1666, 1668, 1676, 1681, 1683–1800); Innholders' Company (1642–3, 1654–70, 1673–1800); Poulters' Company (1691–1729, 1754–1800); Upholders' Company (1704–72); Paviors' Company (1568–1800); Founders' Company (1643–1800); Armourers and Brasiers' Company (1610–1800); Coachmakers' and Coach Harness Makers' Company (1677–1800); Ironmongers'

Company (1655–1800); Dyers' Company (1706–46); Cooks' Company (1654–1800); Masons' Company (1663–1800); Farriers' Company (1619–1800); Carmen's Company (1668, 1678–1800); Curriers' Company (1628–1800); Wax Chandlers' Company (1666–1800); Brown Bakers' Company (1615–46); Apothecaries' Company (1617–69); Plumbers' Company (1571–1800); Plaisterers' Company (1597–1662, 1698–1800); Cutlers' Company (1442–8, 1565–1800); Brewers' Company (1531–1685); Feltmakers' Company (1676–82, 1692–1800); Painter-Stainers' Company (1655, 1666–1800); Tallow Chandlers' Company (1633–1800); Pewterers' Company (1611–1800); Blacksmiths' Company (1605–1800).

Between 1710 and 1811 a stamp duty was levied upon apprentices, with masters having to pay a tax on the money that they received for taking on the apprentice. Registers relating to this stamp duty now form the Apprenticeship Books in TNA: PRO IR 1. An index to these records (1710–74) is available at the SoG, with microfiche copies available at TNA: PRO and the Guildhall Library. Wallis *et al.* (1988) include apothecaries in their list of eighteenth-century medics.

## Architects

Colvin (1995) provides a detailed biographical dictionary of British architects between 1600 and 1840.

## Authors, Artists, Actors and other Stage Personnel

Of the thousands of practising artists and authors that once existed, only a few became famous enough to permit their names to travel down the centuries. The rest, many of whom were best-sellers in their day, remain unsung. Those seeking literary or artistic ancestors have a number of avenues they can try, including trade directories and newspapers (in which many advertised).

The central resource for authors, poets, essayists and other wordsmiths is the *Dictionary of Literary Biography*, which currently runs to over 160 volumes. This is an international project and so it is not just British writers that are covered. Each volume covers a specific genre and date range (e.g. volume 136 is 'sixteenth-century British nondramatic writers'), so you will need to know roughly in what field your ancestor was writing. It may also be worth checking the resources listed under Printers and Publishers (see below), as many authors and artists would self-publish and/or worked in this trade.

For published biographies of artists try Bryant (1903), which is a very comprehensive dictionary of painters and engravers, or Stewart and Cutten (1997), who provide a biographical dictionary of portrait painters to 1920, Fisher (1972), which concerns watercolour artists between 1760 and 1900, and Bryant and Heneage (1994), which concerns cartoonists and caricaturists between 1730 and 1980. In addition, Gunnis (1951) provides a biography of British sculptors, 1660 to 1851, while Beard and Gilbert (1986) provide a biography of English furniture makers between 1660 and 1840.

Those seeking theatrical ancestors, be they actors, actresses, musicians, dancers, managers, playwrights or other stage personnel, should first consult the multi-volume Highfill *et al.* (1973), with comprehensive information on all these people working in London between 1660 and 1800. Less detailed, but useful, is Baker *et al.* (1812), which offers biographies of eighteenth-century actors. If you know roughly when and where your theatrical ancestor was working, then it may be worth checking *The Gentleman's Magazine* or other similar publications (see Section 19.1) for advertisements or reviews of plays in which they were appearing.

The following entry is taken from Bryant (1903), and concerns the brother of a direct ancestor of mine whom I knew to have been an artist but about whom I knew next to nothing.

DEAN, Hugh Primrose, a landscape painter, was born in Ireland towards the middle of the 18th century, and was known as the 'Irish Claude.' Assisted by Lord Palmerston, he spent several years in Italy, returning in 1779. He was of an unprincipled character, and in his latter years his art failed him. He died about 1784. Amongst the works he exhibited at the Spring Gardens Exhibition and at the Royal Academy were: View of the Danube, 1768; View of Naples, 1775.

## Barbers and Barber-Surgeons

Before 1745 both barbers and surgeons had to belong to the Barber-Surgeons' Company of London. After this time the surgeons went their own way, forming the Company of Surgeons, the forerunner to the Royal College of Surgeons. Microfilm copies of the records of the Barber-Surgeons' Company of London are held at the London Guildhall Library and date from 1522 to the mid-nineteenth century. Both the membership and apprenticeship records survive, although the majority concern only those in London. However, between 1705 and 1745 the Company produced certificates for prospective naval surgeons, including those resident outside the capital. TNA: PRO holds the 1696 Association Oath Roll for members of the Barber-Surgeons' Company in C 213/171/17. Young (1890) provides a history of the Barber-Surgeons together with some examples from their records.

*See also* Surgeons.

## Civil Servants

For many years employees of the state could only be of British origin and Protestant, which, on occasion, meant that they had to declare their loyalty. For further information see the oath rolls, especially the Test (or Popish Recusants) Act of 1672 (Section 17.1). Information relating to individual appointments and rewards (such as knighthoods) may also occur in the letters patent (Section 17.2) or be published in *The Gentleman's Magazine* and *The Times* (see Section 19.1). Senior civil servants may be listed in directories such as the *Royal Kalendar* (see Section 19.2) or the *Court and City Register* (between 1742 and 1808) and the *British Imperial Calendar* (between 1809 and 1972).

There are a number of volumes, mostly compiled by John Sainty, that cover British office-holders in the Admiralty (Sainty, 1975b), Boards of Trade (Sainty, 1974), Colonial Office (Sainty, 1976), Exchequer (Sainty, 1983), Foreign Office (Collinge, 1979), Home Office (Sainty, 1975a), House of Lords (Sainty, 1971), Navy Board (Collinge, 1978), the Royal Household (Sainty and Bucholz, 1997, 1998), Secretaries of State (Sainty, 1973) and Treasury (Sainty, 1972) between the seventeenth and nineteenth centuries. In addition, Valentine (1970) provides a biography of British establishment figures between 1760 and 1784 while the *Dictionary of National Biography* will contain biographies of senior or noteworthy civil servants.

## Clergy

### Printed Sources

Before the Victorian era almost all clergymen obtained degrees from either Oxford or Cambridge universities and thus the printed biographical registers from these places can act as a good general source of genealogical information: see Chapter 9 for details.

The *Clerical Guide* is a parish-by-parish list of incumbents (not curates) which gives limited information. There are editions for 1817, 1822, 1829 and 1836, all of which are indexed. Hennessy (1898) contains good biographical information on incumbents in London parishes between 1321 and 1898, while Foster (1890) is a good resource for clergymen working between 1800 and 1840. *The Gentleman's Magazine* (see Section 19.1) often carried reports of church appointments and the death of clergymen.

For the careers of bishops and higher ecclesiastical dignitaries, try Le Neve (1969–2003), who covers the period 1066–1857 (many of Le Neve's volumes are available on line at: www.british-history.ac.uk). Lists of naval chaplains before 1978 can be found in Taylor (1978) and, from 1629 to 1903, in Kealey (1905).

A list of Catholic priests operating in England and Wales between 1558 and 1850 may be found in Anstruther (1968). Details of Methodist ministers may be found in Hall (1897), which contains a list of the ministers attached to each circuit from 1765 to 1896.

Details of many eighteenth- and nineteenth-century priests who undertook missionary work or were associated with the Society of the Propagation of the

Gospel in Foreign Parts (an organisation founded to promote Christianity abroad, especially active in North America, the Caribbean and Africa) may be found in Pascoe (1901). This volume also contains details of the Society's archives, microfilm copies of which may be found at the Billy Graham Center, Wheaton, Illinois. The archive of the Church Missionary Society is currently held at Birmingham University Library; this apparently holds many biographies of missionaries.

Printed local history volumes often contain information on the priests, curates and other workers from individual churches. CROs, local libraries and the Institute for Historical Research are good places to find these.

### Manuscript Resources

The ordination of individual priests plus records of their appointments can be found in the bishops' transcripts for the diocese in which they operated (see Section 4.1). If you know the parish in which your priest lived then further information should be obtainable from the parish's archives (see Section 4.6) or perhaps from the parish registers (see Section 4.1). For information on London clergy contact the Guildhall Library, which holds microfilm copies of many original sources relating to London clergymen including curates, lecturers and wardens (a detailed leaflet is available on their website). The names of clergymen may also be found on many of the oath rolls (see Section 17.1).

The Chancery's Dispensation Rolls held in TNA: PRO C 58 contain information on those clerics who, between 1595 and 1747, received income from more than one source or whose sons wished to succeed them. No indexes exist.

## Customs and Excise Officers

The Departments of Customs and Excise have their origins in the thirteenth century, and for centuries were extensively used by the Exchequer to raise money for foreign wars and other national expenses. Guides to the records of the customs and excise from 1697, most of which are held at TNA: PRO, may be found in the List and Index Society (vol. 20, 1967).

Before the eighteenth century the appointment of customs officers was performed by the issuing of a letter patent (see patent rolls, Section 17.2); the nature of these records is dealt with by HMSO (1913) and Baker (1961) and also in the TNA: PRO 'Domestic Records Information Leaflet 38' (available on line). The letters patent continued to be issued until 1797 and, from 1722, may be found in TNA: PRO C 209, although they are said to be sporadic after 1760.

For customs and excise officers employed after 1714 there is a series of warrant books recording the issuing of letters patent in TNA: PRO C 208 (1714–89, arranged chronologically) with associated indexes in C 202/267–269. Pay lists, arranged chronologically then geographically, may be found in PRO 30/32/15–29

(1673–89), CUST 18 (1675–1813) and CUST 19 (1814–29). Staff lists from 1671 to 1970 may be found in CUST 39 (arranged geographically, then chronologically; available on microfilm) and include details of salaries and disciplinary offences.

In addition there are separate pay lists for excise officers in T 44/16–57 (1705–1835, arranged chronologically), while CUST 109/9 contains a list of all serving excise officers in 1692 with details of salary and place of work.

## Freemen

In medieval and early modern times freemen were a group of people who helped in the political organisation and day-to-day running of a town or city. Being made a freeman was a great honour, and with the title came a number of rights and privileges, many of which were often set out in the city's charter.

Registers of freemen have survived for many towns and cities, some of which go back to the thirteenth century and list thousands of names. Much genealogical information is contained within these registers, including the name, age, trade and parentage of the freeman, as well as the means by which he was made a freeman (usually either by apprenticeship, birth or payment). Also mentioned may be the names of the freemen's apprentices, who were often the sons of a relation or close family friend.

The registers of freemen, where they survive, are usually to be found in local archives, such as CROs, but they have often been transcribed and published by local history societies. This is certainly the case for the towns and boroughs of Canterbury, Chester, Doncaster, Exeter, Ipswich, King's Lynn, Norwich and York, but others may exist. Copies of these publications may be found in local libraries and CROs, but try searching the catalogue of the British Library too.

## Horticulturalists

Desmond (1994) provides a detailed biographical dictionary of British and Irish botanists, horticulturalists, plant collectors, flower painters and garden designers.

## Law Court Officials (Lawyers, Attorneys, Barristers, Solicitors, Judges, etc.)

Lists of practising attorneys and solicitors, including those from provincial towns, were published annually in the *Law List* (which dates to at least 1775). However, those before 1790 are considered by some to be inaccurate, with some names missing, while those after 1790 list only those attorneys and solicitors who were in active practice that year. Some *Law List* volumes also contain lists of other professions, such as auctioneers and bankers. In addition, Giles (1740) provides a list of practising English attorneys from that year.

From 1728 attorneys and solicitors working for the central law courts were, on being admitted, required to sign an oath roll; these are now preserved in TNA: PRO CP 70 (1729–1848, arranged chronologically, no index). Each entry gives the attorney's name, address, date of admission and date of enrolment and the name of the admitting judge. After 1749 attorneys were also required to file an affidavit within three months of their admission; the registers pertaining to these may be found in CP 72 (1740–1875, arranged chronologically; most registers are indexed). Before 1728 a voluntary registration scheme for attorneys operated, the books for which may be found in CP 69 (1656–1761, no indexes). In 1729 and 1730 and from 1785 onwards attorneys and solicitors had to submit an annual certificate of admission, information from which would be entered into the attorneys' certificate books. These are now held in E 109/1–2 (1729–30 and 1785–1841, no index) and were used, from 1790, to create the published *Law List* (see above).

As well as these general registers, many of the central courts held separate admission lists. The TNA: PRO's 'Domestic Records Information Leaflet 36' (available on line) provides a detailed guide to the admission records for the Court of Pleas, King's Bench, Exchequer, Exchequer of Pleas and Palatine courts. Aside from the admission records, many lawyers advertised in trade directories (Section 19.2) and/or would have first obtained a university degree (Chapter 9).

From medieval times barristers were required to train and practise through London's Inns of Court, which are: Lincoln's Inn, Middle Temple, Inner Temple and Gray's Inn. The registers for the Inns of Court can stretch back to the fifteenth century and have been transcribed and published in Cooke (1877; Inner Temple), Foster (1889; Gray's Inn), Baildon (1896; Lincoln's Inn), Sturgess *et al.* (1949–78; Middle Temple).

The Selden Society has published a list of English superior court judges between 1272 and 1990 (supplementary series, vol. 10, 1993) and also a list of English law officers, King's counsel and holders of patents of precedence (supplementary series, vol. 7, 1987).

The following example comes from the *Law List* of 1782 and concerns the attorneys practising in the town of Gloucester. The number at the start refers to the number of MPs returned by the town; then follow details of public transport (to and from London, including the fare) and a list of practising attorneys for the town.

2 – *Gloucester* (Glouc. 101) Lad Lane, every aft. at 3, except Frid., fa. £1, – Tho. Bishop Bonner – Edward Driver – Wm. Hayward – Lane and Jepson – Rich. Pember – Edmund Philips – John Skinner Stock – Jn. Pitt – Wm. Pitt – Th. Rudge – Edw. Wilton.

## Lighthouse Keepers

All lighthouse keepers, light vessel crews and related staff were employed by Trinity House, all of whose records are to be found in the London Guildhall Library. However, no pre-twentieth-century lighthouse keeper records survive, although the names of individual keepers may turn up in some of Trinity House's other employee records, most notably:

Court minutes (1661 to present day; MS 30004). These are indexed and, at certain periods (most notably 1720–47; 1816–51) may list an individual's job.
Board minutes (1746 to present day; MS 30010). These are indexed from 1781 onwards, with lighthouse keepers being separately indexed from 1809 to 1841.
Wardens' minutes (1828 to present day; MS 30025).
   *See also* Trinity House pensioners (below).


## Midwives

Traditionally midwives did not need to have formal medical training, and in many rural areas the local midwife was simply a local woman with experience of childbirth.

There was no formal registration of midwives, but in 1603 it was decided that those practising midwifery should be licensed by their local bishop so that they could baptise stillborn or dying babies. Those taking the bishop's oath would have their names (together with those of local witnesses who would testify to the midwife's skill) entered into the bishop's subscription books, copies of which should be found with the rest of the diocesan records (see Chapter 4). This system of licensing lapsed in the latter half of the eighteenth century. It was not until 1881 that the Midwives' Registration Society was set up. Wallis *et al.* (1988) includes midwives in his list of eighteenth-century medical practitioners. Those interested in the practice of midwifery should read Smellie (1752).


## Physicians and Medics

A physician was a person who would diagnose and treat general illness, diseases and infections of the body (as opposed to a surgeon, who would deal with physical symptoms that required surgery). A good guide to tracing medical ancestors is Bourne and Chicken (1994). Those seeking medics practising in the eighteenth century should first consult Wallis *et al.* (1988), who provide an exhaustive list of practitioners of all kinds and include their dates of practice, name, job, address and other available details such as name of their master/apprentice, qualifications, etc.

From 1518 most English physicians were also Fellows or licentiates of the Royal College of Physicians; biographies of all the College's physicians from 1518 to 1997 are available in *Munk's Roll* (Munk, 1878–1989), although the post-1825 records concern College Fellows only. The early *Munk's Roll* volumes are not generally indexed, but an online index can be found at: www.rcplondon.ac.uk/scripts/munk_index.asp. Baach (1962) provides a directory of English county physicians between 1603 and 1643 and is based upon ecclesiastical records.

The Royal College of Physicians' library (11 St Andrews Place, London NW1 4LE; tel: 020 7935 1174; www.rcplondon.ac.uk/college/library) contains further archives and is open to non-members by appointment.

If you cannot trace your physician ancestors through the Royal College of Physicians, then it may be that they were Scottish (try the Royal College of Physicians of Edinburgh and Glasgow). Many physicians also had university degrees, so try university alumni lists (see Chapter 9). Wallis *et al.* (1988) is an index to eighteenth-century medics whose information largely comes from subscription lists of books including medical treatises and other works but that also includes information on medical apprentices. See also the ecclesiastical licences (see surgeons) and trade directories (see Section 19.2).

For those who have medical ancestors near to the start of the Victorian era, it may be worth checking the *Medical Directory*, which was published annually from 1845 onwards, and the *Medical Register*, which started in 1859. These list the names of all doctors licensed to practise and include their addresses, qualifications and medical school.

If you know the approximate date of death of your medical ancestor, check the obituaries published in *The Lancet* (1823 onwards), *British Medical Journal* (1828 onwards), *Medical Times/Medical Times & Gazette* (1839–85), *Glasgow Medical Journal* (1828 onwards) and *Edinburgh Medical Journal* (1805 onwards).

Although nurses existed before the Victorian era, there was no formal system of training or registration until the 1860s, when Florence Nightingale started her school at St Thomas's Hospital.

Those seeking information about ancestors who might have worked in a hospital should consult Bourne and Chicken (1994), where a summary of the scope and whereabouts of records pertaining to London and provincial hospitals is provided.

The following example is an entry from *Munk's Roll* (vol. 2):

ROBERT BANKES, M.D., was born in London, and educated at Eton, whence he was elected in 1720, to King's College, Cambridge, of which society he was a fellow. He proceeded to A.B. 1724; A.M. 1728; M.D. 1735; and the same year was appointed professor of anatomy in the university. He was admitted a Candidate of the College of Physicians 25th June 1736; and a Fellow 25th June, 1737; was Gulstonian lecturer in 1738; Censor in 1739; and Harveian orator in 1743. Dr. Bankes was chosen physician to Christ's hospital in April, 1737, and died in November, 1746.

## Pilots

In order to qualify for a pilot's licence a person had to be British, under thirty-five years of age, with several years' seagoing experience and a Master Mariner's certificate. However, in some smaller ports the pilots would be fishermen. The licence itself was issued by Trinity House, whose archive is held at the London Guildhall. There are no records before 1808, but MS 30193 does contain a list of those pilots who were working in the outports (i.e. those outside London) in 1808. After this there are the registers of London pilots' licences (1808–1929; MS 30172, indexed in MS 30173A) and the registers of outports pilots' licences (1808–76; MS 30174). These give a pilot's age, residence, qualifications and physical description.

## Police

*Metropolitan Police*

The origins of the modern police force can be traced back to 1748, when Henry Fielding created the 'Bow Street Runners' to reinforce the decisions of London magistrates. Formal police records do not begin until September 1829, when Robert Peel, the then Home Secretary, formed the Metropolitan Police force, whose initial area of operation was limited to any place within a 7-mile radius of London's Charing Cross train station. The size and scope of the police improved with time, but it was not until after 1839 that their jurisdiction increased significantly. As might be expected, all the early police were men; women did not serve in the force until 1919.

The earliest police records are held at TNA: PRO. The only ones that cover the pre-Metropolitan Police era are the entry books held in class MEPO 1, but I am not sure how useful they are to the genealogist.

From 1829 the earliest Metropolitan Police recruits had to be literate, physically fit and 5 feet 7 inches or more in height. On joining, each officer was given a warrant number; these are often referred to in the records. The Metropolitan Police was broken into a number of divisions (each denoted by a letter, e.g. 'K division'), each of which operated within a specific area of London.

An excellent guide to tracing police ancestors is Shearman (2000). Metropolitan Police records may be found under the following classes at TNA: PRO.

MEPO 4/31–32 – Registers that record the appointment of officers between September 1829 and March 1830. They are organised numerically by warrant number (between 1 and 3247), so unless you know your ancestor's warrant number or approximate date of joining, it may be better to look at the alphabetical registers first (see below). If the officer was removed from the force, the reason will be recorded.

MEPO 4/333 – Alphabetical register of police officers joining between December 1830 and December 1842. Includes the officer's physical details and the names and addresses of any referees. (MEPO 4/334–338 cover the years 1843–1933.)

HO 65/26 – Alphabetical register of police officers serving the force between 1829 and 1836. This gives information on an officer's career, including details of promotion and disciplinary action.

MEPO 4/2 – A list of officers who died while on service. It covers October 1829 to December 1889 and lists the cause of death. An index to this exists in MEPO 4/488.

MEPO 5/1–90 – Details of officers' pensions can be found in here, among other financial details and correspondence relating to the Office of the Receiver. The receipt of a pension was not an automatic right before 1890 but was left to the discretion of the police authorities.

MEPO 7 – Annual registers (1829 onwards) of police orders. These contain information on personnel matters including promotions, transfers, dismissals and retirements. Confidential notices are also contained here.

MEPO 2 – This contains general correspondence relating to the running and organisation of the police as well as some of the investigations and special duties they had to perform. It covers the years 1816–1994 and contains over 11,000 files, but before 1882 the correspondence was reorganised under subject headings, which makes searching for individual names difficult. Additional early police administrative and other papers may be found in MEPO 3 and MEPO 4.

The following example is taken from MEPO 4/333 and concerns the entry for John William Jeffries; it gives a brief summary of his career in the police and provides information (such as his warrant number and date of resignation) that can be used when searching further records:

| | |
|---|---|
| DATE OF APPLICATION: | August 22 1830 |
| NAME: | Jeffries John William |
| No. OF WARRANT: | 13,877 |
| REMOVAL FROM FORCE: | Resigned |
| DATE: | 17 Jan 1837 |
| BY WHOM RECOMMENDED: | J L Brown, Briar House, Hackney |
| | WM Bright, 5 Whitechapel Road |

P. Or⁶

22 Feb.
1838

The following Gratuities are allowed by the Commissioners to be received.

| | | | | | |
|---|---|---|---|---|---|
| ✓ PS | F. | Fryer | E. | 15 | 2/6 |
| ✓ PC | James | Robinson | „ | 23 | 2/6 |
| ✓ PS | John | Collison | I. | 12 | 5/- |
| ✓ PC | G. P. | Smith | „ | 143 | 5/- |
| ✓ „ | Thomas | Aylesbury | „ | 156 | 2/6 |
| ✓ PS | Henry | Lupton | „ | 7 | 2/- |
| ✓ PC | J. | Grugeon | N. | 27 | 7/- |
| ✓ „ | George | Hale | „ | 63 | 2/6 |
| ✓ „ | J. | Thompson | S | 53 | 1/- |
| ✓ „ | T. | Bell | „ | 70 | 1/- |
| ✓ „ | T. | Fletcher | „ | 79 | 1/- |
| ✓ „ | C. | Atkins | „ | 91 | 1/- |
| ✓ „ | J. | Rendal | „ | 98 | 1/- |
| ✓ „ | C. | Tombs | „ | 147 | 1/- |
| ✓ „ | S. | Ruggles | „ | 175 | 1/- |

The following Police Constable is
dismissed and will receive Pay till the date a-
gainst his name.
James Pack P. Division.
for being absent from a part of his Beat from
1 6block am. till 4 am. and when found was
in Liquor — 5ᵗʰ Report pay 20ᵗʰ instant.
P. C Thomas W. Earney V. Division is reinstated
without Pay for time Suspended.

*A page from the Metropolitan Police order book for 22 February 1838. It records the dismissal of Constable Samuel Pack for being drunk on duty. (TNA: PRO)*

*City of London Police*

The City of London Police did not come into being until 1839 and were (and remain) a separate body from the Metropolitan Police. Before this the City's streets were controlled by day and night patrols made up of marshalmen and constables. The Corporation of London Record Office (CLRO) holds various records relating to these patrols, including the patrol registers from 1802 to 1816, which contain the names of the constables. Among other records held at the CLRO are warrant books and personnel files (from 1832 onwards), which are indexed and record the name, age, date of joining and marital status of new recruits, and various minutes from the Court of Aldermen (1825–43, not indexed) and the Court of Common Council (1811–1926, indexed). For further details see CLRO Information Sheet 20 or Shearman (2000).

## Postal Workers

The Post Office dates back to 1635, when it was founded by Charles I; in 1656 it was formally incorporated into the government, whereupon it became known as the General Post Office. Few records survive from before 1666 (thanks to the Great Fire of London), and it is really only from the start of the eighteenth century onwards (when the Post Office became more organised) that documents of use to family historians begin to be found.

All documents relating to the Post Office's history are to be found at the Royal Mail Archive, Freeling House, Phoenix Place, London WC1X 0DL (tel: 020 7239 2570; email: heritage@royalmail.com). Entry is free; the search room is modern and well equipped and the staff helpful. Further details can be found on the website: www.royalmailgroup.com/heritage. Comprehensive guides are available on this website and in the search room.

For pre-Victorian times the most useful records for family historians are those relating to postal workers' pensions. Most senior postal workers received a pension but the families of those who died or who were invalided out of the service or (in the case of women) left to marry, also received gratuities. The pre-1860 pension and gratuity information is to be found in annual volumes of correspondence between the Post Office and the Treasury, part of which includes details of the money paid out to pensioned postal workers. These volumes are located under classmark POST 1 and there is an index of those that paid out in this way at the start of each annual volume.

Further information about an ancestor may be obtained from the Post Office's minute books, which date back to 1792 and are to be found under classmark POST 35. The minute books contain details of promotions, appointments, reprimands, accidents at work and dismissals. Minute books were made annually and each contains indexes for names, places, departments and subjects.

It can be difficult to find information about an ancestor working in the postal service before Victorian times. My only attempt was to try to trace a sub-postmaster who operated the post office in Stoke Ferry, a small Norfolk village in the late 1750s, but I could find nothing at all. According to the staff at the Archive, the post office concerned was so small that its accounts were probably incorporated within those of the main branch at nearby King's Lynn.

## Printers, Publishers, Booksellers and Stationers

Before the late eighteenth century many publishers and printers were small businesses that usually operated out of small shops and that would print a mixture of pamphlets, books and newspapers for money.

Published biographical sources include Plomer *et al.* (1907, 1922, 1932) and McKerrow (1910), which between them cover booksellers and printers between 1557 and 1775, and the more generalised Timperley (1889). Other than this, if you suspect that an ancestor was a publisher, you could try searching for works that they may have printed on the British Library's catalogue or (more time-consuming) searching contemporary newspapers for advertisements for published works that your ancestor may have produced.

Between 1554 and 1709 copyright concerning printed works was exclusively handled by the Stationers' and Newspaper Makers' Company, although copyright continued to be registered there until 1923. The current Stationers' Hall library (Ave Maria Lane, London EC4M 7DD; www.stationers.org) holds the copyright registers from 1556 to 1842, with those up to 1709 having been published in Arber (1785–94) and Eyre (1913–14). Other Stationers' Hall records include membership records (1554 to now) and its court record (1602 to now). The entire archive has been microfilmed and is available in a number of British, American and Australian university libraries (see the Stationers' Hall website for a list).

## Psychiatrists

The Association of Medical Officers of Asylums and Hospitals for the Insane was founded in 1841 but later changed its name first to Medico-Psychological Association and then, in 1971, to the Royal College of Psychiatrists. Their membership archive, which is held at their library (tel: 020 7235 2351; email: infoservices@rcpsych.ac.uk), dates back to the 1850s; members were listed in the *Journal of Mental Science* published from 1855 onwards.

## Scientists and Engineers

Before the mid-nineteenth century science was not so much a career as a hobby of the rich and well-heeled. The few professional scientists who did exist had often trained as medics (see surgeons and physicians), were in the Church (see above) or had obtained university degrees in other fields (see Chapter 9).

Good general resources containing biographical information on early scientists include Taylor (1956, 1966), who provides biographies of mathematicians between 1485 and 1840, many of whom had influence in other scientific fields such as instrument making, surveying, astronomy, etc., and Yolton *et al.* (1999) and Pyle (2000a, 2000b), who provide biographies of seventeenth- to nineteenth-century philosophers, a field in which many early scientists practised. For a biographical dictionary of civil engineers between 1550 and 1830 see Skempton (2002).

For centuries the Royal Society (6–9 Carlton House Terrace, London SW1Y 5AG; www.royalsoc.ac.uk) was one of the world's foremost learned institutions, with many of Britain's leading scientific brains among its ranks. Its archive dates back to 1660 and contains many papers, letters and minutes related to its administration and its members; it is searchable through the website.

From the sixteenth century it was possible to safeguard the intellectual rights to an invention by enrolling details (specifications) of it with the Chancery. If accepted, the Chancery would issue a letter patent (see Section 17.2) to the inventor, granting him or her exclusive rights to exploit it. TNA: PRO has several indexes (by subject, chronology and patentee name) to the whereabouts of individual patent specifications within the Chancery records. The British Library holds a printed list of all patent specifications filed before 1853.

## Stockbrokers and Jobbers

The London Stock Exchange received its familiar name in 1773, although its roots date back to the seventeenth century; its archive is housed in the London Guildhall Library. In addition to much information about the companies, it also contains an archive of applications made by brokers (who bought shares from jobbers to sell to the public) and jobbers (who sold them only to brokers on commission) to become members of the Stock Exchange (classmark MS 17957) as well as an annual list of approved members (classmark MS 19311). Both of these date back to 1802. Further information about access can be obtained from the library staff or from its website.

## Surgeons

A surgeon is traditionally a person who performed invasive operations (such as the removal of Samuel Pepys's famous 'stone'), although in practice many different styles of medical practitioner adopted the term; it was often also adopted by those completely unqualified in medicine as a means of enhancing their status. Wallis *et al.* (1988) includes surgeons in his list of eighteenth-century medical practitioners (*see* Physicians, above, for more details). Before 1745 all London surgeons belonged to the Barber-Surgeons' Company of London (*see* Barbers and Barber-Surgeons). After this time they formed the Company of Surgeons, which, in 1801 became the Royal College of Surgeons. Power (1930–81) contains biographical information on members of the Company of Surgeons (1745–1800) or the Royal College of Surgeons (1801 onwards).

The post-1745 records are held at the Royal College of Surgeons' library (see above); it will undertake a search of its records for a fee (£15 in 2006) but generally discourages this unless there is a clear connection between an ancestor and the College.

From the early sixteenth century some ecclesiastical authorities had the right to license surgeons operating within their jurisdiction. Some of their records survive. Those for the Bishop of London can be found at the Guildhall Library (1627–1767) and the London Metropolitan Archives (1529–1685) and are listed in Bloom and James (1935). Those for the Dean and Chapter of St Paul's Cathedral (1700–13) are also at the Guildhall Library, while those covered by the Archbishop of Canterbury (1535–1775) are indexed in an unpublished manuscript, 'A Directory of Doctors and Surgeons Licensed by the Archbishop of Canterbury' (by M. Barber), held at Lambeth Palace library.

Biographies of surgeons who served in the army between 1660 and 1960 can be found in Peterkin *et al.* (1968). (For naval surgeons from 1793 see *Naval List*, Section 11.1.) A good general resource for eighteenth-century medics is Wallis *et al.* (1988), but also try university biographical registers (see Chapter 9).

## Surveyors and Mapmakers

Those seeking information on land surveyors or local mapmakers should consult Bendall (1997), which provides biographies of those working in Britain and Ireland between 1530 and 1850.

## Trinity House Pensioners

Those who were employed by Trinity House could petition the corporation for a pension or for the use of one of its almshouses. These petitions survive in the Trinity House archive now held at London's Guildhall Library. They may provide much detail about an individual's life, including information on career, circumstances and close family members.

The main resources are the series of petitions 1787–1854 (MS 30218A and MS 30218B, respectively). Both are indexed in *Trinity House Petitions*, a copy of which is available in the reading room. Another resource is the registers of almspeople and pensioners (1729–1946, MS 30218), which give the applicant's age and a description of their circumstances. There is no index to this.

## Victuallers' Records

The licensing of brewers and sellers of alcohol has long been a problem. In medieval times the quality and sale of alcohol were regulated by the manors on which it was brewed, but from 1552 publicans were required to get a licence to sell alcohol from a Justice of the Peace. The licence required them to run an orderly establishment, and from 1619 this licensing became an annual affair.

Alcohol sellers generally had to apply for their licences through the local courts, which means that details of their applications can be found in the records relating to the quarter sessions, petty sessions and assizes (see Chapter 12), as well as in more local parish records (Section 4.6). Gibson and Hunter (2001) provide a detailed guide to the intricacies associated with the licensing of alcohol sales and the whereabouts of surviving records, while Fowler (2003) describes records relating to brewers and publicans.

## Watermen and Lightermen

The existence of the London watermen dates back to the times when the capital city had few permanent bridges, thus forcing people to travel from shore to shore by boat. As the city grew in size, so there was also a need for boats to ferry people up and down the river to and from London's satellite villages.

The increased number of permanent bridges saw a decline in the number of watermen but, as the Port of London grew in size, so many former watermen were employed to ferry goods from cargo ships to the shore; such people were known as lightermen.

Like many urban trades, that of watermen and lightermen was regulated by a guild, in this case the Company of Watermen, which was founded by an Act of Parliament in 1566 (although watermen had been regulated since the twelfth century) and which, in 1700, incorporated the Woodmongers' Company, which had hitherto represented the lightermen.

To become a waterman or lighterman involved undergoing a period of apprenticeship during which the individual would be bonded to a master. At the end of the apprenticeship period the master and his apprentice had to undergo an examination before finally being given the Freedom of the Company. In the majority of cases it was traditional for an apprenticed waterman to be bonded to his father or some other close male relative. In a few instances a boy would be bonded to his mother, especially if the father died during the apprenticeship period. It was not uncommon for several successive generations of a family to be watermen.

Records for the Company of Watermen and Lightermen are held at the Guildhall Library, London. Most have been microfilmed and are on open access; there is a guidebook to the records available at the library (see also Harvey, 1998). These include:

Apprentice bindings 1688–1908 (MS 6289)

Apprentices' affidavit books 1759–1897 (MS 6291) – these include birth and baptism details

Quarterage books 1764–1917 (MSS 6402 and 6819) – these include people's addresses, mooring details, subscriptions paid and dates of death

Also available are separate records relating to the regulation and discipline of company members (these include records from the Court of Complaint), records of individual ferry services (including the names of the watermen who operated them) and a register of lighters, barges and passenger boats, which gives people's names and addresses. A further register (MS 30335) of ex-mariners who became watermen between 1829 and 1864 exists from the Corporation of Trinity House (*see also* Trinity House Pensioners).

Many of the watermen apprenticeship records are available to buy on microfiche or CD-ROM from Trueflare Ltd (hometown.aol.com/rjcindex/trueflare.html; 19 Bellevue Road, Bexleyheath, Kent, DA6 8ND), which also offers a consultation service. Those wishing to know more about the lives of watermen and lightermen in general should consult Mayhew (1983).

On my father's side of the family I am descended from a family called Smith, a name that is so common that it has caused me many headaches. Using the civil registration records I was able to trace my Smith ancestry to James John Smith, who started life as a waterman in London's Limehouse district. Using the apprenticeship records (bindings and affidavits) at the Guildhall, I discovered that James had been apprenticed to his father, James William Smith, in 1869. James William Smith's apprenticeship was to a John James Parkinson, but two of his brothers (whom I traced using the 1841 census) had been apprenticed to their father, John Thomas Smith, of Greenwich, Kent. John Thomas Smith had been apprenticed to his father John in 1816 and he to his father John in 1780. Thus the Smiths' association with the Company of Watermen has made tracing their ancestry a great deal easier than it would otherwise have been.

# CHAPTER NINE

# EDUCATION RECORDS

Before the Victorian era education was neither compulsory nor paid for by the government, which meant that a sizeable proportion of the population had little or no education and were functionally illiterate. Among my ancestors I have some who were, to judge from their writing on various documents, literate in the 1550s and yet, strangely, in the 1700s some of their descendants could sign only by making a mark. Some of my other ancestors, who worked as labourers, were unable to sign their names in the 1840s.

During the medieval era the Church was responsible for much of the education in the country, although it mostly taught only recruits to its monasteries. The sixteenth century saw the establishment of fee-paying grammar schools, which would educate the sons of the local middle-class families. The grammar schools increased in numbers until every large town had at least one, a good many of which are still in existence today. For those children whose parents could not afford the grammar schools (or whose children could not get a scholarship to one) there were always Church and charity schools, many of which were wholly or partly funded by the benevolence of the rich: if all else failed, there was always the local Sunday school. Those who excelled at school and who had career ambitions in law, the Church, civil service or other elite fields could apply to university. A general discussion of education records may be found in Chapman (1999).

## School Records

All schools, whether grammar, charity or other, kept a register of their pupils that normally contained details about their background and other information. Unfortunately, the survival of such school registers is not great, especially from more community-based schools, which often moved location and could be short lived. None the less it may be worth checking with CROs or the Access to Archives website to see if any registers or other documents have survived. Among fee-paying grammar schools the situation is slightly better, as many of these institutions have been little interfered with over the centuries. Some grammar schools, including one for which a relation of mine worked, hold registers and other information going back to the sixteenth century. However, in most cases you will need to get in touch with the school itself, as few of these records are ever published.

For a list of schools that exist or existed in the region where your ancestors lived, try the VCH series or, if this is not available, local history guides. Some registers have been published, especially from the more established and wealthy schools (e.g. Eton and Harrow). The SoG and Institute of Historical Research hold many of these. The following example has been selected at random from the published register of Giggleswick, a grammar school dating back to the fifteenth century, and gives an idea as to the sort of information that these registers may contain:

Goodread, Thomas, son of John Goodread, Giggleswick; Christ's Coll., Camb., March 1656–7; B.A. 1660–1; M.A. 1664. Thos. Goodread M.A., became Headmaster of Ashbourne Grammar School, 17th Dec. 1666; was removed 17th April, 1672. Vicar of Ashbourne, 1669–1702. He had trouble with his parish: on 14th July 1696, he was suspended on articles presented by the churchwardens and parishioners: suspension removed 29th July, on his giving a bond to repair his houses, and on promising not to be seen in any public house in Ashbourne or Mapleton. Died 1702. Buried in Ashbourne Church. M.I. 'The memory of the just is blessed.'

## University Records

Before 1832 the only two universities in England were Oxford and Cambridge. In response to the demands of historians and genealogists, published biographical registers have been compiled that give details of the students who attended both universities from their earliest times to around 1900. For Oxford see Foster (1891–2) and Emden (1974); for Cambridge see Venn and Venn (1922–54; now available on CD-ROM) and Emden (1963).

These volumes contain much information about each student, including age, date of matriculation (admission to the university), college attended, plus other details such as previous schooling, father's name, age, further career details and date of death.

Many of the individual colleges have also published their own registers containing biographical information. The SoG and Institute for Historical Research libraries hold copies of these.

University College London, founded in 1826, the University of Durham, founded in 1832, and the University of London, founded in 1836 have not published their registers and so they remain part of their archives.

If your ancestor does not appear in an English university, try looking at the records of Scottish universities or Trinity College, Dublin, some of which have their own published registers (e.g. Addison, 1898; Burtchaell and Sadlier, 1924).

In my own pre-Victorian family history there is a remarkable lack of university graduates. However, in the 1640 will of Elizabeth Chambers (who was the widow of Robert Chambers, brother to my ancestor Samuel) she makes reference to her 'sister Mary Bainbrigg, now wife of Thomas Bainbrigg D^ct. in divinity and Master of Christ's College in the University of Cambridge'. I checked Venn and Venn (1922–54) and found an entry for Thomas Bainbridge and, as Elizabeth Chambers's will mentions that Thomas had a son called Edward, was able to confirm that this Thomas was Mary's husband. Using the information given, I was able to confirm from parish registers that there was a Bainbridge family resident in Kirkby Lonsdale in the mid-sixteenth century, although the only baptism for a Thomas Bainbrigg was in 1543, which is probably too old for Mary's husband but possibly the right age for his father or an uncle. The volume also contained an entry for Thomas's son Edward, who matriculated in 1642 and gained his MA in 1650.

**BAINBRIDGE, THOMAS.** Matric. pens. from CHRIST'S, 1593. Of Westmorland, Probably of Kirkby Lonsdale. B.A. 1596–7; M.A. 1600; D.D. 1616. Fellow, 1599. Master of Christ's, 1622–46. Received the King when he was Vice-Chancellor in 1627–8. Incorp. at Oxford, 1603. Died in College, 1646. Buried Sept. 9. Donor to Christ's College. Will proved (V.C.C.) 1646. Father of Edward (1642). (*D.N.B.*; *Peile*, I, 207.)

CHAPTER TEN

# ARMY RECORDS

From medieval times England and Wales have had a periodic need for large numbers of soldiers and commanders in order to defend against enemies from abroad but also from within the state. Such armies would be raised only on an ad hoc basis and would be disbanded again as soon as the trouble passed (see Chambers, 2005, for details of medieval soldiery). As Britain entered the early modern era, so long-standing rivalries with neighbouring countries created a need for a more permanent and better-trained army. This began to occur in the seventeenth century, and by the eighteenth century the British Army was one of the largest in the world. Men from all sections of society joined the army, with the wealthy buying their way in as officers and the poorer people joining as soldiers. It is therefore not unusual to discover an ancestor who served in the British Army. This chapter will show how to obtain further information about a military ancestor. In addition, Fowler and Spencer (2000) provide a guide to the army records held at TNA: PRO, while Kitzmiller (1988) provides a general history of the British Army, a discussion of its genealogical records and gives some case studies in tracing British Army ancestors.

## 10.1. SOLDIERY BEFORE 1660

### Muster Rolls

Before the English Civil War, England and Wales did not have a regular peacetime army; instead, in times of war troops would be drawn from the general population. From 1522 onwards local sheriffs and large landholders were required to make lists of able-bodied men who could be drafted into local militia in the event of war. These lists are known as muster rolls and they may contain the names of many local men, usually aged between fifteen and sixty, and often include those who are disabled or who are known draft-dodgers. Before the Civil War (see below), the muster rolls represent one of the few reliable means of finding out whether an ancestor was in the army.

Muster rolls were not routinely collected by any official body. The TNA: PRO muster rolls are found in a number of archives relating to the Exchequer and state, including E 101, E 36 and E 315, but many have found their way into county record offices and other archives; some are in private hands. Gibson (1989) provides a list of the whereabouts of most of the known muster rolls; use this to find out whether there are any rolls that might cover areas where your ancestors lived. Gibson's list includes those muster rolls that have been transcribed and published by local history societies and others. For resources relating to medieval soldiery see Chambers (2005).

The following example concerns the muster roll for foot soldiers raised from parishes within Flitt Hundred in Bedfordshire in 1683 (taken from Bedfordshire Historical Record Society, vol. 71).

Flitt Hundred Militia Foote
Capt. Palmers Company

*Silsoe* 2 M [muskets] 1 C [corslet]
Jo. Bland
Wm. Whittamore
Tho. Godfrey
Tho. Layton

*Flitton* 4 M
Rich. Honnor
Tho. Astry
Robt. Meyne
Wm. Lake

## The Civil War and the Interregnum, 1642–60

The outbreak of hostilities between Parliamentary and Royalist armies occurred in 1642, but the chaotic way in which army regiments would be created and disbanded at short notice led to few formal records being created. However, some references may be found to officers serving on both sides of the war.

Peacock (1983) provides a list of Royalist and Parliamentary officers at the outbreak of war, while Newman (1981) is a biographical dictionary of Royalist officers from 1642 to 1660. Other references to officers, including appointments and commissions, may be found among the state papers (see Chapter 16) and in Green (1875–86; 1888; 1889–93). An original pamphlet from 1663 entitled *A List of Officers Claiming to the Sixty Thousand Pounds* is available at the British Library; it refers to a specialist payout to Royalist army officers made by King Charles II. Laurence (1990) provides a list of Parliamentary army chaplains before 1651.

The sources for ordinary soldiers are scarcer, although some muster rolls do exist for the Parliamentary forces (see above and Gibson, 1989). In 1649 the government began to sell off former Royalist property in order to raise enough money to give the army its back pay. In TNA: PRO E 121 each royal property has a certificate relating to its sale, attached to which is a statement of arrears that lists the names of soldiers (usually belonging to regiments local to the sale) who would be paid from the proceeds. The certificates are arranged by county and are not indexed. For other more obscure resources relating to the Civil War and interregnum try Aylmer and Morrill (1979).

## 10.2. ARMY OFFICERS' RECORDS

Army officers could hold their rank only after receiving a royal commission, which could be either awarded (usually for having undergone suitable training or as a promotion) or, more commonly, purchased. The ability to purchase a rank meant that most officers came from well-off backgrounds, with promotions from the normal soldiery being rare. Even after the abolition of purchased commissions in 1871, officers still tended to be drawn from the minor gentry, with those who 'came up through the ranks' subjected to much prejudice.

Before hunting for original documents associated with an officer, it is best to establish something of that person's career using the army lists. These may give you all the information you need; at least they will provide valuable details that will make any further searching much easier.

### Army Lists

Lists of the names of army officers, arranged by regiment and rank, were made at regular intervals from 1702 onwards and can be found in TNA: PRO WO 64; a name index to the years before 1754 is available on microfilm.

From 1740, annual printed lists of army officers were produced that, although appearing under several slightly differing titles, are usually referred to simply as the *Army List*. Many larger libraries hold sets of these, but they may also be found in TNA: PRO WO 65. Each volume is arranged by regiment and contains the officer's name, rank and date of promotion; after 1766 the volumes are indexed by name. The *Army List* represents the most convenient means of finding and tracing information about an officer. For earlier years, lists of commissioned officers from 1661 to 1727 have been compiled by Dalton (1892–1904; 1910–12).

In addition to these national army lists, there are many individual publications that give biographical information on the careers and lives of the officers belonging to a particular regiment. For example, Edwards (1898) lists all the officers in the Royal Engineers from 1660. To find such publications try searching the online catalogues of the British Library and other large libraries using the regiment name as a keyword. The British Library website (www.bl.uk/collections/social/srvlists.html) holds a separate and detailed list of its publications that list army and navy personnel.

The example below is from the *Army List* of 1798 and shows the officers of the 32nd Cornish Foot Regiment.

| Rank | Name | Rank in the Regiment | Army |
|------|------|------|------|
| Colonel | Ralph, Earl of Rofs. | 17 May 1781 | Gen. 3 May 96 |
| Lieut. Colonel | Richard Northey | 5 Nov. 1793 | Col. 26 Jan. 97 |
| | Arthur Forbes | 21 Jul. 96 | 6 Jul. 96 |
| Captain | Will. Aug. Johnson | 7 Jan. 1795 | 23 Apr. 94 |
| | John Wood | 9 do. | 12 Nov. 94 |
| | John Hicks | 9 Feb. | |
| | Edward Baynes | 25 Mar. | Major 9 Nov. 96 |

## Documents Relating to Commissions

Records relating to the issue of a commission can be found in the commission books held in TNA: PRO WO 25/1–88 (series 1: years 1660–1873) and WO 25/89–111 (series 2: years 1728–1818). These are not indexed, although a series of commission books held in WO 25/112–117 (years 1760–1805) do have indexes attached to them (see the online Catalogue for details). Biographical and career details tend to be sparser in the later books.

The written correspondence of the Secretary at War, which includes many letters relating to individual commissions and the circumstances relating to their issue, can be found in WO 4/513–520 (years 1704–1858); these are indexed and are noted as a good source of biographical information for commissioned officers. Another good source is the Commander in Chief's memoranda in WO 31, which hold information on appointments, promotions and resignations, and include the letters of application relating to this. It is sometimes possible to find summaries of an individual's army career and/or information concerning family background. The memoranda are not indexed.

For those officers commissioned before around 1700 it may be worth checking among the published calendars relating to the state papers.

## Service Records and Personal Information

Summaries of officers' service records from 1764 onwards may be found in WO 76 (years 1764–1915). These contain a great deal of useful information, including a list of the different ranks held, where the individual served and, if applicable, the names of his wife and children. An index to these records exists at TNA: PRO. Reports of officers' marriages from 1830 onwards (although some certificates date to 1799) may be found in WO 25/3239–3245; an index exists for those marriages before 1851.

## 164    Thirty-second (or the Cornwall) Regt. of Foot.

| Rank. | Name. | Rank in the Regiment. | Rank in the Army. | |
|---|---|---|---|---|
| Colonel - - | Ralph, *Earl of* Rofs | 17May1781 | Gen. 3May | 96 |
| Lieut. Colonel { | Richard Northey | 5Nov.1793 | Col. 26Jan. | 97 |
| | Arthur Forbes | 21July 96 | 6July 96 | |
| Major - - { | William Maxwell | 29July1796 | 7Nov. 94 | |
| | James Manfergh | 1Aug. 97 | | |
| Captain - { | Will. Aug. Johnfon | 7Jan.1795 | 23Apr. 94 | |
| | John Wood | 9do. | 12Nov. 94 | |
| | John Hicks | 9Feb. | | |
| | Edward Baynes | 25Mar. | Major 9Nov. | 96 |
| | John White | 20May | | |
| | Webfter Harrifon | 24Aug. | | |
| | George Evans | 2Sept. | 19Apr. 94 | |
| | John Bennet | 9do. | | |
| | William Davis | 1Oct. | 18Sept. 94 | |
| | John Prieftley | do. | 31May 95 | |
| Captain Lieut. and Captain { | Robert Coote | 4Oct.1797 | 29May 96 | |
| Lieutenant { | Thomas Crawley | 2Oct.1794 | | |
| | Annefley Gore | 3do. | | |
| | Henry White | 29July 95 | | |
| | Jonas Fitzgerald | 1Oct. | | |
| | ——— Sherfton | 4Nov. | | |
| | John Rowland | do. | | |
| | William Harrifon | 20Jan. 96 | | |
| | Jonathan Short | 10Feb. | | |
| | Matthew Evans O'Brien | 4Apr. | | |
| | William Handcock | 12do. | | |
| | Alexander Mackay | 13July | | |
| | Archibald Boyd | 3Aug. | | |
| | Andrew Douglas | 15Sept. | 7July 93 | |
| | Henry Rofs Lewen | 24May 97 | | |

*A page from the* Army List *volume for 1798 detailing the rank and basic career information for officers from the 32nd Regiment of Foot.* (Author's collection)

Probably the greatest resource of family information relating to officers is to be found in WO 42, where copies of officers' baptism, marriage and death certificates may be found, together with other documents such as personal papers and, in the case of those who died in service, wills, administrations and their widows' or children's pension applications. These records cover the years 1755–1881 and are for the most part arranged alphabetically by surname. They are available only on microfilm and are indexed.

In the absence of an army pension, officers could either sell their commission to someone else (and be free of the army forever) or keep their commission and go on to half-pay, which meant that they were still available for duty should the need arise. A dead officer's widow also had the right to apply for a pension from the army, although she could lose this if she remarried.

Documents pertaining to half-pay may be found in PMG 4 (years 1737–1921, arranged by regiment) and WO 24/660–747 (years 1713–1809, arranged chronologically). Details of widows' pensions are in PMG 11 (years 1808–1920) and WO 25/3020–3045 for full-pay officers (years 1735–1811, arranged chronologically with gaps) and WO 25/3046–3058 (years 1755–78, arranged chronologically) for half-pay officers. Other miscellaneous documents relating to the Paymaster General's army accounts may be found between PMG 1 and PMG 14; see the TNA: PRO online Catalogue for details.

Most of the other valuable personal information relating to officers is to be found in WO 25 (some of which is covered above), although unfortunately the only practical means of seeing what is held in this vast collection is to browse through it using the TNA: PRO online Catalogue.

## 10.3. SOLDIERS' RECORDS

Individual soldiers serving in the army were not subject to the same level of record keeping as their officers, which makes finding information about them more difficult. Especially problematic are a lack of general army indexes in the pre-Victorian era and, between around 1660 and 1730, a general lack of decent records at all.

Most pre-Victorian soldiers' records are arranged first by regiment and then by year. Thus, in order to trace an individual soldier's career it is helpful to know to which regiment he belonged and roughly when he was serving. However, this chapter will assume that you do not know your ancestor's regiment and so starts by looking at records that relate to the end of a soldier's career, as these are easier to search. This means that you should begin by looking for a soldier's discharge and/or pension records or records that relate to his death or desertion. Those seeking further information about soldiers' records should consult Fowler and Spencer (2000) and Kitzmiller (1988).

## Tracing a Soldier's Pension Records

From 1681 soldiers who served their full term of service or who were invalided out of the army could receive a pension from the Royal Hospital, Chelsea. (A second Royal Hospital also existed in Kilmainham, Ireland, for Irish army soldiers; see Bevan, 2000, for more details.) Most soldiers received an out-pension (i.e. they were not resident at the Royal Hospital itself), but the Hospital did also take permanent inmates, known as in-pensioners.

The majority of the Royal Hospital's pension records are held in TNA: PRO WO 97. This is the best place to begin your hunt for a soldier's records, as they are searchable using the TNA: PRO online Catalogue. These records cover the years 1760–1913 and contain information on the careers of soldiers who became pensioners of the Royal Hospital, Chelsea. Try searching for your ancestor using The Catalogue (but make sure you restrict your search to class WO 97). If your ancestor is there, this will tell you his name, place of birth, regiment, age at discharge and service years. For example:

WO 97/161/24: CHRISTOPHER CHAMBERS Born CAMBRIDGE, Cambridgeshire Served in 2nd Foot Guards Discharged aged 40; 1824–1844

If your ancestor has a pension record in WO 97, you may not need to go any further, as these are an excellent source of family history material, especially the pre-Victorian records. A typical soldier's papers might include his attestation papers (from when he signed up), discharge form (from when he left), plus various records of service, affidavits and other evidence needed to obtain a pension. In among these you should find your ancestor's age, birthplace and an outline of his career, including commendations and medals awarded. Details of next of kin may also be included.

There may be several reasons why your ancestor cannot be found in these records. It may be because his pension/discharge details are in another index. Those awarded Chelsea Hospital out-pensions between 1787 and 1813 might have records in WO 121/1–136; these are also searchable using The Catalogue.

Information on out-pensioners, including some not in WO 97, may be found in the admission books held in WO 116 (invalided soldiers, years 1715–1882, arranged chronologically, indexed from 1832) and WO 117 (service pensions, years 1823–1913, arranged chronologically). These give details of the soldier's age, regiment, birthplace and reason for discharge. In addition there are admission books held in WO 120 (years 1715–1857) that list pensioners by regiment. TNA: PRO holds an index for some of the foot regiments.

If your ancestor was in receipt of a pension and was without next of kin, he could, if aged fifty-five or older, apply to become a resident (or in-pensioner) at the Royal Hospital. Records relating to in-pensioners can be found in WO 23/124–134 (years 1702–1813, arranged chronologically) and include muster rolls for the Hospital (1702–89) and inventories of residents (1795–1813). From 1824 admission books were kept: WO 23/162.

Although I turned out not to be related to him, I tracked down the Royal Chelsea Hospital's service record for Christopher Chambers, who shared the same name as a member of my family and who lived in the same region. Christopher's service record covers several pages and includes many details of his army career in the Coldstream Guards, including promotions, a physical description, a medical report, his discharge and the proceedings of the regimental board. From this it is possible to find that, before he entered the army, Christopher was a labourer in Wicken parish and that he was discharged from the army because of disability. The surgeon notes that 'his habits are bad from dishonesty', something borne out by a period of imprisonment noted on his record.

## Other Discharge Records

If your ancestor's pension records cannot be traced, this may be because he did not receive a regular army pension. Instead he may have purchased his discharge, the records for which are in WO 25/3845–3847 (years 1817–24, arranged by regiment, no index), or he may have requested a discharge, WO 25/3848 and 3849 (years 1830–8, arranged by regiment, no index) or he may have received a pension under special circumstances, WO 25/3850 (years 1830–56, arranged by regiment, no index).

It is also possible that your ancestor was one of those unfortunate soldiers who died on active service. If so, then his next of kin may have received a payment and/or the soldier's personal effects. Registers of the authorities to deal with a dead soldier's possessions are in WO 25/2966–2971 (years 1810–22, arranged chronologically) and give the soldier's name, regiment, death date, list of effects and details of next of kin. A register of deceased soldiers can be found in WO 25/2972 (years 1824–58, arranged chronologically).

It is, of course, possible that your ancestor may not have left the army in an honourable fashion. An index of army deserters compiled from bounty certificates (i.e. documents that were issued to the person that turned in the deserter) is located in TNA: PRO E 182. The index covers deserters captured in London, Middlesex, Bedfordshire, Berkshire, Buckinghamshire and Cambridgeshire between the years 1689 and 1830. It gives the man's name and regiment and an approximate reference to the resulting bounty certificate's location within E 182. Trying to trace bounty certificates relating to those deserters who were not caught in one of the above indexed counties is prohibitively time-consuming.

Other references to deserters include a register of those who surrendered to the authorities (WO 25/2955, years 1803–15, arranged chronologically) and registers of captured deserters in WO 25/2952–2954 (years 1813–45, indexed before 1833).

## Courts Martial

Those officers and soldiers who committed criminal offences or behaved in a manner that contravened the army's rules and regulations could find themselves placed in front of one of the military courts, which are collectively referred to as courts martial. There were several different courts martial depending on the seriousness of the offence and/or the soldier's rank; for a summary of these see McArthur (1813) or Cole (1997).

Court martial records were generated and filed by the Office of the Judge Advocate General, which was created in 1666 to act as the army's legal representative to the Crown and whose job it was to prepare the case for trial. To find out whether a soldier was subject to a court martial check the registers of court martial cases held in TNA: PRO WO 90 (cases heard abroad, years 1796–1960) and WO 91 (cases heard at home, years 1666–1704; 1806–1960; an index for the years 1806–33 exists in WO 93/1A). The register gives the soldier's name, rank, regiment, trial location, charge and sentence.

For those years not covered by the registers, try looking among the after-trial reports compiled by the Judge Advocate General. These are in WO 71/34–64 (years 1715–90, arranged chronologically).

If your ancestor was subject to a court martial, it is possible that some of the court papers may still survive. The proceedings and papers are all in WO 71, with the earliest dating to 1668. For a breakdown of these records either use the browse function in the TNA: PRO online Catalogue or consult *An Alphabetical Guide to Certain War Office and other Military Records Preserved in the Public Record Office* (List and Index Society, vol. 53, 1931), which also contains some other little-used resources referring to the courts martial.

## Other Resources

Between 1708 and 1878 each regiment was required to produce a monthly muster roll and pay lists that carried an inventory of all the serving soldiers together with their rank. A soldier's first entry will normally contain his age, while his last entry may give his birthplace and date of enlistment. The majority of muster rolls are in WO 12, where they are arranged by regiment and then by year. Those pertaining to the artillery regiments are in WO 10 and WO 69, and the engineers' regiments in WO 11 (years 1816–78).

Further information may be found in the regimental description and succession books held in WO 25/266–688 and WO 54/260–316 (years 1756–1900, arranged by regiment and then alphabetically by name). These carry details of the soldier's age, birthplace and service.

After 1761 many regiments kept records of those children born to married soldiers. Indexes to these records are available at TNA: PRO, but copies of any certificates have to be ordered from the Office for National Statistics. Details on army medals can be found in WO 100, but the lack of an index makes finding an individual's name difficult.

Some regimental records are filed separately. These include records relating to the Life and Royal Horse Guards and Household Battalion, which are to be found in WO 400/1–4 (years 1801–56, arranged by name), the Royal Artillery before 1855, which are in WO 69, and the Coldstream, Grenadier, Irish, Scots and Welsh guards, whose records are held at the Guards' Regimental Headquarters, Birdcage Walk, London SW1E 6HQ.

For a guide to where and when British regiments were operating in the past, try Kitzmiller (1988), which lists the whereabouts of each regiment between 1640 and the Second World War. As this volume explains, knowing whereabouts in the world your ancestor's regiment was stationed can be of assistance in discovering further genealogical information (e.g. entries in local church registers, etc.).

## Militias and Conscription Records

The establishment of a standing army after the English Civil War ended the practice of raising an army from the general population. However, in 1757 an Act was passed that required every county in England and Wales to establish its own militia regiment (in theory made up of volunteers) that could be trained in basic soldiery and then drawn on to help the professional army in times of crisis. This tradition lasted until after the First World War. For general guides to militia records consult Spencer (1997) or Gibson and Medlycott (2004).

To facilitate the creation and continued stocking of these regiments each parish was required to provide an annual list of all its resident males aged between eighteen and forty-five. These militia lists would be used to select able-bodied men who could serve in the county's militia regiment. Those who were selected for duty had their names entered onto a separate enrolment list. These militia lists generally give a man's name and his occupation or apprenticeship, but they may also note other circumstances, such as whether he was a poor man, whether he had children and whether he was able-bodied (sometimes a clue to any disability or injury is given; e.g. 'lame' or 'broken-bodied'). The list was usually verified by the local priest and constable.

Because (in theory) they contain the names of all a parish's adult males, militia lists are useful not just to military historians but also to the genealogist trying to find out general information. The majority of militia lists are lodged in CROs (which may also hold other militia records), but some are also to be found at TNA: PRO. For a detailed list of what records survive and where they are to be found see Gibson and Medlycott (2004). Some local history societies have published transcripts of individual or multiple militia lists. For example, Hertfordshire Family and

Population History Society has been steadily publishing the surviving militia lists for the county on a parish–by–parish basis (e.g. Hill, 1994).

Detailed information on the careers of individual militia soldiers and officers is hard to come by. Probably the best resources are to be found in TNA: PRO WO 68 (years 1759–1925), which holds such useful items as payment records, casualty lists, monthly returns and enrolment books, as well as a miscellany of other correspondence. The records are arranged by regiment and then chronologically (use the TNA: PRO online Catalogue to browse these). Additional militia pay lists and muster rolls may be found in WO 13 (1780–1878), arranged by county and then chronologically. Some militiamen were able to qualify for pensions; try checking the Chelsea Hospital admission books (see above).

# CHAPTER ELEVEN

# NAVAL AND RELATED RECORDS

## 11.1. ROYAL NAVY SERVICE RECORDS

Much of Britain's wealth and international notoriety is as a consequence of its strong and powerful navy, which through much of the early modern era was the largest and most feared in the world. Although the origins of the navy go back centuries, the first recognisable fleets did not appear until the time of Henry VIII, and it was not until the end of the English Civil War that the Fleet Royal was taken under Parliamentary control and transformed into the permanent Royal Navy. From then until the Second World War the Royal Navy was the strongest fleet in the world and was responsible for such famous victories as the Battle of Trafalgar in 1805.

During its existence the Royal Navy has employed thousands of people (almost exclusively men) as officers, ratings (ordinary seamen) or associated dockyard workers. Not all these people were there voluntarily, and in the eighteenth century shortages of sailors led to unfortunate (but often drunk) individuals being grabbed off the street and 'pressed' into service. Even so, the navy offered a good career to many poor people or to the sons of the lesser gentry, and most people with British ancestry will find that a family member was once a sailor.

Although the Royal Navy has been in existence since late medieval times, few records are preserved before the eighteenth century. Those seeking references to naval ancestors before around 1690 should try looking through the calendars associated with the state records (see Chapter 16), although for the most part only the names of senior officers are recorded.

From the late seventeenth century the majority of Royal Navy personnel records are held at TNA: PRO, although they are patchy in places. There are also significant historical records relating to individual ships and officers held at the National Maritime Museum (Greenwich, London SE10 9NF; www.nmm.ac.uk), which has online guides to its collections and an online library catalogue. The importance of the navy means that there are several detailed guides to tracing naval ancestors, including Rodger (1998) and Pappalardo (2001, 2003).

## Naval Officers' Records

There were two types of officer within the Royal Navy: commissioned officers, who held ranks (in order of increasing seniority) of Lieutenant, Master or Commander, Captain, Commodore, Rear-Admiral, Vice-Admiral and Admiral; and the more specialist warrant officers who brought with them specific skills reflected in their titles such as surgeon, carpenter, sail-maker, master and gunner. For a general guide to officers' and other naval records try Rodger (1998) and Pappalardo (2001, 2003).

*Published Resources*

There are many published biographies and lists of naval officers from the early modern era, most of which are available at the British Library, TNA: PRO, SoG library and larger institutional libraries. The standard published annual lists of officers are *Steele's Navy List*, published from 1782 and the *Navy List*, published from 1814. These provide the officer's name, the ship, port or other place where he was serving, rank and date of last promotion. The lists are ordered by rank and then by year of commission, although later *Navy List* volumes also have alphabetical lists by rank. For senior naval officers (those above the rank of captain), from 1805 onwards the Admiralty produced the annual *List of the Flag Officers*.

To follow an officer's career may mean searching through many volumes of the *Navy List*. However, it may be possible to save some of this legwork by consulting one of the many specialist published volumes containing biographical information on Royal Navy officers. The best of these is Syrett and DiNardo (1994), which gives abbreviated career information on all commissioned sea officers between 1660 and 1815, listing dates of promotion and discharge. The following entry relates to Henry Collins Deacon (the abbreviations are explained in the volumes):

DEACON, Henry Collins

| | |
|---|---|
| L | 24 Feb 1808 |
| CR | 7 June 1814 |
| CA | 2 Apr 1817 (PRO) |
| Ret CA | 1 Oct 1846 (PRO) |
| Ret RA | 16 June 1851 (PRO) |
| Ret VA | 30 July 1857 (PRO) |
| Ret A | 10 Nov 1863 (PRO) |
| d | 9 Nov 1869 (PRO) |

Less useful are Charnock (1794–6) and Marshall (1823–30), which cover officers in the periods 1660–1794 and 1660–1823 respectively, but which are not indexed. The only published list covering the period before 1660 is Anderson's (1964) list of naval captains, 1642–60. For the careers of those who joined in the nineteenth century, try O'Byrne (1849), which provides detailed biographies of all the living officers in 1845 such as this one:

### BAKER. (Lieutenant, 1824. F-P., 32; H-P., 5.)

GUSTAVUS SPICKER BAKER, born 25 July, 1796, is brother of Lieut. Chas. Henry Baker, R.N.

This officer entered the Navy, 1 May, 1810, as Fst.-cl. Vol. on board the UNICORN 32, Capt. Alex. Robt. Kerr, and assisted in blockading the French ports in the Bay of Biscay. During the whole of the American war he was very actively employed with the same officer, as Midshipman, in the ACASTA 40 . . . Since 31 March in the latter year he has served uninterruptedly in the Coast Guard. We should not omit to mention that, in March 1830, while in discharge of his duty, Lieut. Baker encountered a band of smugglers, and, in a desperate conflict which ensued, received several severe wounds on the hand and in different parts of the body; and that his conduct on the occasion was reported in the most flattering terms to the Admiralty.

More specialist lists and biographies include a general list of lieutenants between 1760 and 1764 (Admiralty, 1760–4), biographies of distinguished officers from the reign of George III (Ralfe, 1828), admirals between 1660 and 1816 (Campbell and Stevenson, 1917), naval chaplains between 1626 and 1903 (Kealy, 1905) and naval commissioners from 1660 to 1760 (Duckett, 1889).

*Documentary Sources*

Before consulting the original naval records, it is worth looking at the above published sources, as knowing something about your ancestor's service career will save you a great deal of time and effort.

The majority of original documentary evidence relating to naval officers' careers is to be found at TNA: PRO. Assembling details of an individual may mean having to search through several classes of record. It should be noted that before the nineteenth century the records become scarcer and more difficult to use.

Detailed descriptions of the Navy Board documents held in ADM 106 are being added to the TNA: PRO online Catalogue. These contain the names of many commissioned and warrant officers and are worth searching (restrict your search to ADM or ADM 106), as they often give details of the ship on which your ancestor may have been serving.

Written summaries of an individual officer's career are held in the registers of officers' services in ADM 196 (available on microfilm at TNA: PRO). The registers cover officers' dates of entry starting from 1777 and contain information on warrant and commissioned officers. A typical entry will contain the date of the officer's entry

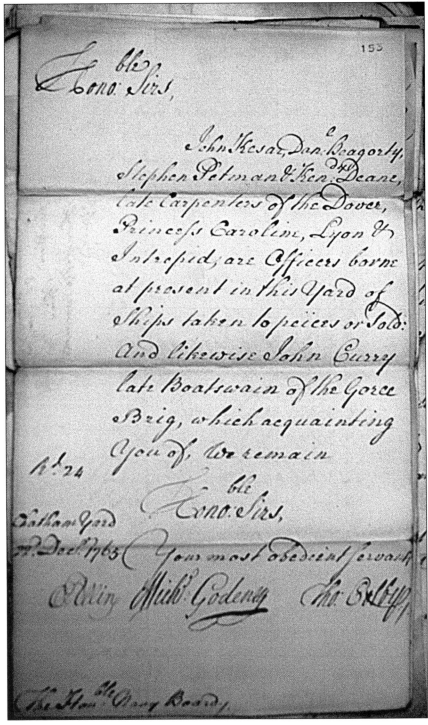

This letter from the records of the Navy Board was able to tell me which ship Kennedy Deane, the brother to an ancestor, had served upon. Knowing this allowed me to find further records relating to this navy carpenter. (TNA: PRO)

into and discharge from the service and also his date of birth, rank, seniority, orders and commissions, awards, distinctions and examinations. A general index to officers in the registers is on open access at TNA: PRO but it is not always reliable. Other indexes exist as part of the registers themselves and may be found in ADM 196/7, 26, 27, 28, 33 and 57. It is advisable to read the TNA: PRO 'Military Records Information Leaflet 30' (available on line) regarding issues associated with these indexes.

For older records, it is necessary to turn to the pay registers held in ADM 22–25 (arranged by full or half pay, then chronologically). These date from c. 1693, are divided into 'full pay' and 'half pay' and list the officer's name and the amount paid to him. An officer on half pay was not on active service and was effectively held on a retainer. Before 1795 only the half-pay registers survive.

Other useful records include officers' passing certificates, which were issued to those who passed the examination that permitted them to accept a rank. These may contain other genealogical information such as date of birth or previous naval experience. The best accessible of these records are the lieutenants' passing certificates in ADM 6, 13 and 107, which date from 1691 and were recently indexed by name in List and Index Society (vols 289 and 290, 2001). Pre-Victorian warrant officers' passing certificates relating to boatswains (1810–13), gunners (1731–1812) and pursers (1813–20; index in ADM 6/193) may be found in ADM 6. The certificates for masters (1660–1863) and surgeons (1700–1800) may be found in ADM 6 and ADM 106. An index showing dates of qualification and appointment of naval surgeons is on open access at TNA: PRO. Before enlisting, naval surgeons had to receive a certificate from either the Barber-Surgeons' Company or, after 1745, from the Royal College of Surgeons (see Chapter 8). Naval surgeons are also usually listed in the *Navy List* volumes; a more detailed description of their records can be found in Bourne and Chicken (1994).

Records relating to an officer's pension or to charity payments made to his next of kin may be found across a broad range of TNA: PRO classes. The only nominal index covers the certificates and other evidence submitted in support of a claim from the Charity for Sea Officers' Widows in ADM 6/335–356 (years 1797–1818). For details of other pension records see Pappalardo (2001) or the TNA: PRO 'Military Records Information Leaflet 30' (available on line).

In 1817, 1828 and 1846 the navy conducted surveys of the careers of its commissioned officers, the returns for which may be found in ADM 9, with an index on open access at TNA: PRO. Some stray and duplicate returns are in ADM 6/66. The returns (1817 only) for gunners, boatswains and carpenters may be found in ADM 11/35, 36 and 37.

## Naval Ratings' Records

There are no published lists or biographies concerning ordinary seamen, which makes tracing information relating to them a more difficult task than for their officers. One of the main obstacles in the pre-Victorian era arises from the navy's policy of attaching individual seamen to a particular ship. Because most of the records are organised by ship, if you do not know the name of the ship on which your ancestor was serving, finding information about him will be problematic. Other than laboriously searching the muster and pay records (see below), there is no easy way of finding out the name of an ancestor's ship. However, before resorting to the muster books, it may be worth checking to see if your ancestor received a pension from the Chatham Chest or Royal Greenwich Hospital, as this should give you his ship details (see below).

If you know the name of your ancestor's ship, then finding information on his naval career is a matter of checking the ship's muster books, which are held in ADM 36, 37, 38, 39, 41, 119 (arranged by ship, then chronologically). (To search for the ship use the TNA: PRO online Catalogue, restricting your search to class ADM.) Musters of the entire ship's crew would be entered into the books every two months and also annually. The books date back to 1688, although the earliest books contain only a minimum of information, such as the individual's name, rations and pay, plus information on where the ship has been. From 1764 the seamen's age and place of birth may be listed, and in later books further information, such as a visual description, may be included. Once you can find a reference to your ancestor, it is then a matter of searching forwards and backwards in time in the muster records, tracing his career.

Similar to the muster records are the naval pay books, which are also organised by ship and may be found in ADM 31–35, 117. These contain the names of the ship's crew and their pay, but, as they are based upon the muster records, they are unlikely to give you any further information, although they may be used to fill in years when the muster books are missing. The oldest books date from 1691.

The will of Kennedy Deane, the brother of one of my ancestors, showed that he had been a carpenter in the navy. The TNA: PRO online Catalogue revealed a letter concerning him in ADM 106, which mentioned that in 1765 he was stationed in Chatham Dockyard, but that he had until recently been with the ship *Intrepid*. Using The Catalogue I found the pay books relating to HMS *Intrepid*, and several entries relating to Kennedy Deane. The one below is from 1762. I was, however, unable to trace any pension records relating to him, probably because he was still serving in the navy on his death, or widow's payment, probably because he left his wife a comfortable sum of money in his will.

ENTRY:          7th Oct 1762
MENS NAME:      Kennedy Deane
QUALITY:        Capt.
FULL WAGES:     26. 19. 3.

## Naval Dockyards

The Royal Navy's dockyards are justifiably famous, with some, for example Portsmouth, Plymouth, Chatham and Sheerness, still in use. However, at the height of its imperial power Britain had dozens of dockyards and other naval establishments (such as victualling yards) not just in Britain but around the world. These dockyards employed hundreds of people, including various clerks, agents, shipwrights, craftsmen, labourers and others. The dockyards and other naval properties were not under direct control of the Admiralty but instead were the responsibility of the Navy Board, a civilian-run organisation (although often staffed by ex-officers) over which the Admiralty had little control. (For an account of the corruption and disorganisation associated with Deptford dockyard in the 1660s see Samuel Pepys's diaries.) Many warrant officers who were tired of life aboard ship would end up working in the dockyards.

Like the ships, the dockyards kept muster and pay books that give lists of their employees, sometimes including further biographical information. These records are arranged by the dockyard's name and spread across a variety of classes at TNA: PRO, but most are in ADM 32, 36, 37 and 42. A catalogue of the whereabouts of each yard's records (including foreign yards) can be found in the TNA: PRO 'Military Records Information Leaflet 41' (available on line).

There is a Naval Dockyard Society (www.hants.gov.uk/navaldockyard), which produces a regular newsletter and which has initiated a project to catalogue all the Navy Board letters held in TNA: PRO ADM 106.

## Naval Pensions and Widows' Payments

Before the Victorian era a pension was not an automatic right for naval personnel, although the navy often put its unemployed officers on half pay as an alternative (see half-pay book above). The records of the navy's pensions, charities and other funds are complex and are explained fully in Rodger (1998). For warrant officers and ratings, pensions can be a useful means of finding out the name of the ship on which an ancestor was serving.

### Officers

The widows of naval officers (commissioned and warrant) who found themselves in distress could apply to the Charity for the Relief of Officers' Widows. The Charity's pay books are in ADM 22/56–237 (years 1734–1835, arranged chronologically), and there is an index at TNA: PRO. After 1835 the records are arranged alphabetically in PMG 19/1–94. The pay books may include references to the officer's death and/or marriage.

Widows and next of kin of those commissioned officers (not warrant officers) who died or were killed while still serving could also apply to the Admiralty's Compassionate Fund, which was established in 1809. The Fund's register of applications, which covers 1809–35, provides the most information and will list the officer's name, rank, death date, length of service, marriage date and place as well as the applicant's address and relationship. The registers are in ADM 6/323–328 and are arranged chronologically with no index. For those whose applications were successful, the Fund's pay books record the name of the recipient and the dead officer, plus their age and relationship. They are in ADM 22/239–250 (years 1809–36, arranged chronologically) and afterwards in PMG 18. The widows and next of kin of warrant officers could apply for money from the Chatham Chest (see below).

## Chatham Chest

The Chatham Chest was a centrally administered fund that paid out pensions to warrant officers, ratings and dockyard workers who were wounded in service or to the families of those who were killed in action. The fund dates back to Elizabethan times, but the earliest preserved records date from 1653 and are continuous from 1675 to 1799. The pay books, which give details of the officer's career and death/wounding, are in ADM 82/12–119. They are arranged chronologically, with an annual index of names.

## Royal Bounty

The relatives, especially widows and orphans, of those killed during battle were entitled to apply to the Royal Bounty. Successful applicants would receive a one-off payment of a year's wages. Records relating to Bounty payments date from 1675 to 1822 and are found in ADM 106/3023–3034 (arranged chronologically); there is an index at TNA: PRO.

## The Royal Greenwich Hospital

By far the most abundant naval pension records are associated with the Royal Greenwich Hospital, an institution that was founded in 1694 to relieve the distress of wounded, elderly or poor pensioners.

Like the army's Chelsea Hospital, the Royal Greenwich would house and care for distressed or disabled sailors who had no family or other means of support. The details relating to such 'in-pensioners' are all held in ADM 73 and include individual sailors' admission papers in ADM 73/1–35 (years 1790–1865, arranged alphabetically), which give details of their naval career and medical condition and may also include a sailor's certificate of service with details of their career. The full information on a series of additional certificates held in ADM 29 (years 1802–1919) has been entered into the TNA: PRO online Catalogue and is searchable on line by

| Mens Names | Age | Service | When Disch.d | Remarks |
|---|---|---|---|---|
| Ryan Edw.d | 47 | 6 | Feb.y 95. | Wounded in arm |
| Sloan Isaac | 48. | 15. | Oct.r 93. | Disabled |
| Bell And.w | 70. | 11. | Dec.r 94 | Worn out |
| Gaar Tho.s | 65. | 14. | May 95. | Lost a leg P. |
| McCleaoD Hugh | 63. | 9. | Apr.l 99 | Infirm |
| Baillie Forbes | 66 | 12. | Dec.r 90. | Worn out |
| Scott John | 74 | 8. | Feb.y 61. | D.o |
| Scott Alex.r | 64 | 15 | July 83. | D.o |
| Baker Dav.d | 41. | 13. | Dec.r 93. | Infirm |
| Lawrence John | 67 | 22 | Feb.y 03. | Worn out |
| Connel Patrick | 32 | 12 | May 95. | Disabled |
| Edwards Wm | 22 | 2 | Feb.y . | Bad Leg |
| Smith Wm. | 50 | 16. | Nov.r 94 | Rheumatism |
| Donaldson James | 51. | Out Pensioner | | |
| Harding Dennis | 50. | 8. | Sept. 94 | Infirm |
| Pinhorn John | 46 | 23. | Oct.r 92 | Consumptive |
| Ward Zach.l | 67. | 9 | Dec.r 90. | Infirm |
| Alford Edw.d | 60. | 8. | Aug.t 63. | Worn out |
| Butcher Tho.s | 55. | 11. | June 95. | Deaf |
| Vowell Corn.s | 60. | 10. | Feb.y . | Worn out |
| Ward Joseph | 42 | 4 | Jan.y 01. | Bad Leg |
| Sinclair Tho.s | 41. | 4 | Sept. 90. | Fractured Skull |
| Hayley Morrice | 42 | 6. | Jan.e 03. | Lost a leg P. |
| Ross And.w | 62 | 6. | Aug.t 01. | To bring his Ticket Worn out |
| Knight Wrigh.t Barg.tn | 50 | 3. | Sept. 07. | Deaf & Blind |

A page from the register of applicants to Greenwich Hospital that lists the names of sailors who have been discharged from the navy and are seeking admission to the hospital, a pension or some other form of financial relief. (TNA: PRO) name and place of birth. The papers associated with applications to the Hospital are preserved in annual registers in ADM 6/223–266 (years 1737–1840) with an index in ADM 6/223–247 (years 1737–1840); and the Hospital's entry books in ADM 73/51–69 (years 1704–1869, arranged chronologically). In addition the Hospital's church registers, which contain death records, may be found in RG 4/1669–1679 (years 1705–1864).

As well as dealing with in-pensioners, the Royal Greenwich Hospital also provided meagre pensions to hundreds of ordinary sailors and Royal Marines. These pensions were paid to sailors who had been discharged and would continue to be paid unless the individual died or re-entered the navy.

The Hospital's registers of out-pensioners begin in 1789 and are in ADM 6/271–320 (years 1789–1859, arranged chronologically) and contain the names and details of many naval ratings. The Hospital's pay books are in ADM 73/95–131 (years 1781–1809, arranged chronologically) and ADM 22/254–443 (years 1814–46, arranged alphabetically).

The following example comes from the Greenwich Hospital's out-patient register for July 1795, which gives the names of individual sailors, their age, years of service, when discharged and the reason:

| NAME | AGE | SERVICE | WHEN DISCHARGED | REASON |
|------|-----|---------|-----------------|--------|
| Ryan Edw. | 47 | 6 | Feb 95 | wounded in chest |
| Bell Andw | 70 | 11 | Oct 93 | worn out |
| Gower Tho | 65 | 14 | May 95 | lost a leg |
| Pinhorn John | 43 | 26 | Oct 92 | consumptive |

## Other Naval Records

Individual ships' logbooks were more concerned with the weather and the state of the ship and are not good sources of information. They may be found in TNA: PRO ADM 50–55; copies of some logbooks and personal journals may be found in the National Maritime Museum (see above).

From 1786 a considerable number of sailors' wills were lodged with the Navy Pay Office for safe keeping. These may be found in ADM 48/1–105, with associated registers in ADM 142/1–14. Many seamen had their wills proved in the Prerogative Court of Canterbury (see Section 4.2) and so it may be worth searching the TNA: PRO's online database of PCC wills.

## 11.2. ROYAL MARINES

In October 1664 the first dedicated naval infantry unit, known as the Admiral's Regiment, was formed. Within decades these naval soldiers were being called

Marines but they remained part of the British Army until 1755, when they came under control of the Admiralty. The Royal Marines did not receive their current title until 1802 and have, since the mid-eighteenth century, been headquartered at the naval towns of Chatham, Portsmouth and Plymouth.

For much of their history the Marines were not a popular career choice and so they were often understaffed and full of people who had joined through no other choice or because they were escaping debtors, family problems, etc. Many Marines found it difficult to transfer to the other armed forces, especially the officers. However, in the nineteenth century the Marines became more established and are currently held in highest regard.

The personnel records of the Royal Marines are mostly held at TNA: PRO but the Royal Marines Museum (Southsea, Hampshire, PO4 9PX; www.royalmarinesmuseum.co.uk) also holds a significant amount of information on the history of the Marines, individual regiments and related records. Thomas (1995) provides a guide to the records of the Royal Marines, while Lowe (1990) gives a guide to the pre-1800 records associated with the Portsmouth division.

## Royal Marines Officers' Records

Unlike the army and navy, the commissioned officers of the Royal Marines did not need to buy their way into the senior ranks and so were frequently drawn from poor families. This made it next to impossible for a Marine officer to transfer into other branches of the armed forces, especially the army.

There are no published biographies of Marines commissioned officers of which I am aware, although Edye (1893) contains a collection of pre-1701 records, including information on the service records of some commissioned officers. From 1740 the annual *Army List* (see Section 10.2) and, from 1755, the separate *Marine Officer List* (copies available at the Royal Marines Museum and at TNA: PRO) contain lists of serving officers, their rank and location, but no genealogical information.

Registers containing details of officers' commissions between 1703 and 1713 can be found in ADM 6/405 and between 1755 and 1814 in ADM 6/406, but there is no index, and no details of age, next of kin or place of birth are included. The service record of those officers who entered in 1793 or later are in ADM 196/58, with an index in ADM 313/110. These can be a better source of information and, as well as career details, include birth dates and places and the name of wives, parents or other next of kin.

Apart from this, the only other records are the half-pay books (for those Marines who had left service but were being paid a retainer) in ADM 6/410–413 (years 1789–93 and 1824–9, arranged chronologically, no index).

The example below is taken from the *Army List* of 1798, which lists the officers of the Royal Marines in order of rank and then date of promotion:

376 OFFICERS OF THE MARINE FORCES.

| | | | |
|---|---|---|---|
| Captain | 105 | William Buchan | 13 June 1796 |
| | | John M— Macnamara | 15 do. |
| | | John Victor | 18 July |
| | | John Clark | 6 Oct. |
| | | David Wilson | 28 do. |
| | | Thomas Hopper | 29 do. |
| | | Charles Stanser | 7 Nov. |
| | | Abraham J— Tregent | 18 do. |
| | | John Dunsmure | 19 do. |
| | 110 | John Lodington | 20 do. |
| | | John Simpson | 23 do. |
| | | John Burdwood | 24 do. |

| | | | | |
|---|---|---|---|---|
| Captain Lieut. and Captain | 5 | James Jardine | 25 Nov. 1796 | |
| | | William Minto | 26 do. | |
| | | George Kempster | 27 do. | |
| | | Joseph Morrish | 28 do. | |
| | | John Long | 29 do. | |
| | | Henry Elliott | 1 Dec. | |
| | | William Darley | 2 do. | |
| | | Andrew Macintosh | 25 do. | |
| | | James Malcolm | 1 Jan. | 97 |
| | 10 | James Knox | 19 do. | |
| | | Gilbert Patterson | 28 do. | |
| | | Simeon Busigny | 7 Feb. | |
| | | James Maxwell | 1 Mar. | |
| | | Palmer Westroppe | 3 do. | |
| | 15 | Robert Roe | 13 Apr. | |
| | | Trevor Hull Letham | 26 do. | |
| | | Philip Sturgeon | 27 do. | |
| | | William Faddy | 24 July | |
| | | Edward Parke | 30 Aug. | |
| | 20 | Paul Hunt | 28 Sept. | |
| | | Robert Johnston | 1 Oct. | |
| | | John Richardson | 20 do. | |
| | | Lawford Miles | 17 Nov. | |
| | | William Reding | 18 do. | |

| | | | |
|---|---|---|---|
| First Lieut. | 5 | Ephraim Bomford | 18 Apr. 1793 |
| | | Benjamin Dickinson | do. |
| | | George Wolfe | do. |
| | | William Barry | do. |
| | | Alexander Mackenzie | do. |
| | | Robert Torkington | do. |
| | | William Marke Combe | do. |
| | | John Short | do. |
| | | William Hollier Allen | do. |
| | 10 | John Wardlaw | do. |

*A page from the* Army List *volume for 1798 showing the names of the officers for the Royal Marines, who were an army unit that served on naval ships.* (Author's collection)

Captain

| | |
|---|---|
| William Buchan | 13 June 1796 |
| John M Macnamara | 15 do. |
| John Victor | 18 Oct |
| John Clark | 6 Oct |

. . .

First Lieut.

| | |
|---|---|
| Ephraim Bomford | 18 Apr. 1793 |
| Benjamin Dickinson | do. |
| George Wolfe | do. |
| William Barry | do. |

## Other Royal Marines' Ranks

When tracing other ranks it is useful to know the individual Marine's Division, as this is how most records are organised. The various Marines' Divisions were based in Chatham, Portsmouth, Plymouth and, between 1805 and 1869, Woolwich.

If you do not know their Division, then the first place to try is the card index of names to the Royal Marines' attestation records at TNA: PRO. On enlisting, each Marine would fill in an attestation form to which further information would be added as his career progressed. The forms can contain very valuable information such as age, place of birth, next of kin, previous trades and career details, including Division. The forms began in 1790 and are filed by date of discharge, with the index covering the years 1790–1883.

If you cannot find your ancestor's attestation form, you will need to find a ship on which he served using the ships' muster and pay books (see Section 11.1). Then use other records, such as the *Naval List*, to find out where that ship was based; it is likely that your ancestor's Division will be in the same place.

The other useful records for Marines are held in ADM 158; these include description books that contain details of each Marine's age at enlistment, place of birth and a simple description of height and complexion but no details of career service. These records begin in 1750 and are arranged by Division and then alphabetically. Other registers held in ADM 158 include recruit books, which hold similar information to the description books and discharge books.

## Pensions

Royal Marines were entitled to apply for pensions from the Chatham Chest, Royal Bounty and Royal Greenwich Hospital (see Section 11.1). In addition, the Royal Marines Pay Office also made pension payments to widows, documents relating to which are in ADM 96/523 (years 1712–1831, no index). Wills and administrations relating to Marines are in ADM 96/524 and are searchable using the TNA: PRO online Catalogue.

## 11.3. MERCHANT SEAMEN AND SHIPPING RECORDS

In addition to a formidable military fleet, Britain also had one of the largest and best-organised merchant navies. The merchant navy was not a centrally organised fleet but instead consisted of a myriad of shipping companies and individual ship owners who ferried merchant goods and people from port to port. Given the size and extent of the British Empire, the number of ships needed to service the domestic and commercial needs of such far-flung locations as India, America, Africa and Australia was vast. Everything from spices, fruit, minerals, textiles and, shamefully, slaves was shunted about the globe and, naturally enough, such a large operation required large numbers of people to staff it. As a consequence many of us will have ancestors who went to sea as merchant seamen. Aside from TNA: PRO, two other particularly good resources for information about the history of merchant ships and the companies that owned them are the National Maritime Museum (www.nmm.ac.uk) and the Guildhall Library, London. For a detailed guide to the records of the merchant navy see Watts and Watts (2004).

### Merchant Seamen Records

Unlike the Royal Navy, which was controlled by the Admiralty and Navy Boards, the merchant navy had no such central organisation, so the hiring and firing of seamen were left to the discretion of individual companies, merchants, boat-owners and captains. This casual arrangement left few permanent crew records and makes tracing individual seamen in the early modern era problematic.

Before 1835 there was no central register of people serving on merchant ships but, thanks to the Act for the Relief of Disabled Seamen, from 1747 ships' captains were required to keep muster lists of all the crew serving on a particular voyage. On reaching the destination port, the captain would deposit the muster list with the Collectors of Customs. Some of these muster lists survive; most may be found in TNA: PRO BT 98, although some are in CUST 66/227 (Plymouth) and CUST 91/111–12 (Scarborough). The musters are filed by port and then alphabetically by ship's name; some port records date back to 1747, but most begin sometime around 1800. Some muster rolls are very detailed and give the names and addresses of the seamen, their date of engagement and discharge and the name of their previous ship; others just list the number of crew on board. There is no index to these rolls, and during the course of his career a seaman could serve on dozens of different ships, so, unless you know details (i.e. ship's name, voyage date and destination) of a specific voyage on which your ancestor was serving, searching the muster records is a prohibitive task. If you do know the name of the ship on which your ancestor was serving, it might be possible to use *Lloyd's Register* (see below) and its associated records to gain more information about the ship's voyages.

If your ancestor was involved in piracy or was a privateer (a form of state-sanctioned piracy), try looking in Downie (2000). If he was a sea officer associated with the East India Company (see Section 15.2), try Farrington (1999).

## Ships' Records

If your ancestor was the master or owner of a merchant ship, it may be possible to trace him through the published records associated with the insurance company Lloyd's of London. Naturally, Lloyd's was concerned about the seaworthiness of the vessels that it might have to insure and so, from at least 1764, it published an annual register of British merchant ships. Copies of *Lloyd's Register* are available at many academic libraries, but a complete set of volumes (1764, then 1768 onwards) is available at the Guildhall Library, London, giving details current at the time of publication. Between 1800 and 1833, as a result of the dispute, two separate registers were produced (the 'Red Book' published by the Society of Mainly Shipowners and the 'Green Book' by the Society of Underwriters).

*Lloyd's Register* contains the following information: the vessel's name; any previous names; description; tonnage; load-draught (1785 onwards); date and place of building; name of owner; name of master; number of crew (1764–71 only); port of survey; class; 'Postings' of casualties (1775 onwards); destined voyage.

*Lloyd's Register* only contains information on the ships that it surveyed and gives little other information. For fuller details about individual shipping movements or incidents at sea it is necessary to consult *Lloyd's List*, which was first produced in 1741 and published twice weekly until 1837 when it went daily (again, the Guildhall Library, London, holds a set). *Lloyd's List* contains information on the movements of ships from home ports and around the world. Arrivals and sailings for each port are listed, giving details such as vessel's name, master's name, date and the destination port. Any attacks, shipwrecks or other disasters are also given, together with casualty lists, although the names of individual seamen are rarely given. Unfortunately, before 1838 *Lloyd's List* has no index, which makes tracking the movements of individual vessels and/or their masters a tedious process. Those trying to track vessel movements or trying to gain information on an incident at sea (e.g. a shipwreck) after 1786 might try searching for the ship's name in *The Times Digital Archive* (see Section 19.1). Larn (1995–8) provides a list of British shipwrecks.

Further background information on individual ships may be obtainable from the registers of shipping. These were created in 1786 and contain lists of individual ships, the names of their masters and the names and addresses of their owners (sometimes individual ships could be owned by dozens of people, a bit like modern racehorses) as well as the date of ship's building and basic technical details. The ships (which had to be over 15 tonnes) were registered with the Customs at their home port, but copies of the registers were filed in the Custom House at London or Edinburgh.

The Custom House registers are now filed in TNA: PRO BT 107, arranged by geographical region and then by port, although a fire in 1814 means that before this date only London records survive. The original local Customs registers (including some older than 1814) may sometimes be found in the CRO covering the port concerned.

References to ships, their masters and owners may also be found in the more specialised port books, shipping returns and customs letters. These are covered in detail by Watts and Watts (2004).

CHAPTER TWELVE

# COMMON LAW RECORDS

The English system of common law is ancient and complex. In 1744 Giles Jacob defined English common law as being 'grounded upon the general customs of the realm; and includes in it the law of nature, the law of God, and the principles and maxims of the law; it is founded upon reason; and is said to be the perfection of reason, acquired by long study, observation and experience, and refined by learned men in all ages'.

In its most basic form, common law is a set of rules and regulations that were needed to ensure that the people of England had certain fundamental rights safeguarded and that the country could run smoothly on a day-to-day basis. In the twelfth century the common law was divided into two main categories: (1) offences committed by a citizen against the Crown or against the king's peace. These include treason, riot and almost all criminal offences such as assault, murder and other felonies. Such actions were known as pleas of the Crown; (2) offences committed by one citizen against another. These include debt, trespass and rights of ownership. Such actions were known as common pleas.

The highest common law courts were in London, but to ensure that justice was available to those living in the countryside there was also a system of local and itinerant common law courts.

## 12.1. THE ASSIZES

The lack of permanent criminal courts outside London led to a system of itinerant or wandering courts, which saw London judges and other court officials periodically saddle up and ride out into the countryside. At key provincial towns the court would be established, and those accused of committing crimes brought before it and tried by jury. However, they were notoriously infrequent and reached some parts of England only every few years or so. In late medieval times a better-organised type of wandering court evolved known as the assizes (derived from *assise*, Old French for a court session). The assizes existed for more than six centuries and were abolished only in 1971 (1956 in Liverpool and Manchester). During this time they were England's principal criminal courts and gained important functions concerning local administration and the supervision of local officials. To facilitate their organisation, the assizes were grouped into six regional circuits. These are:

| The Home Circuit | Essex, Hertfordshire, Kent, Middlesex, Surrey and Sussex |
| The Midland Circuit | Derbyshire, Rutland, Leicestershire, Lincolnshire, Northamptonshire, Nottinghamshire and Warwickshire |
| The Norfolk Circuit | Bedfordshire, Buckinghamshire, Cambridgeshire, Huntingdonshire, Norfolk and Suffolk |
| The Northern Circuit | Cumberland, Northumberland, Westmorland and Yorkshire |
| The Oxford Circuit | Gloucestershire, Herefordshire, Shropshire, Staffordshire and Worcestershire |
| The Western Circuit | Berkshire, Cornwall, Devon, Dorset, Hampshire, Oxfordshire, Somerset and Wiltshire |

In addition, until the nineteenth century Bristol, Chester, Durham and Lancaster had their own separate assizes jurisdictions, while Wales had its Court of Great Sessions (see below).

Twice a year, usually in late February/March and July/early August, two Westminster judges would mount their horses and ride an assigned circuit. Accompanying them were a small number of clerical staff, including a clerk of the assize. The place, date and time for the trials would have been decided in advance by the issuing of a writ to the county sheriff. When the judicial party reached the appointed place (usually the county's principal town or another large central urban centre), the judges would establish a court where they would hear civil pleas and try any suspected criminals. Criminal trials could be heard under one of two main categories.

The first, and most important, were criminal cases held under the commission of gaol delivery. This permitted the assizes court to hear the cases of people who had been accused of a crime, apprehended and then placed in prison. Only when the assizes court tried their case could their fate be decided. This sometimes meant a wait of several months, although many would be given bail after their committal.

The second criminal category was the commission of oyer and terminer (from Old French, meaning to 'hear and determine'), which gave the assizes court permission to enquire, hear and determine any other outstanding criminal cases within the county.

Civil cases (such as trespass) could be heard by the assizes, while civil cases awaiting trial in Westminster could also be heard by the assizes by the issuing of a writ of *nisi prius* which gave the judge permission to hear the case concerned.

The earliest preserved assizes records are from the late thirteenth century; the last is from 1971. Coverage is patchy throughout the entire medieval period, with no records at all preserved before 1559. Records written before 1733 will almost certainly be in Latin. For a general guide to the assizes see Cockburn (1972).

Cockburn (1973–95) remains the best guide to the assizes, especially the introductory volume. Hawkings (1992) contains several examples of assizes cases.

## The Survival of Records

Because the assizes courts were neither local nor fully centralised, many of the written documents related to the trials were not filed centrally or locally, and so went missing or were destroyed.

The Home Circuit records have the best survival rate, with some counties going back to 1559; the records for most other counties begin in the seventeenth or eighteenth century, with the survival from particular years being patchy until the start of the nineteenth century. The records relating to all the assizes are to be found at TNA: PRO. The scope and location for the records for each county's assizes records can be found in Hawkings (1992) and also the TNA: PRO Research Guide 'Legal Records Information Leaflet 14' (available on line). Hawkings (1992) also provides a list of the whereabouts of the calendars of prisoners relating to the assizes and the quarter sessions (see below).

Records relating to the Bristol assizes are at the Bristol Record Office, and the Welsh records are housed at the National Library of Wales, Dyfed. Records relating to the City of London are held in the Corporation of London Record Office, while those for London and Middlesex are in the London Metropolitan Archives. After 1834 all the London assizes were held at the Old Bailey, whose records are held at TNA: PRO under classes CRIM 1–13 (see below).

There are no indexes to the assizes, and very few of these records have been transcribed and published. The exception is the records for the Home Circuit (Essex, Hertfordshire, Kent, Surrey and Sussex), whose early records (1559–1625; to 1684 for Kent) have been transcribed and published by Cockburn (1973–95).

## How to Use Assizes Records

A lack of indexes and published transcriptions and the patchy survival of records make the random searching of the assizes records a very difficult task. Realistically, to find the records relating to a particular trial it is necessary to know the rough date of the trial, in which county it took place and, of course, the name of your ancestor. The county of the trial will tell you which assizes circuit it came under (see above); this, together with the approximate date, will enable you to use the TNA: PRO 'Legal Records Information Leaflet 14' (available on line) to find where the relevant records are stored.

Assuming that the records you want have survived, the next step is to look within the assizes calendar (see below) for the relevant documents. In most cases these contain a list of the prisoners due to be tried, together with a brief summary of their offences and, in some cases, also the court's verdict and any sentence. If your ancestor's name is to be found within any of these documents, you should look within the Indictments for the individual record that relates to your ancestor's trial. This will usually give you a detailed description of the defendant and the alleged offence, and such information as the defendant's name (plus any aliases), occupation, place of residence, and details of the alleged offence including the name of any victims. These can often be lengthy documents, especially if the offence was a serious one.

## Assize Trial Procedure

The following gives a generalised outline of a typical assize procedure; for further examples see Cockburn (1973–95).

### Indictments

Before the start of the trials the county sheriff was compelled to assemble a grand jury (see below), whose chief function was to examine each indictment and to decide whether the charges it contained were true (*billa vera*) or false (*billa ignoramus*). Some records reveal that there was frequently a high degree of tension between the grand jury and the judge.

As well as details of their crimes and their sentences, indictments can contain useful information about named individuals such as their address and occupation, and family information such as a spouse's name. The following examples come from the Maidstone Assizes for 21 March 1661 (see Cockburn, 1973–95):

Indictment of Thomas Wrangham of Deptford, labourer, for bigamy. On 5 Dec. 1654 at St George's, Southwark, Surrey, he married Martha Page, spinster, while Juliana Full, whom he had married at Brixham, Devon, on 21 Feb. 1652 was still alive.
Not guilty.

Indictment of Thomas Thomson of Deptford, labourer, for cozening. On 17 Sept. 1660 at Deptford he deceitfully told Thomas Fallowfield of Deptford that Joan Fallowfield, his wife, who was a nurse in Leadenhall Street, London, had asked him to carry to her in London a chest of clothes. Thomas gave him the chest, which he unlawfully carried away.
Guilty; to be pilloried.

### The Assizes Calendar

The most useful record is the assizes calendar, a series of documents that, at the end of the assizes, would be bundled together as a record of the proceedings. Many assizes calendars still survive and can be a good source of genealogical information.

Once a place, date and time for an assizes court had been issued, the local sheriff would be tasked with drawing up several lists (known as the sheriff's returns), which together form the so-called assizes calendar. These are:

1. The *Nomina Ministrorum*, simply a list of all the county's officials including its mayors, justice of the peace, coroners, bailiffs and stewards.
2. A list of grand jurors who were eligible to stand at the assizes. Grand jury members were freemen of the county who would be compelled to come to the assizes to perform jury service. The size of the jury was variable and the original list of names was usually obtained by the sheriff issuing instructions to manorial bailiffs.
3. The gaol calendar (also known as a gaol book). This was a list of the prisoners held on remand in the county's prisons plus a brief outline of their alleged crime(s). In earlier calendars there would often be little differentiation between crimes (especially varieties of assault and robbery), with such cases often being described simply as 'a breach of the King's peace'.
4. The gaol delivery roll or roll of prisoners. This document lists the names of all the prisoners brought before the assizes, together with a note of their crime and fate at the hands of the court (i.e. their sentence, remand in prison or release). The gaol delivery calendar was the final part of the proceedings and usually provides the best information for the case (see Section 13.1).

*Coroners' Records*

The coroner's office was originally created in 1194, and in cases of murder or suspicious death a coroner would be asked to undertake an inquest into the matter, later returning a statement to the assizes court confirming whether or not the death was unlawful. This statement would then be used as part of the proceedings against any individual accused of that murder. The coroner would also be asked to examine the death of anybody who died in prison or of any other type of unnatural death, including suicide, drowning, etc. Coroners' inquest rolls may contain information about people and places connected with the death of an individual.

Before 1926, coroners themselves were elected locally and, while they had to be freeholders, they did not need to have either medical or legal training. Coroners' inquests were carried out using juries, and until 1860 the coroner would be paid per inquest undertaken.

Coroners' records generally reside with the assizes records (see above) and also with the records of the King's Bench in TNA: PRO KB 9–11 (years 1294–1845). Mentions of coroners' inquests can also be found within the pardons issued as letters patent in C 66 (see Section 17.2). Gibson and Rogers (1992) provide a list of the whereabouts of medieval, modern and local coroners' records.

*Assizes Writs*

There are several types of writ that may be preserved relating to the assizes trials. They are of little genealogical interest (unless you are interested in the career of one of the judges or court officials). The writs are: the patent of assize (this gives permission for the assizes to take place); the patent of association (this empowers some of the local officials, e.g. the clerk of assizes, to hear civil cases); the writ of admittance (this identifies those people who were empowered by the patent of association); the writ *si non omnes* (this allows clerks of the court temporarily to take the position of judge); the commission of oyer and terminer (this empowered the assizes court to hear and decide over criminal cases); the commission of gaol delivery (this empowered the assizes court to hear the cases of those on remand in prison); the writ *venire facias* (summoning people for the next assizes); and the writ *capias* (requesting those defendants who failed to appear at these assizes to be present at the next). Few of these writs survive.

## Other Records Associated with the Assizes

In situations where the assizes records do not survive, it might be worth checking TNA: PRO E 389/241–257, which contains sheriffs' assize vouchers from 1714 to 1832. These contain information about expenses relating to the assizes and the sentencing of prisoners, including the costs associated with hanging, whipping, imprisonment, transportation and the pillory. These records may include the names of individual criminals, the verdict of the court and details of their sentence.

Civil courts, such as the King's Bench or Common Pleas, would often refer civil cases (e.g. trespass, etc.) to the assizes. These cases often leave little or no record in the assizes, as, once a decision had been reached, the documents relating to the civil case would be returned to the civil court that referred it in the first place. Thus the records relating to civil cases tried by the assizes are usually to be found with the court that initially referred the action.

The assizes would also have to deal with some local administrative matters such as the upkeep of local roads, poor relief, buildings or gaols, as well as the licensing of local public houses. Written orders would be made on such administrative matters and often resulted in individuals or communities being told to take responsibility for certain matters such as road repair. These orders would be filed with the rest of the assizes documents. Cockburn (1959) has published many of the administrative orders relating to seventeenth-century Somerset.

## The Great Sessions of Wales

Wales was not subject to the assizes courts but twice a year between 1542 and 1830 each Welsh county did play host to the Court of Great Sessions. Like the English Assizes, the Great Sessions operated around four circuits:

| | |
|---|---|
| Chester Circuit | Denbighshire, Flintshire and Montgomeryshire |
| North Wales Circuit | Anglesey, Caernarfonshire and Merioneth |

Brecon Circuit          Brecon, Glamorgan and Radnorshire
Carmarthen Circuit      Cardiganshire, Carmarthenshire and Pembrokeshire

The Great Sessions were primarily common law courts, but civil cases were heard as well. The Court's records are all housed at the National Library of Wales, Aberystwyth; some date back to the Court's inception in 1542. There is no overall index to the records (which are written in English), which means that the surviving calendar rolls and docket books (in the case of civil pleas) have to serve as finding aids. There is a detailed breakdown of the Library's Great Sessions holdings on its website (www.llgc.org.uk/lc/lcs0040.htm) and in Hawkings (1992) and List and Index Society (vols 4 and 40). For information using these records see the aforementioned website or Parry (1995).

## Palatine Courts

Before 1830 the Palatine Court of Chester held precedence over the assizes and Court of Great Sessions (see above). Records relating to this court may be found in TNA: PRO CHES 20, 21 and 25. Likewise Durham and Lancashire also had Palatine Courts that operated until 1876; their records are in DURH 15–19 and PL 25–28 respectively.

## 12.2. COURTS OF QUARTER SESSIONS

The courts of quarter sessions date back to 1363, when Justices of the Peace were given the power to hear and determine local criminal cases, although more serious offences (such as those warranting a death sentence) would usually be referred to the assizes (see Section 12.1). In addition the sessions were responsible for certain administrative matters such as the upkeep of local roads or the condition of the county gaol. In time many civil cases (e.g. trespass, bad debts, etc.) were also heard by the sessions.

The quarter sessions were so called because they would meet four times a year, with the individual sessions being called, respectively, Epiphany, Easter, Midsummer (Trinity) and Michaelmas. They were local courts and so were administered at a county or borough level and would convene at a large town where two or more Justices of the Peace would sit in judgment. (The exception to this is Middlesex, which instead had the monthly Old Bailey sessions; see below.)

During the nineteenth century the sessions' work became overburdened with administrative duties, which, in 1889, led to their administrative functions being transferred to the recently created county councils. Under the 1971 Courts Act the jurisdiction of the quarter sessions was transferred to the Crown Court.

The aim for each session was to try to hear all the outstanding cases in a single day, but during the early nineteenth century this was increasingly difficult to achieve and often necessitated the re-formation of the court on a subsequent occasion (usually the following week or month). Court procedure broadly followed that of the assizes (see above), resulting in a similar collection of documents relating to the trial of individuals. As with the assizes, the most useful tool for finding an ancestor's name is the calendar of prisoners produced as part of the trial process (see Sections 12.1 and 13.1). Emmison and Gray (1967) and Hawkings (1992) provide general guides to the quarter sessions records.

## Documents Generated

The records generated by the quarter sessions bear a similarity to those of the assizes, as do many of the criminal cases that were brought before it (although the quarter sessions include many more local issues concerning debts, poorly repaired bridges, etc.). There are three main categories of record.

### Judicial Records

These include sessions rolls and files that contain a written summary of an individual court session. A typical roll may contain a list of the court officials, including the jury, a list of 'presentments' (which normally concern parish matters such as the failure to repair roads, although other matters, such as complaints against alehouses, may also be included), a list of 'indictments' (accusations against individuals for larceny, assault, poaching, etc.), 'depositions' (the examination of defendants) and convictions. In addition, the sessions rolls may contain other documents such as calendars of prisoners (see Section 12.1), reports from coroners, petitions against the parish and removal orders against unwanted parishioners (usually vagrants; see Section 4.6). The sessions rolls are the documents that are probably of most interest to genealogists, as it is within these that the names of criminals (or those accused of crimes and found not guilty), victims, informers, etc., are to be found. Some CROs hold indexes to their sessions rolls.

### Order Books

The order books record the formal proceedings of the court and tend to focus more on administrative matters. Included may be reports on the state of local infrastructure (e.g. roads, gaols, etc.), records of new appointments and expenditure as well as enquiries into local events such as fairs, alehouse licensing, suspicious fires, etc. The order books may be of interest to those whose ancestors were in business locally, as they may at some time have had cause to apply to the court for a licence. Many order books are indexed.

*Account Books*

The imposition of rates on parishioners in the early seventeenth century led to a need for the parishes to be accountable for the money that they were spending. From 1739 the County Treasurer was required to submit quarterly accounts to the quarter sessions, which would detail the county's expenditure on salaries, repairs, gaols, etc. These are probably of more interest to local historians than to genealogists.

The following example concerns a presentment made in 1747 at the Flintshire Quarter Sessions and illustrates that, in addition to criminal cases, these courts had jurisdiction over local matters:

> Holywell, 16 July 1747
> County of Flint. The presentment of Wm Jones and John Williams, high constables of the hundred of Ruthland in the said county . . . We the high constables forenamed, do humbly certify and present unto this honourable court that all things within the sd hundred are in good order and repair, save and except the bridge known by the name Pontydd Newydd nigh Llannerch, and the road leading from the sd bridge to the common commonly called Waen y Goleygod . . . Wm Jones and John Williams.

## Finding Aids

Being local courts, all surviving documents relating to the quarter sessions are held in CROs, with some dating back to the sixteenth century. Gibson (1982) provides a summary list of all the surviving records in England and Wales and their whereabouts. Hawkings (1992) provides a list of the whereabouts of the calendars of prisoners for the sessions.

*An entry in the Middlesex Quarter Sessions roll for February 1825 in which Jane Finley is found not guilty of the assault on Mary Murphy.* (London Metropolitan Archives)

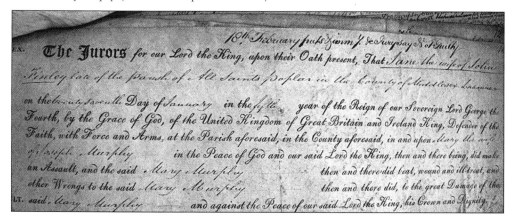

No central finding aids exist for the quarter sessions, but some local history societies have published calendars or indexes to their records and unpublished guides may also exist; consult your CRO or local library to see what is available.

For example, Manning (1996) provides an index to all the persons listed in the Kent Quarter Sessions from 1639 to 1677, while Allen (1974) provides a transcription of the order books relating to the Essex sessions between 1652 and 1661.

## Petty Sessions

The workload of the quarter sessions became so great that it was often necessary for some of the more minor offences and matters concerning licensing etc. to be heard at a further session held in between two of the main quarters. These are known as petty sessions, and, where they survive, documents relating to them can usually be found with the quarter sessions at CROs. Before 1848 (when Clerks of the Justice at the petty sessions were ordered to send details of their cases to the Clerk of the Peace) records relating to the petty sessions are rare.

## 12.3. THE COURT OF THE KING'S BENCH AND HIGH COURT OF ADMIRALTY

### The Court of the King's Bench

Around the twelfth century the Court of the King's Bench evolved from the medieval King's Court and, by the fifteenth century, had become a fixed central court based in Westminster. Other than Parliament, the King's Bench (*coram rege*) was the most powerful court in the land. It tended to handle more serious cases where a person had either committed an offence against the king (e.g. treason) or his property, which, by definition, included the bodies of his subjects. This meant that cases of assault, murder and rape were also heard in this court, although it did also hear a limited number of equity cases. The King's Bench remained the highest court in England and Wales until the establishment of the High Court in 1875.

### Surviving Records

The early plea rolls, from 1272 to 1701, are preserved in KB 27, but only the docket books have been indexed (IND 1/1322–1384 and IND 1/604–26096). The series continues to 1852 in KB 122 (years 1702–1852, no index). A list of the rolls can be found in List and Index Society (vol. 4, 1910).

For examples of the King's Bench plea rolls see the Selden Society (vols 74, 76, 82, 88, 1955–71) or some of the treason cases covered by Howell (1816–28).

As an example, Howell (1816–28) provides details of the case of Anne Turner, who was tried before the King's Bench on 7 November 1615 for her part in a conspiracy to murder Sir Thomas Overbury. The Judge's closing remarks underline the seriousness of her situation. She was afterwards found guilty and hanged.

> Then the Lord Chief Justice told Mrs Turner, that she had the seven deadly sins: *viz.* a whore, a bawd, a sorcerer, a witch, a papist, a felon, and a murderer, the daughter of the Devil Forman; wishing her to repent, and to become a servant of Jesus Christ . . . She desired the Lord Chief Justice to be good unto her, saying, that she was ever brought up with the countess of Somerset, and had been of a long time her servant . . . She desired only favour but could not speak anything for weeping . . . Then Judge Crook made another grave speech exhorting her to repentance, and to prepare herself ready for death; and that the little time which should be assigned to her to live, she should not spend it either in hope or in imagination to get life, for that hope was but a witch.

## The High Court of Admiralty

Operating between 1535 and 1834, the High Court of Admiralty was authorised to deal with crimes (such as piracy, murder and sodomy) committed at sea and also in larger harbours and estuaries. During its history the court met at the Guildhall, Southwark and Old Bailey courts and followed standard common law procedure as outlined above.

The most useful court records are held in TNA: PRO HCA 1 (years 1535–1834), which contains the oyer and terminer records and includes minutes of session, minute books, calendars of prisoners, warrants, bails, pardons, petitions and orders. These are not indexed, although some of the post-1700 cases held in the Old Bailey are included among the *Old Bailey Proceedings* (see Section 12.4). For biographies of many famous pirates, buccaneers and privateers see Downie (2000).

## 12.4. LONDON CRIMINAL JURISDICTION

### The Old Bailey, pre-1834

The City of London and the county of Middlesex were not covered by an assizes circuit; instead criminal justice was administered chiefly by sessions of the peace and gaol delivery sessions. (For exceptional trials, e.g. state trials, a special session of oyer and terminer would be held at the Guildhall; see Price, 1886 for further details.)

Before 1834, sessions of the peace, which frequently took place at the Guildhall, would hear minor offences such as fraud, perjury and assault, most of which would be referred up to the Old Bailey for trial. The gaol delivery sessions dealt with more serious cases and concerned those people who had been imprisoned (often in

Sessions House or Newgate Gaol) and were awaiting trial on a variety of charges from treason through to rape and murder. Their cases would also usually be referred to the Old Bailey for trial.

The trial process at the Old Bailey followed that of other courts, and consisted of depositions, indictments, examinations and verdict. When in session, the court was set up to process cases as quickly as possible. There were two juries (one to hear cases from the City of London; the other, cases from Middlesex), so that, while one jury was deliberating, the other could be in court hearing trials. Each jury would hear several cases at a time before retiring to offer their verdict. It is reckoned that an average Old Bailey trial would last for a little under nine minutes.

At the end of the trial any relevant documents would be returned to the body that referred the case, which means that surviving records are now to be found in two locations. Those concerning the City of London may be found at the Corporation of London Record Office, while the Middlesex trial records are held by the London Metropolitan Archives. Both organisations have leaflets explaining their holdings and note that their records are incomplete and usually consist only of the minute books and some sessions papers. The oldest records date back to the late seventeenth century. Some Old Bailey sessions papers from 1801 to 1834 are held in TNA: PRO PCOM 1/1–30; some examples of these are given by Hawkings (1992).

For those trials that reached the Old Bailey it is probably better to use the printed *Old Bailey Sessions Papers* (see below).

## Central Criminal Court

In 1834 the role of the gaol delivery sessions was expanded, leading to the establishment of the Central Criminal Court at the Old Bailey. The CCC was centrally administered and would try serious offences (e.g. murder, rape, burglary and assault) originating in London, Middlesex and parts of Essex, Kent and Surrey; it could also try cases arising at sea. The records of the CCC are all held at TNA: PRO and are arranged chronologically in CRIM 4. A calendar of indictments, which can act as a finding aid, may be found in CRIM 5, while the court books (containing summary details for each trial) are in CRIM 6. Further records relating to the proceedings in court (e.g. original depositions) may be found in CRIM 1; these tend to refer to more serious trials and are searchable by defendant name using the TNA: PRO online Catalogue.

### Old Bailey Sessions Papers

In October 1678 an account of all the trials at a single Old Bailey session was published. The publication quickly became established and for many years went under the unwieldy title of *The Proceedings of the King's Commission of the Peace and* of him, and would have trusted him with all I was worth without dispute.

*Mr. Butler.* I have known the prisoner about two years, and never heard of a blemish in his character before this. I have done work for him, and he was very punctual to his time of payment.

*Anne Rider.* I have known the prisoner between five and six years, and never heard any thing but what was very good and honest. His character was exceeding good.

*Mary Howell.* I have known him ever since December last, and I always heard he was a very sober, honest, and industrious young man. Guilty, Death.

---

## MISDEMEANORS.

345. John Harding, and Jane his wife, were indicted for wilful and corrupt perjury, in falsely swearing on the trial of Silas Dowling, last sessions.
*See Number* 260.
No evidence appearing, they were acquitted.

---

346. Thomas Stanley was indicted for wilful and corrupt perjury.
No evidence appearing, he was acquitted.

---

The trials being ended, the Court proceeded to give judgment as follows.

Received sentence of death, 2.

*Thomas Womersly,* and *George Watson.*

Transportation for seven years, 19.

*Lucy Skeyte, John Walker, James Lee, Mary Low, Joseph Commings, Richard Smith, John Munk, Mary Taylor, Elizabeth Oldman, George Foster, Eleanor Hine, Charles Farring, Anne Car, Anne Collins, Thomas Biggs, Thomas Fulham, Catharine Scott, Thomas Cardinal,* and *James Tobin.*

Whipped, 2.

*Elizabeth Barret,* and *Elizabeth Knott.* The first was ordered to be publickly whipt near St. Bartholomew's Hospital Gate.

*Elizabeth Canning,* convicted last Sessions for wilful and corrupt perjury, was ordered to be imprisoned a month in Newgate, and after that to be transported for seven years.

*John Parry and David Edom,* capitally convicted in April sessions, were executed on Wednesday the fifth of June.

The Right Honourable THOMAS RAWLINSON, Esq; Lord Mayor.

God save the King,

The next ensuing Sessions to begin on Wednesday the seventeenth of July.

*An image from the* Old Bailey Sessions Papers *for 30 May 1754 in which Elizabeth Canning, a notorious London trouble-maker, is sentenced to a month's imprisonment followed by seven years' transportation to America. (Author's collection)*

*Oyer and Terminer, and Gaol-Delivery of Newgate, held for the City of London and the County of Middlesex, at Justice-Hall, in the Old Bailey.* The publication was published continuously until 1913, during which time it went under several titles: most people now refer to these collectively as the *Old Bailey Sessions Papers*.

After each session the *Old Bailey Sessions Papers* would be published as a small commercial pamphlet designed initially to titillate the masses but which, in time, became a useful legal resource. The descriptions of each trial can be very detailed and include not only names, ages, etc., but also transcripts of questions asked and answers given as well as lurid details of the crime committed.

Individual pamphlets from the *Old Bailey Sessions Papers* can be found in many libraries, but there is a complete edition (1684–1913) at the Guildhall Library, London. However, a recent project by the Universities of Sheffield and Hertfordshire has seen the digitisation of those publications from 1674 to 1834 (covering roughly 100,000 trials). These have been made available free on line (www.oldbaileyonline.org) and can be searched by name, place, date and keyword (among others). This fantastic resource is by far the most convenient means of accessing and searching the Old Bailey records and should be consulted before trying to track down original documents. There are apparently plans to continue digitising the pamphlets through to 1913.

The following example is taken from the *Old Bailey Proceedings* and reports on the trial of Elizabeth Canning for perjury on 24 April 1754 after having wrongly convicted a gypsy named Mary Squires of imprisoning her. The case had the whole of London in uproar, and in this section Mary Squires's son proves that his mother was not in London at the time she was supposed to be holding Elizabeth Canning prisoner. The original transcript runs over several pages and contains much detail about the lives of the defendants, plaintiffs and witnesses.

George Squires, the gypsey's son, deposed that he, his mother, and sister Lucy, were at South Parrot on the 29th of December, 1752; they went to Litton the next day, and on the 31st to Abbotsbury; where they staid from the 1st of January to the 9th, on which, day they went to Portsham, and from thence to Ridgway, and on the 11th to Dorchester; from whence they set out and walked almost all night, and got to another village, and the next day they lay at Morton in a barn; and on the day after they lay at Coome; after which he could not recollect where he lay till he came to Basingstoke, where he was directed to lodgings at a house at Old Basing; then they travelled to Bagshot and lay there, and after that to Brentford, and from thence to the Seven-sisters at the two Brewers near Tottenham; and from thence to Mother Wells's at Enfield-wash; that his business was to tarry there till he could get a debt, which was due to him in London, of 7 l. 15 s. being afraid of going to his own lodgings, where he had goods of his own at Newington Butts, for fear of being arrested; that they had been there but a week and a day before his mother was taken up and committed. On his Cross-Examination he gave a very lame account how he went from Newington to South Parrot and named as many counties he went through as towns; but could not name a sign or inn that he lay at.

# 12.5. CRIMINAL TRIALS: OTHER RESOURCES

## Published Details of Trials

From its earliest days the printed media has had an obsession with reporting trials, and from the seventeenth to nineteenth centuries it was common practice for reporters to sit in a court room taking notes that would later be published in the form of a pamphlet. Many of these pamphlets were bestsellers, and original copies of them are to be found in the British Library or other major archives. Others have been reproduced in local or national newspapers of the day. If you know the approximate date and place of a trial, it may be worth checking the newspapers of the day to see if they carry any further details (see Section 19.1).

The original notes of some court reporters also seem to have survived in some local and county archives. When researching a historical book I was amazed to find that the Corporation of London Record Office held a twelve-page transcript of the trial of several of the central characters that had taken place at London's Guildhall in July 1762.

However, probably the best collection of such trial reports is to be found in *British Trials*, a commercial collection of microfiches that contain copies of thousands of trial reports from 1660 to 1900. The sorts of trials covered include anything from serious criminal trials involving rape, murder and larceny through to civil cases concerning sexual scandals. Many of these cases involved ordinary members of the public, although obviously the more sensational the crime, defendant or victim, the more likely it is that it would be written about. Most of the descriptions provide far more detail about people, crimes and trials than can be found in the official court records.

A series of nine indexes allows searching by the name of defendants, plaintiffs, victims and judges, as well as by location, subjects and date. Only the largest libraries will have *British Trials* (e.g. Guildhall Library, London).

Those whose ancestors may have been involved in famous state trials (for treason, murder, witchcraft, forgery and so forth) could try searching Howell (1816–28), which gives descriptions of state trials from the twelfth century to 1783 or Salmon (1730), which contains much the same information. Harrison (1991) provides a list of all the prisoners ever to be held at the Tower of London from 1100 to 1941, and includes brief details of their crime and fate.

It may also be worthwhile searching the British Library's online 'eighteenth century short title' catalogue, which contains information on trial pamphlets and transcripts that do not form part of the above collections.

CHAPTER THIRTEEN

# CRIMINALS AND PUNISHMENT

## 13.1. TRACING PRISONERS HELD IN ENGLAND AND WALES

In pre-Victorian times every county had to have a prison or gaol which could be used to hold those prisoners who were awaiting trial (such prisons were not generally used as places of punishment). The prisons were usually privately run and pretty terrible places. This chapter describes the resources available to those seeking an ancestor who may have had to spend time behind bars. For more information see Hawkings (1992), Bevan (2000) and Paley (2001).

### Calendars of Prisoners

Before the criminal registers (see below) in the late eighteenth and early nineteenth centuries, there is no centralised index or register of those people held on remand and/or convicted of a crime. The only reliable source of information on such people is the calendar of prisoners (also known as gaol calendars and gaol delivery rolls), which would be drawn up before the sitting of an individual court. These calendars contain details such as the names of the accused, their age, occupation, residence and the nature of the crime they were alleged to have committed (see Section 12.1 for more details).

Calendars of prisoners are filed with other documents that relate to the court in which the prisoners were placed on trial and can be found at CROs and TNA: PRO. Hawkings (1992) contains a comprehensive list of the calendars held by CROs. Within TNA: PRO those calendars relating to the assizes and quarter sessions (Sections 12.1 and 12.2) can be found in PCOM 2, while those for the Old Bailey are in HO 16, CRIM 5 and CRIM 9, and those for Newgate Prison in HO 77. A special assize held on 18 December 1830 (to deal with an agricultural riot) may be found in HO 130. For a more detailed breakdown of these records use the 'browse from here' facility in the TNA: PRO online Catalogue or consult Hawkings (1992).

From the end of the eighteenth century it was common for many calendars to be published. Copies of these may be found at CROs or among the court records at TNA: PRO (see above). From 1868 calendars were often printed after the trials so that the sentence could be added; copies of these may be found in TNA: PRO HO 140. See also sheriffs' assizes vouchers (Section 12.1).

## Criminal Registers

From 1791 onwards Middlesex began producing an annual register of all those people who had been charged with a criminal offence within the county. These registers recorded the person's name, age, alleged crime, place of trial, the sentence and any other remarks. Some of the earliest registers contain additional information, such as a physical description and place of birth. From 1805 similar annual criminal registers were produced for all the counties of England and Wales. They are held at TNA: PRO, although many county records hold copies or similar documents, some of which date back to the late eighteenth century. A detailed list of those registers held by CROs may be found in Hawkings (1992).

Within TNA: PRO the Middlesex criminal registers (referred to as 'Series I') are all filed under HO 26. No indexes exist for these. The criminal registers for other counties are referred to as 'Series II' and are filed under HO 27, where they are arranged chronologically (1805 onwards) and then alphabetically by county name (some counties are arranged differently in certain years; see the notes in the TNA: PRO online Catalogue). A set of indexes to the criminals listed in the registers is available on microfiche at TNA: PRO, although these mostly cover only the years 1805–16 (the exceptions are Anglesey, Cornwall and Dorset, which run to 1840). There is also an index to treasons, executions and machine breakers, 1805–17. From 1849 the 'Series I' (i.e. Middlesex) and 'Series II' registers are combined in HO 27. For a more detailed breakdown of these records use the 'browse from here' facility in the TNA: PRO online Catalogue or consult Hawkings (1992).

The following example was taken from the Middlesex criminal registers for 1838:

| | |
|---|---|
| NAME OF OFFENDER: | Medhurst, David |
| DEGREE OF INSTRUCTION: | Imp |
| AGE: | 16 |
| AT WHAT SESSIONS TRIAL: | Central Criminal Court, 27th November |
| OFFENCES OF WHICH TRIED: | Larceny before committed of felony |
| SENTENCES: | Transportation – 7 years |
| AQUITTALS: | – |
| EXECUTIONS: | – |

## Prison Hulk Registers

Male prisoners awaiting transportation would be held on disused ships moored at major ports such as Chatham, Sheerness, Plymouth, Portsmouth and Woolwich, or

## No. 3111.

### REPORT *of the Proceedings and of the Informations received at the several* POLICE OFFICES, *on Wednesday, the 3rd day of January, 1838; and of Informations received at the Metropolitan Police Office, on the same day, relating to Offenders and Stolen Property.*

*Containing the Substance of all Informations received in Cases of Felonies and Misdemeanors of an aggravated nature, and against Receivers of Stolen Goods, Reputed Thieves, and Offenders who may have Escaped from Custody, with the Time, the Place, and any particular Circumstance marking the Offence. The Names of Persons not in Custody, who are charged (if known), or, if not known, their Appearance or Dress, or any other Mark of Identity that can be described, the Names of Accomplices or Accessories, with any other Particulars which may lead to their Apprehension. The Names of all Persons brought before the Magistrates in the course of the Day, charged with any of the Offences above-mentioned, and whether committed for Trial, Re-examination, or how otherwise disposed of. Also, a description of Property that has been Stolen, with as much particularity as can be given, with every Circumstance that may be Useful for the purpose of tracing and recovering it.*

### BOW STREET OFFICE.

#### INFORMATIONS.

Stolen, on Monday night, the 1st instant, or early the following morning, from a field at North Stoneham, a Chesnut Blood Mare, four years old, with switch tail and white blaze on her face. She has been fired on her near fore foot, for a ring bone, and each side of her inside hoof also fired. She has a very rough long coat. Information to be given to I. T. Enright, superintendent of police, Southampton.

A Woman, named WINIFORD POWELL, stands charged with robbing a man at Abergavenny of Forty Pounds. She is a street-walker, and a native of Abergavenny. Fair complexion, good-looking, genteelly dressed, wears feathers in her bonnet, about five feet seven inches high, twenty-five years of age, light hair, and walks very upright, and generally wears a green stuff cloak. Whoever will apprehend and lodge her in any of Her Majesty's gaols, shall receive Two Pounds Reward by applying to Mr. Richards, near Abergavenny, or to Patrick Cusack, police-officer, Abergavenny.

#### PERSONS CHARGED.

LOUISA POWELL, re-examined, with stealing two pair of stockings, and other articles, the property of Michael Barton, her master and employer, in Duke-street.—Discharged.

MARY ANN RAWLEY, re-examined, with stealing two hats, the property of Esther Bennett, in Bedfordbury.—Discharged.

ROBERT GRAVES, with stealing a quantity of lead, the property of some person unknown, in Lincoln's-inn-fields.—Committed for further examination on Saturday next.

JOHN FITZGERALD, and PATRICK BRYAN, with frequenting High-street, Saint Giles, with intent to commit felony.—Discharged.

### QUEEN SQUARE OFFICE.

#### PERSONS CHARGED.

WILLIAM ROBINSON, on re-examination, with stealing a book, and other articles, the property of John Hayward, his master.—Committed to Newgate for trial.

JOSEPH BEASMORE, on re-examination, with stealing fifteen pieces of brass, the property of some person unknown.—Remanded till Monday next.

JANE RIDLEY, on re-examination, with obtaining, by false pretences, of and from John Smith, three shawls, the property of Richard King Thomas, with intent to cheat and defraud him thereof.—Remanded till Wednesday next.

HENRY ADAMS, with stealing part of a cart-harness, the property of William Lawrence, at Fulham.—Discharged of the felony ; but convicted of unlawfully disposing of the said harness, and fined five pounds and the value.

MARY ANN PRENDERGAST, with stealing two pillows, and other articles, the property of Joseph Sumpter, in Clifford-row, Pimlico.—Discharged.

*A page from the* Police Gazette *for 3 January 1838, a useful resource when searching for ancestors who may have landed themselves in trouble with the law.* (Author's collection) at the foreign ports of Gibraltar and Bermuda. These 'prison hulks', as they were known, were run by private companies, which would receive their funding from the Treasury. In order to reclaim their money, these companies were obliged to return quarterly registers of their prisoners, giving details such as their name, age, place of conviction and, if applicable, date of transportation or removal to another prison hulk. In addition, there are some early nineteenth-century registers of prisoners from the prison hulks that may contain supplementary information, such as a physical description, place of birth, marital status, etc.

All prison hulk records are held at TNA: PRO. The early quarterly registers of prisoners (1802–18) are held by the Treasury in T 38/310–338 (arranged by ship), with later ones (1824 onwards) being filed in HO 8/1–150 (arranged chronologically and then by ship).

Individual registers of prisoners may be found in TNA: PRO HO 7/3 (Bermuda; 1823–9); HO 9/1–16 (1820–45); ADM 6/418–423 (1814–35) and PCOM 2/105, 131–137 (1837–60). In addition, some registers reside in T 1/653–6848, but there is no modern index to these records, and finding individual records is notably problematic.

In all cases these records are arranged by ship name and then chronologically. For full details of all the above records see the TNA: PRO online Catalogue or Hawkings (1992). For more details on the history of the prison hulks see Johnson (1970); see also Section 13.2.

## Criminal Entry Books

From 1782 onwards the Home Office kept copies of outgoing letters and warrants concerning prisoners' remissions, respites, pardons and movements. They are held in TNA: PRO HO 13; each volume has a name index associated with it.

## Petitions, Warrants and Correspondence Relating to Prisoners

Petitions to the Secretary of State concerning individual prisoners are held in TNA: PRO HO 17 (covering the years 1819–39). These include petitions from prisoners (or their representatives) requesting some form of leniency. The registers of criminal petitions, in HO 19 (covering the years 1797–1853) act as an index to the records in HO 17.

Books containing copies of warrants issued regarding prisoners (e.g. free pardons) are held in HO 38 (covering the years 1782–1969). Only a minority of these warrant books are indexed. Other official correspondence relating to individual prisoners may be found in HO 42 (Domestic Correspondence to George II, 1782–1820); HO 47 (Judges' Reports, 1784–1829); HO 48 (Attorney and Solicitor Generals' Reports, 1782–1871); and HO 54 (Civil Petitions, 1783–1854). See the TNA: PRO online Catalogue for further information.

## Other Resources for Criminals

For those prisoners sentenced to death in the period before the creation of the criminal registers, probably the best resource is local newspapers and other publications (see Section 12.5), although TNA: PRO HO 334/1 apparently contains a central register of prisoner burials from 1834 to 1869.

HO 62 contains printed daily reports from the London Metropolitan Police Offices, which include lists of crimes committed, the names of victims, of persons charged and tip-offs received by the police between 1828 and 1839. MEPO 4/12–30 contains a similar handwritten list (1828–39).

A miscellaneous collection of papers sent to the Home Office by individual judges and court recorders may be found in TNA: PRO HO 47 (1784–1829) and HO 6 (1816–40). These may contain comments on individual cases, recommendations for mercy, etc. They are filed by year of conviction but there is no index.

The survival and whereabouts of criminal records held by the prison service and in police archives are listed in Hawkings (1992).

Another resource is the *Police Gazette* (called *Hue and Cry* in its earlier editions), which was first published in 1772 by Sir John Fielding. It contains notices relating to unsolved crimes in London and includes the names of suspects, victims, police officers and also of criminals who were on the run. Unresolved cases would be listed for several issues in a row. TNA: PRO holds copies (in HO 75), as does the British Newspaper Library.

*An extract from the 1838 Middlesex register for persons charged with indictable offences. As well as the person's, name, age, place of trial and offence, the registers also list the trial outcome, including any sentence. (TNA: PRO)*

| Names of Offenders | Degree of Instruction | Ages | At what Sessions Tried or Discharged without Trial | Offences of which those Tried where Convicted or Acquitted—and of which those discharged without Trial where charged on Indictment or Commitment |
|---|---|---|---|---|
| Morris, Sarah | Imp | 20 | Central Criminal Court 22nd October | Larceny |
| Mahon, Robert | Imp | 17 | Do | Larceny by Servant |
| Miller, Joseph Christ. | Imp | 28 | Do | Larceny on a port |
| Martin, Nicholas | N | 29 | Do | Larceny |
| Mitchell, Thomas | N | 42 | Do | Maliciously Wounding with intent to do bodily harm |
| Morgan, Louisa | Imp | 15 | Westminster Sessions 15th November | Larceny |
| Matthews, Henry | Well | 25 | Central Criminal Court 27th November | Do |
| Miller, Charles | N | 14 | Do | Do |

## 13.2. TRANSPORTATION TO THE COLONIES

By the late sixteenth century the inflexibility of the law meant that increasing numbers of people convicted of felonies such as theft, assault, burglary, etc. were being handed out mandatory death sentences. In many cases this sentence could be avoided if the defendant could exploit a loophole in the law that decreed that a clergyman could opt to be sentenced under canon (i.e. Church) law rather than that of the king; this route usually led to a pardon. To be declared a clergyman, all one had to do was to be able to read out in court Psalm 51 from the Bible (many illiterate people simply learned it). This loophole (called 'benefit of clergy') meant that dozens of people were able to escape the death sentence and, in many cases, any form of punishment at all.

To rectify this, an Act of Parliament in 1597 created an alternative to the death sentence; convicted criminals could now be exiled from England and Wales, with the threat that any who returned would be hanged. In 1615 this was amended so that the courts were permitted to sentence criminals to deportation to the newly emerging colonies along the American east coast and to the West Indies. Those sentenced to 'transportation' (as it was known) would be loaded onto ships and taken to Virginia, Maryland and elsewhere, and there sold to plantation owners to work on tobacco and other farms. Initially transportation was simply offered as a means of escaping the death sentence, but from 1718 sentences were standardised to fourteen years for serious felonies, and seven years for more minor ones. After serving this time, the criminal could return to England. To the ships' captains transportation was highly lucrative, as they were not only paid to take the criminals abroad but once there they could sell them and then load their empty ships with tobacco and other cargo for the return journey.

The American Revolution meant that from 1776 transportation to America was no longer an option. However, the sentence was still used by the courts, leading to hundreds of prisoners being stored on floating prison hulk ships (see Section 13.1). In 1787 the problem was solved by the decision to turn Australia into a penal colony. The first fleet of ships departed that year and in the following decades were joined by dozens of others. Those convicted had to serve at least five years, although it was often longer, and many did not bother to return at all, as many living Australians will tell you. The use of transportation was popular in the early nineteenth century, but, as the law became more sophisticated and the range of sentences available to the court increased, so transportation became less frequently used. By the time of its abolition, in 1868, it had been effectively redundant for several years. It is estimated that around 60,000 people were transported to America and around 160,000 to Australia.

## Transportation to America, 1615–1776

Until recently tracing the names of those transported to America and the West Indies was time-consuming and problematic. However, in the late 1980s the genealogist Peter Wilson Coldham published *The Complete Book of Emigrants in Bondage: 1614–1775* (1988), later followed by two supplemental volumes (1992a, 2002). These books were recently superseded by *British Emigrants in Bondage: 1614–1788* (Coldham, 2005), which is available on CD-ROM and at a reasonable price.

Coldham's work is acknowledged to be a near complete record of all the people who were sentenced to transportation to America and should be the first port of call for those seeking to find information on an ancestor. Information given includes the ancestor's name, crime, where he or she lived, where and when he or she was tried and, where available, the name of the convict ship, where he or she ended up and any other details such as pardons, escape attempts, etc. The new edition (Coldham, 2005) also has details about the movements of the individual convict ships used to transport the criminals. Coldham's records will tell you where and when your ancestor was tried. Use this information to obtain their trial records (see Chapter 12); with luck these will tell you whereabouts your ancestor lived and so permit you to start searching more local records. An alternative to Coldham's works is Filby and Meyer (1981), which draws its list of passengers from other published works, including Coldham's.

For those who want to search manually, lists of transported criminals may be found among the Treasury Board Papers in TNA: PRO T 1 and T 53. Records of sentences are to be found among the court records (Chapter 12). Some CROs may hold documents such as transportation bonds (agreements with ships' captains), delivery of prisoners to agents and ships, transportation agents' papers and landing certificates.

I had an interest in the case of Elizabeth Canning, a woman who was at the centre of a scandal in London in 1753 and whose case was subsequently brought before the Old Bailey court (see Section 12.4); she was sentenced to transportation. Coldham (1988) confirms that she was transported from London to America in July 1754 but offers no further information. However, as her sentence was for seven years, I checked the newspapers for 1761 and discovered a small entry in the *Gentleman's Magazine* for November that year announcing her return to England.

## Transportation to Australia, 1787–1868

To many Australians, being able to trace their ancestry to a transported criminal is a matter of pride. Unlike the American convicts, there is as yet no single index to all those who were transported to Australia, which means that in order to trace an ancestor's transportation records it helps to know roughly when and where he or she was transported.

The easiest way of doing this is to try to find a record of your ancestor after transportation to Australia. There are a number of published records from the early part of the nineteenth century that may be of help (see Sainty and Johnson, 1980; Fidlon and Ryan, 1981; Ryan, 1982 and Baxter, 1987a and b, 1988a and b, 1989, 1999). Many of these records contain details of which ship a person arrived on and also details of the trial. The original census returns are held in TNA: PRO HO 10, with the one for 1828 being considered the most useful, as it contains much personal information (age, religion, residence, occupation) and, more importantly, how the person arrived in Australia (i.e. as a freeman, convict or born there), including details of the ship and date of arrival (see Sainty and Johnson, 1980).

There is also an increasing number of online databases that hold information about transported convicts; a good starting point is the links page at www.convictcentral.com. In addition, the State Library of New South Wales holds many computer databases that cover early immigrants (including convicts) to Australia, although many of these are not available for use on line (see www.sl.nsw.gov.au).

If you can find a reference to a person's date and place of trial, you can use it to find the relevant court records relating to the trial (Chapter 12). Many convicts were imprisoned for months before being transported, so it may be worth checking the prison records, especially those for prison hulks (Section 13.1).

For those who have to search manually, Hawkings (1987) is a good, if now out-of-date, guide to the available records; see also the TNA: PRO Research Guide 'Legal Records Information Leaflet 17' (available on line). For further information on Australian genealogy see the online fact sheets provided by the National Archives of Australia (www.naa.gov.au). The following records relate to the transportation of convicts to Australia.

*Transportation Registers*

Located in TNA: PRO HO 11 are records from individual convict ships that list the names of those transported, their date and place of conviction and their sentence. They cover the whole period (1787–1867) and are arranged by year and then by individual ship. If you know roughly when or on which ship your ancestor was transported, then these are worth searching.

Additional registers of convicts' names (covering 1842–67) relating to paperwork generated by the ships' owners can be found in TS 18/460–515; those relating to 1308–61 with some slightly earlier ones are in PC 1/2715–2719. The names of the ships are searchable using the TNA: PRO online Catalogue and are listed in Hawkings (1987, 1992).

*Petitions*

Given that many men were breadwinners, their families would often petition against transportation. Their petitions may be found in TNA: PRO HO 17, 18, 48, 49, 54 and 56. A register of petitions relating to HO 17 and 18 can be found in HO 19. (See also other resources relating to prisoners in Section 13.1.)

It was possible for wives to apply to accompany their husbands. These petitions, usually in the form of letters (from 1819 to 1844), may be found in PC 1/67–92 and HO 12 (registers relating to HO 12 may be found in HO 14).

*Other records*

Medical records relating to the convict ships may be found in the Admiralty records in TNA: PRO ADM 101, while individual captains' and ships' logs are located in ADM 51 and 53.

## 13.3. LUNACY AND IDIOCY

### Commissions and Inquisitions of Lunacy

Traditionally the affairs of those classed as idiots (those born with a low intelligence) and lunatics (those who suffered from periodic mental ill health) came under the realm of the Chancery. Relatives of those with mental health problems would often apply to the Chancery in order to get power of attorney over their land and financial affairs. Such an application needed to be supported by two affidavits declaring the person to be insane. If all was in order, the Lord Chancellor would commission an inquisition of lunacy (*de lunatico inquirendo*), which would determine if the person was insane or not. If so, then the lunatic would be committed to custody (before 1828 all asylums were privately run), a survey of his or her estate undertaken and, finally, control over the estate given to a relative, solicitor or other interested party to administer. Those who were given control over the estate are referred to as the 'committees'.

From 1540 to 1646 documents relating to commissions of lunacy may be found among the Court of Wards' records in TNA: PRO WARD 7. From 1646 onwards they are to be found in C 211, where they are arranged in alphabetical order by the name of the accused lunatic. (Those for the palatine of Lancaster are in PL 5.) Generally the earlier documents contain more information, especially concerning the property holdings of the individual. The last documents were deposited in 1932, by which time the commission had been reduced to a more formal petition and report. Appeals against the findings of the commission are to be found among the Chancery's common law pleadings in C 206, but there is no finding aid.

Registers of the bonds given by the committee to the Clerk as security for the administration of the property can be found in J 103 (these run from 1817 onwards and are arranged chronologically). Annual reports submitted by the committee to the Chancery may be found in C 101; this is searchable by name using the TNA: PRO online Catalogue. For further information on lunacy see the TNA: PRO Research Guide 'Domestic Records Information Leaflet 105' (available on line).

## Criminal Lunacy

Provision for criminal lunatics did not exist before 1800; before this the criminally insane were treated identically to other prisoners (see Section 13.1). After 1800 it was possible for the courts to acquit a defendant by reason of insanity, although this invariably meant that the accused would be committed to an asylum for an indeterminate length of time. It was shortly after this that the government began building special asylums for the criminally insane.

A set of registers of patients admitted to some private asylums between 1798 and 1812 may be found in TNA: PRO MH 51, while, from 1846, the registers of county asylums may be found in MH 94 (the records are arranged annually and then alphabetically by patient name). The LMA holds records of asylums from Middlesex and the CLRO those for the City of London, while CROs may hold records relating to local asylums. The Bethlem Royal Hospital Archives and Museum (Monks Orchard Road, Beckenham, Kent BR3 3BX; www.bethlemheritage.org.uk) holds many mental health records, including those of the Old Bedlam asylum founded in 1247; a catalogue is available on their website. For other more obscure references to tracing lunacy records see Faithfull (2002).

## 13.4. DEBTORS AND BANKRUPTS

Technically there were two classes of insolvent person: a bankrupt, an insolvent trader (i.e. businessman) who had legally been declared bankrupt (see below), and a debtor, who was simply an insolvent person who owed money. As we shall see, it was better to be declared a bankrupt than to be classified as a debtor, a situation that often led to debtors trying to pass themselves off as traders.

## Debtors

Debtors were usually declared as such after having been taken to court by their creditors. The recovery of debts was subject to civil litigation, which means that any trial records relating to debtors will usually be found in the equity courts (see Chapter 14), although most common law courts were able to try civil cases as well, especially the quarter sessions (see Section 12.2).

Once declared a debtor, the individual would be slung in prison and left there until his or her debts were paid or the creditors were agreed upon a release. In some cases this would be a death sentence, and some debtors spent the remainder of their life behind bars.

Outside London, debtors would be put into the local prison with other criminals, and so information about a debtor ancestor should be sought among those records that relate to prisons and prisoners (outlined in Section 13.1). Inside London, there were several debtors' prisons that would contain just the insolvent and no criminals. Some of these institutions, such as the Fleet and King's Bench Prisons, are famous, while others, such as the Marshalsea Prison, are less well known. The records for these prisons are all preserved in TNA: PRO PRIS 1–11 and in some cases date back to the early seventeenth century. A list of the locations of other prison registers for England and Wales may be found in Hawkings (1992).

The establishment of the Court for the Relief of Insolvent Debtors in 1813 accepted petitions from imprisoned debtors; these are to be found in TNA: PRO B 6, with an accompanying index in B 8. The *London Gazette*, the official newspaper of the government (1665 to present day), would also routinely carry lists of debtors who were applying for release (TNA: PRO ZJ 1). After 1861 the bankruptcy laws (see below) were extended to cover debtors, which meant that they could no longer be imprisoned for their insolvency, although they were still subject to legal proceedings regarding fraud, etc. See also Fleet weddings (Section 4.1).

## Bankrupts

Traders and businessmen who owed more than £100 could legally be declared bankrupt under an Act of Parliament passed in 1571. Bankruptcy proceedings were designed to help the bankrupt person find a legal means of discharging his debts by distributing money from any remaining assets among his creditors. This would, in the eyes of the law, wipe out the debts and permit the bankrupt to begin trading again.

In order to enact bankruptcy proceedings the creditors would issue a petition to the Lord Chancellor (under whose jurisdiction bankruptcy fell), who would in turn enact a Commission of Bankruptcy. An independent commissioner would then assess the debtor and his financial situation to see if he qualified for bankruptcy. If he did, then a notice would be inserted in the *London Gazette* (held in TNA: PRO ZJ 1; indexed after 1789) so that any further creditors could make themselves known and submit formal claims to the commissioner. If, after a period of time, an arrangement could not be made between the creditors and the debtor, he would be declared bankrupt and his goods and assets sold and the money passed on to the creditors.

Bankruptcy records are all in TNA: PRO B 1–12 (1–8 covers the pre-Victorian period) and date back as far as the early eighteenth century. Registers of commissions of bankruptcy are in B 4 (covering the years 1710–1849), which are arranged chronologically and are either indexed or ordered alphabetically by the name of the bankrupt. These should provide you with the bankrupt's name, the names of his or her creditors and the legal representatives plus other details such as an address and trade. The files relating to some of these cases may be found in B 3. The enrolment books relating to commissions of bankruptcy are in B 5 (covering the years 1710–1859) and are arranged chronologically, with each volume indexed. Certificates relating to the bankruptcy proceedings (certificates of conformity, declarations of insolvency, etc.) are in B 6 (covering the years 1733–1925) in chronological order. Information relating to appeals is in B 7. See the TNA: PRO online Catalogue for further information on these and other classes. Some bankruptcies (from 1702 onwards) are also included in the patent rolls (see Section 17.2 for details).

When searching for a bankrupt ancestor, first check for notices in the *London Gazette* (see above), *The Times* or local newspapers (see Section 19.1), as these are generally considered to hold a more complete list than the TNA: PRO records. The SoG holds a microfiche index of bankrupts between 1774 and 1786.

The following example of a bankrupt comes from an advertisement placed in *The Times* newspaper on 3 January 1785. It concerns the aftermath of the bankruptcy of Roy Glover, whose property is being sold off to raise money for his creditors.

By Mr Elderton (by order of the assignees)
On Wednesday next the 5th inst.

The neat and genuine household furniture, linen, place and china; a harpsichord; of Mr ROY GLOVER, late of Cornhill, bankrupt, removed for the conveniece sale to No. 49 Lothbury consisting of exceedingly good featherbeds and bedding, mahogany wardrobe, double and single chests of draws, large and other looking glasses . . .

# CHAPTER FOURTEEN

# THE COURTS OF EQUITY

## 14.1. THE EQUITY COURTS

Although the common law courts could deal with criminal actions (such as assault, robbery, etc.), there were other cases for which common law made no provision. Such cases usually took the form of a dispute between two individuals (or parties) in which no crime had been committed against the king or his property and which usually involved one party trying to recover something (such as money or land) from the other or compelling the other person to do something (such as moving a boundary, annulling a contract, etc.).

Such personal disagreements had to be resolved somehow, and so in medieval times a separate series of courts was set up specifically to deal with these cases where the 'equity' (meaning fairness) of the law would decide the outcome.

An equitable lawsuit was usually initiated by one private individual against another. Thus, because it was a person and not the state that was bringing the case to trial, such suits were regarded as being 'civil' in origin. Typically, civil lawsuits would concern such matters as trespass, debt recovery, divorce, inheritance, etc., and their records may contain a great deal of useful information.

In the early modern era a total of five courts were empowered to hear civil lawsuits, the most important of which was the Chancery. These courts are dealt with below; for further information on them and their history see Gerhold (1994) or Bevan (2000).

**Equity Procedure**

All the various courts of equity had a broadly comparable procedure, which, unlike that in the common law courts, was heavily reliant on the submission of written documents. This is to the genealogist's advantage, as it means that much of the minutiae associated with the lawsuit is preserved, including important personal information.

*The Pleadings*

A civil lawsuit begins with the aggrieved person (the plaintiff) filing a bill of complaint (or usually abbreviated to 'bill', but it may also sometimes be called a petition) with the court. The bill was a document, usually drawn up by somebody with legal training, that named the accused person (the defendant) and set out the details of the dispute. A bill of complaint will usually provide much valuable information about the plaintiff (who would refer to himself as the 'orator' in the bill), including his occupation and place of residence.

Next the defendant would be compelled to reply to the plaintiff's bill of complaint by filing an answer. This was a written document that had to address the points raised in the bill.

If the plaintiff felt that the defendant had not addressed all the points raised in the bill of complaint, he could submit a further written document, called a replication, addressing any outstanding points raised by the defendant's answer. The defendant also had a right of reply to this in the form of a rejoinder. Replications and rejoinders could fly backwards and forwards several times until both parties had agreed on a set number of issues that were still in dispute. This whole process is known as the pleadings (sometimes also called the proceedings); after this the court would order the gathering of evidence in preparation for the actual trial.

*The Depositions*

Next both the plaintiff and the defendant (or, more likely, their lawyers) would draw up a list of questions (called interrogatories) to be put to an agreed list of witnesses (called deponents) under oath. This questioning would not take place in court, but would normally be undertaken by people appointed by the court. They would put the questions to the deponents, writing down their answers in the form of a deposition, which would then be submitted to the court. Depositions can be very useful documents as they usually contain detailed information on the lives of the deponents (i.e. witnesses), including their place of abode, age and family status.

*Decrees*

With the pleadings and depositions complete, all the written documents would be brought before the court, together with any supporting evidence such as sworn affidavits or physical exhibits such as wills, deeds, etc. The court would consider all the evidence before it and then issue a final judgment or decree. The court's judgment and the orders it issued would be recorded in the decree and order books. A plaintiff could, for an extra fee, have his decree copied into a separate document known as a decree roll.

It should be noted that many cases did not make it as far as the decree stage, the matter being settled out of court beforehand. Even if a case was abandoned, the documents relating to the pleadings and depositions should still be preserved in the archive.

The following bill of complaint was filed in 1761 by John Lynes against his brother-in-law William Kent, whom he accused of owing him money. Aside from making it apparent that there was bad blood between Lynes and Kent, this document contains a wealth of genealogical information. It gives a basic outline of the Lynes' family history and lists John Lynes's parents, brothers and sisters and their spouses. It also tells us the approximate death dates and ages of some of these people and where they lived. In addition it lists the family's landholdings and gives references to some of the family's wills. The original document (in C 12/1489/4) is lengthy, so the following is an abbreviated extract:

Lynes vs. Kent

31st October 1761

Humbly complaining showeth unto your Lordship your orator John Lynes of Litcham in the County of Norfolk Butcher that Thomas Lynes late of Litcham in the said County of Norfolk grocer deceased was in his Lifeform in the year one thousand seven hundred and twenty five entitled to be admitted to a copyhold estate lying within the Manor of Grossenhall in the said county of Norfolk . . . the said Thomas Lynes and Susan his wife died several years ago leaving Thomas Lynes their eldest son and your orator John Lynes, their youngest son, and Susan Catherine Frances and Ann their daughter and no other child upon whose death the said Thomas Lynes entered upon the said copyhold premises and was seized thereof and continued so seized till the nineteenth of August one thousand seven hundred and fifty nine when he departed this life . . . [the land was willed to] Samuel Rash and Thomas Node and the said Catherine Lynes, Susan the wife of the said Thomas Node, William Kent the executor of the will of the said Frances Lynes who was then deceased and the said Ann Lynes . . . the said William Kent absolutely refuses to pay to your orator any sum of money whatsoever on the account aforesaid the said William Kent pretending that he has applied the sum of money that he so received in payment of the debts of the said Frances Lynes without notice of the said mistake . . .

## 14.2. CHANCERY EQUITY PROCEEDINGS

The Chancery's ability to try equity cases dates to the fourteenth century. It became the most important of the equity courts, handling the majority of civil cases in England and Wales. If you are searching for a civil case, the Chancery is the first place to look.

The proceedings of the Chancery court are an excellent hunting-ground for the genealogist as the thousands of records preserve information about people who would not normally make their mark in history in any other way. The detail provided by the documents can shed vital light on the past lives and actions of our ancestors. For example, Chancery suits could involve family members contesting wills, marriage settlements, debts, etc., sometimes over several generations. Family and social historians highly value the Chancery proceedings not least because the majority of the documents are written in English and not Latin.

The earliest preserved Chancery equity proceedings date from *c.* 1386 and the court remained until the nineteenth century, by which time it had become notorious for lengthy delays (Dickens's *Bleak House* satirises this). After much wrangling, the Court of Chancery was replaced by the Supreme Court of Judicature in 1875.

For further details on the Chancery equity courts and their records see Horwitz (1995) or Moore (2003).

## Chancery Procedure

The general Chancery procedure follows that given in Section 14.1 but with a couple of notable differences. The first is that in the early modern era the depositions are filed under one of two categories based on where the evidence for the case was taken.

If the evidence was gathered in London or within approximately 20 miles of London, the documents will be filed as town depositions. If, however, the evidence was gathered from outside London, they will be filed under country depositions. These differences are reflected in the way in which the documents are currently filed at TNA: PRO (see below).

The second difference concerns especially complicated Chancery cases which were sometimes referred to a master in Chancery to examine further. He would

*A detail from a 1761 bill of complaint filed with the Court of Chancery in which John Lynes alleges that his ex-brother-in-law William Kent owes him money. The bill gives information about John Lynes's parentage, brothers and sisters and their financial circumstances. (TNA: PRO)*

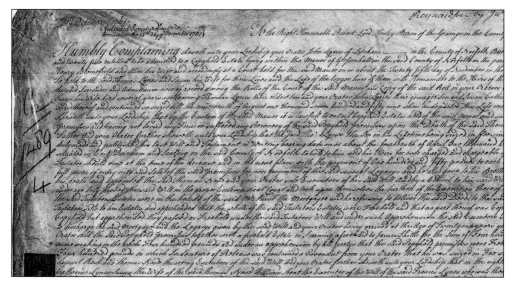

then offer a written report back to the judges to help them when making a decree. The results of these examinations were a master's report, filed separately from the other suit documents (see below).

## Locating Chancery Equity Documents

All the original documents relating to the Chancery equity court are preserved at TNA: PRO. The arrangement of documents is complicated, with the pleadings, depositions, affidavits, decrees and masters' reports all filed separately. This means that to find all the documents relating to a case it is necessary to search across several different categories, a task that is far from easy.

Despite their potential usefulness to genealogists, the Chancery records are not particularly easy to search. The majority of the indexes, catalogues and calendars that exist for the post-medieval Chancery suits are not coordinated and lack vital details such as individuals' first names. Ironically, the best catalogued and readily searchable records are those made before 1558, which can be searched using the TNA: PRO online Catalogue (see Bevan, 2000, or Chambers, 2005, for more details).

When attempting to find a Chancery suit, it is best to start by searching the pleadings, as these mark the initiation of the suit. If you find the pleadings, you can move on to search the depositions to see if the case went any further (often cases were resolved during the pleading process, in which case no depositions will exist). Generally the pleadings and depositions provide the most useful genealogical information, but those who wish to see the process through can carry on and try to locate the decree or any other associated records such as affidavits or exhibits.

### Equity Pleadings Project

TNA: PRO has initiated the Equity Pleadings Project, which is designed to rectify the problems associated with finding Chancery suits. This is a database, accessible through the TNA: PRO website, which permits searching by personal name, location and subject. The project is still in its infancy but at the time of writing the details of around 30,000 cases have been entered from TNA: PRO C 6 (equity suits between c. 1625 and 1714), although further additions are planned.

### Bernau Index

Currently the most comprehensive unpublished finding aid to the Chancery proceedings is the Bernau Index, a card index prepared by C.A. Bernau containing the names of over four and a half million people (mostly plaintiffs and defendants, but also some witnesses) listed in Chancery proceedings up to around the year 1800. The index is in alphabetical order based on a person's surname, then first name. The index is available to view only on microfilm in the SoG or through Mormon Family History Centres. The best guide to the Bernau Index and some of its eccentricities is Sharp (2000).

*Indexes and Catalogues*

The list below reflects the complex arrangement of Chancery equity records and the myriad of different indexes and catalogues pertaining to them. Some of these indexes are now searchable on line through the TNA: PRO online Catalogue (as indicated).

The following lists are organised by their classification at TNA: PRO, but please be aware that there is chronological overlap between many of these categories.

## Chancery Pleadings

Before 1714 the pleadings are split across several categories, which overlap in terms of date.

C 2 (*c.* 1558–*c.* 1660; arranged by reign, then in rough alphabetical order using the plaintiff's surname). Some of the records from James I are searchable on line using the plaintiff's and defendant's surname. Published indexes for James I records include a series of articles in *The Genealogist* (new series, vols 4, 6–9, 1887, 1889–92), which cover surnames A–L and List and Index Society (vol. 47, 1922), which covers surnames A–K. For Charles I there is Phillimore and Fry (1889–1904). Defendants' names for Charles I are also in the Bernau Index.

C 3 (*c.* 1558–*c.* 1660; arranged by the reign of each keeper of the Great Seal and then in rough alphabetical order using the plaintiff's surname). Searchable on line by the surname of the first plaintiff and defendant and also by county. Published catalogues can be found in List and Index Society (vols 7, 26 and 30; 1896, 1908 and 1909). All parties are in the Bernau Index.

C 5 (1613–1714; alphabetical order by first plaintiff's surname). Searchable on line by the surname of the first plaintiff and defendant and also by county. Published catalogues are in List and Index Society (vols 39, 42, 44 and 45; 1913, 1914, 1915 and 1917; these are arranged by plaintiff surname). All parties are in the Bernau Index.

C 6 (1625–1714). Searchable on line using the Equity Pleadings database (see above). No published indexes. The Dwelly Index at the SoG library includes the names of plaintiffs and defendants.

C 7 (1620–1714). Not searchable on line. An unpublished index of first plaintiffs' surnames is available at TNA: PRO.

C 8 (1570–1714). Not searchable on line. An unpublished index of first plaintiffs' surnames is available at TNA: PRO.

C 9 (1643–1714). Searchable on line by the surname of the first plaintiff and defendant and also by county. Published catalogues are Fry (1904). Defendants' names are in the Bernau Index.

C 10 (1640–1721). Searchable on line by the surname of the first plaintiff and defendant and also by county. An unpublished index of first plaintiffs' surnames is available at TNA: PRO.

C 11 (1700–58). Searchable on line by the surname of the first plaintiff and first defendant. An unpublished index exists at TNA: PRO, arranged by clerk and then by the name of the first plaintiff. The names of all parties are included in the Bernau Index.

C 12 (1758–1800). Searchable on line by the surname of the first plaintiff and first defendant. An unpublished index exists at TNA: PRO, arranged by clerk and then by the name of the first plaintiff. The names of all parties are included in the Bernau Index.

C 13 (1800–42). Searchable on line by full name of plaintiff and defendant. No published or unpublished indexes exist.

## Chancery Country and Town Depositions

Country depositions between 1714 and 1880 are filed with the pleadings in C 11, C 12, C 13 and C 14. They are usually filed separately from the pleadings to which they relate but can be searched using the same indexes and databases. The SoG has an index of locations in these depositions between 1714 and 1744.

C 21 (country depositions; 1558–1649). Searchable on line by surname of first plaintiff and first defendant. An unpublished index exists at TNA: PRO. The names of deponents and their place of residence are included in the Bernau Index.

C 22 (country depositions; 1649–1714). Searchable on line by surname of first plaintiff and first defendant. An unpublished index exists at TNA: PRO. Names of deponents and parties are included in the Bernau Index. Suit titles are included in the Great Card Index at the SoG library.

C 24 (town depositions; 1534–1867; arranged by year, legal term and then by plaintiff's surname). Partially searchable on line (C 24/2450–2508). An unpublished index to the title of suit exists in IND 1/9115–9121, but it is said to be unreliable and difficult to use.

## Chancery Affidavits

C 31 (1611–1875, arranged chronologically). Not searchable on line. An unpublished index exists at TNA: PRO in IND 1/14545–14567 (to 1800) and IND 1/14575–14684 (1801–75). A register of all affidavits exists in C 41, which includes information on some documents that are now missing.

## Chancery Decrees

Decrees are difficult to find and rarely contain any information of use to the genealogist.

C 33 (1544–1875). Decree and order books. Not searchable on line. Unpublished indexes of suit titles exist at TNA: PRO.

C 79 (1534–1903, arranged in two series). Decree rolls. Not searchable on line. No indexes exist.

## Masters' Reports

Masters' reports are even more rarely sought out than decrees.

C 38 (1544–1875). Not searchable on line. Unpublished indexes covering 1606–1875, arranged annually and then by suit title, can be found in IND 1/1878–2028 (1606–1759), IND 1/10700/1–41 (1760–1800), IND 1/14919–14993 (1801–75).

Assorted documents, such as affidavits, are associated with the masters' reports. To find these you will need to know the name of the master who heard the case. Documents before 1852 are arranged by the master's name in C 117–126, with associated indexes in IND 1/6617–6627. An article in *Genealogists' Magazine* (vol. 20, 1980, pp. 257–60) explains how to search these effectively.

## 14.3. EXCHEQUER EQUITY PROCEEDINGS

During the reign of Elizabeth I, the Exchequer, which already had the common law court of pleas, was given the right to try equity cases where the outcome could be of financial interest to the Crown.

In practice this usually meant that the cases that came before the court concerned land disputes, debts, legacies or wills. Often plaintiffs would exaggerate the Crown's interest in their cases in order to get them tried in the equity court as opposed to the more rigid common law courts. Like those of the Chancery, the Exchequer equity proceedings can be a good source of family history; and they are almost exclusively written in English. The earliest Exchequer records are from 1558, and the court carried on hearing cases until 1841, when its remit was transferred to the Chancery equity courts.

## Exchequer Procedure

Cases going through the Exchequer followed the same basic procedure as was outlined in Section 14.1, with the exception that the depositions are filed under one of two categories based on where the evidence for the case was taken.

If the evidence was gathered in London or within approximately 10 miles of London, the documents will be filed as barons' depositions. If, however, the evidence was gathered from outside London, they will be filed under depositions by commission. These differences are reflected in the way in which the documents are currently filed at TNA: PRO (see below).

In addition to the resources listed below, there are other more minor records associated with the Exchequer courts. For a full list of these see Bevan (2000).

## Exchequer Pleadings

The Exchequer pleadings are notoriously tedious to search, so much so that it is probably best to begin by searching the depositions on line. If you find the depositions, you can perhaps think about trying to find the bills and answers that preceded them.

E 112 (1558–1841, arranged by reign then county). Not searchable on line. Two sets of bill book indexes exist arranged by regnal year and then county in IND 1/16820–16853. They list the full names of the parties and are in Latin before 1738.

The first series of indexes covers the counties of Bedford, Buckingham, Cambridge, Cheshire, Cornwall, Cumberland, Devon, Essex, Hampshire, Hereford, Hertford, Huntingdon, Kent, Lancashire, Lincoln, Middlesex and Welsh counties. They begin at IND 1/16820 and then continue as even numbers (i.e. 16822, 16824, etc.).

The second series of indexes covers Berkshire, Dorset, Durham, Leicester, Monmouth, Norfolk, Northampton, Northumberland, Nottingham, Oxford, Rutland, Shropshire, Somerset, Stafford, Suffolk, Surrey, Warwick, Westmorland, Wiltshire, Worcester and York. They begin at IND 1/16821 and then continue as odd numbers (i.e. 16823, 16825, etc.).

## Exchequer Depositions

The depositions are more easily searched than the pleadings and are the best place to start when searching for an Exchequer equity suit. Affidavits associated with these cases are in E 103 (1744–1951, filed by legal term), but there are no finding aids before 1841.

E 133 (barons' depositions, 1558–1841). Searchable on line by the surname of first plaintiff and first defendant; the entries after 1603 are undated.

E 134 (depositions by commission, 1558–1841). Fully searchable on line by names of all parties, subject and location. Unpublished partial indexes of location and deponent name are available at TNA: PRO.

## Exchequer Decrees

The decrees and orders are notably difficult to search.

E 123–131 (1559–1842, arranged chronologically). These are not searchable on line and there are many unpublished indexes covering various aspects. For a list of these check each class's description in the TNA: PRO online Catalogue.

## 14.4. COURT OF REQUESTS

Gaining access to the justice system was traditionally more problematic for women and poor people. It was with this in mind that, in 1483, the Court of Requests (sometimes nicknamed the Court of Conscience) was founded as an independent branch of the King's Council. Its remit was to provide easy access to civil litigation for the poor and for women, although other classes of people frequently ended up using the Court as well. The Court was designed to keep the costs of the procedure to a minimum and would hear claims that concerned only small sums of money (like modern small claims courts) and in time became very popular.

Many cases involved disputes over small debts, property, rights of access, wills or marriage contracts. Because the Court of Requests was used by a section of society traditionally under-represented in the records (i.e. the poor and women), it can be a useful resource for the genealogist.

The earliest records date from 1483 through to the Civil War in 1642. After this time people were referred to small claims courts. The procedure follows that of the other equity courts (see Section 12.1), including pleadings, depositions and decrees. Some early records are in Latin but the majority are in English.

## Finding Aids

The Court of Requests documents are in class REQ 2 at TNA: PRO. Most of the preserved documents are from the pleadings stage, although some decrees and other papers are occasionally enrolled with the bill of complaint. The documents are arranged in chronological order in bundles. The only finding aids are List and Index Society (vol. 21, 1906; and supplementary series 7, vols 1–3, 1964–6), which cover the period from the Court's formation through to the Elizabethan period.

The books are held in class REQ 1 and are arranged in series in chronological order. No indexes exist to these records, but because they are in chronological order, if you are aware of the existence of a case from the pleadings documents in REQ 2, it may be possible to find further information here.

Further miscellaneous material from the Court of Requests has been placed in class REQ 3, but it has not been indexed and the documents are not organised.

## 14.5. COURT OF STAR CHAMBER

The Court of Star Chamber was a court of law that evolved from meetings of the King's Council (which used to meet in a room with stars inlaid into the ceiling). The Court became a separate entity only during the reign of Henry VII, although its roots lie further back in the medieval period.

The Court was chiefly tasked with overseeing the actions of other courts, and would sometimes deal with allegations of judicial corruption, bribery and jury rigging. Henry VIII would often use the Court as a political weapon, bringing actions against his opponents. However, most of the cases heard there involved public order offences including assault, riot, aggravated trespass, abduction, etc. Proceedings could be initiated either by the Crown or by private individuals. As with the other equity courts, ordinary disputes involving property, inheritance, etc. were often exaggerated by the plaintiff so that they qualified for the Court of Star Chamber.

The Court became independent in 1485, but some records from earlier proceedings in the King's Council, dating back to around 1461, are also enrolled in its archive. The proceedings for the Star Chamber follow those of the other equity courts (see Section 12.1). Most documents are in English.

Fewer cases were dealt with by the Court of Star Chamber than by other courts, but its popularity did grow with time. It was often abused by the reigning monarch, especially during Stuart times, and was abolished by Parliament in 1641. Records from the Court of Star Chamber may contain the same type of genealogical information as is found in the other equity courts.

### Finding Aids

Documents relating to the Court of Star Chamber are in classes STAC 1 to STAC 9 at TNA: PRO. They are arranged chronologically and categorised by monarch. The records are searchable by name (for both plaintiffs and defendants), subject, place and county. Should you need them, other unpublished indexes and calendars exist at TNA: PRO (see class descriptions on the Catalogue). A typical example from the Catalogue is shown below:

**STAC 8/96/1** Chambers v. Cooke: Cambridge. 04/03/1603–27/03/1625

## 14.6. PALATINE COURTS

### Palatine Equity Courts

The palatine counties had their own equity courts, the records from which are all housed at TNA: PRO. Few finding aids exist for these courts, but the majority of documents have been separated to reflect the equity procedure and are then in chronological order. For further details on the contents of the various classes of document listed below, either view the description for each class in the TNA: PRO online Catalogue or consult Bevan (2000).

*Palatine of Chester*

Records stretch from *c.* 1297 to 1830 and may be found in classes CHES 9 and CHES 11–16.

Records from CHES 15 (pleadings in cases relating to real property) are indexed in an appendix in *The Twenty-Fifth Annual Report of the Deputy Keeper of Public Records* (pp. 23–31, 1864).

*Palatine of Durham*

Records cover the period 1557–1958 and may be seen in classes DURH 1, DURH 2 and DURH 4 to DURH 7.

*Palatine of Lancaster*

Records cover the period 1474–1858 and may be seen in classes PL 9 to PL 12 and PL 30.

*Duchy of Lancaster*

Records cover the period 1472–1872 and may be seen in classes DL 1, DL 3 to DL 6, DL 8, DL 9, DL 48 and DL 49.

Calendars and indexes covering documents in DL 1 (pleadings, 1485–1800s) and DL 3 (depositions, 1485–1818) may be found in *Ducatus Lancastriae* (Record Commission, London, 3 vols, 1823–4).

# 14.7. EXHIBITS FROM EQUITY AND OTHER COURTS

There exists at TNA: PRO a collection of unclaimed exhibits (i.e. private papers that were submitted as evidence during litigation) that come from the Chancery and other courts. Although most exhibits are relatively recent, some date back to the twelfth century. These unclaimed exhibits are a random collection and can be anything from original wills, deeds and charters to personal correspondence, manorial rolls, etc.

Exhibits are a good source for social historians, but the chances of finding something relating to an ancestor are slim. The following is a guide to the location of exhibits relating to various courts; indexes are available to some of these at TNA: PRO.

*Chancery*

Classes C 103 to C 114; indexes are available.
See also: C 115, Duchess of Norfolk Deeds (1085–1842), records from the Scudamore estate; C 116, manorial rolls (1294–1808) extracted from the Chancery exhibits; C 171, additional exhibits from the Chancery court.

*Exchequer*

Class C 106 (1216–1853), indexed.
Class E 140 (1319–1842), indexed.

*Prerogative Court of Canterbury*

Class PROB 35 (1529–86). No index, but entries are subdivided into five categories based on the nature of exhibits.

*Court of Wards and Liveries*

Class WARD 2 (*c.* 1200–1645). No index.

*Chester Court*

Class CHES 11 (1200–1673). No index.

# CHAPTER FIFTEEN

# EMIGRANTS AND IMMIGRANTS

## 15.1. THE NEW WORLD COLONIES

Within a century of the discovery of North America various seafaring European nations were beginning to lay claim to its territories and, from the early sixteenth century onwards, colonise its shores (often to the chagrin of the native American tribes). England had a long-standing seafaring tradition and soon laid claim to several sections of America's east coast plus many of the Caribbean territories. By the early seventeenth century some of these areas, most notably the states along the east coast, and several Caribbean islands, were home to pioneering colonists who took advantage of the wide open spaces to plant vast crops of tobacco and sugar cane that could be harvested, exported home and sold at vast expense. To help in these ventures, prisoners were sometimes exiled to the plantations to work as cheap labour (see Section 13.2 for further details). At times the pioneering farmers were also joined by others who sought to escape persecution in England, the most famous being the 'Pilgrim Fathers', who sailed aboard the *Mayflower*, landing in Massachusetts in 1620. This section gives a brief outline of the sources available to those who suspect that their ancestors may voluntarily have left for the Americas from England (convicts are dealt with in Section 13.2) and/or have been resident there as early colonists.

### North America

*Original Documents*

From the moment of their founding, most of the North American colonies were autonomous, usually with little connection with the English government. Consequently the majority of records were made and stored locally and it tends to be only correspondence (letters, reports, petitions, instructions, etc.) between the Privy Council, Secretary of State and the Board of Trade and individual colonists that is preserved in the British archives. For a guide to what records exist in Great Britain and Ireland and where they are to be found see Andrews (1912, 1914), Griffin (1946), Scottish Record Office (1976), Raimo (1979) and Minchinton and Harper (1983). A more general guide to colonial records can be found in Pugh

(1964) and Thurston (1995). For documents in European archives, see Matteson (1925) or one of the many volumes relating to the whereabouts of foreign historical American documents produced by the Carnegie Institution of Washington in the early twentieth century (e.g. the Institute of Historical Research holds most of these).

The largest collection of records relating both to North America and the Caribbean is to be found in the TNA: PRO Colonial Office archives. Those records before 1688 were gathered together in CO 1, where they are arranged chronologically. All these papers have been calendared in *Calendar of State Papers, Colonial Series* (38 vols, HMSO, 1860–1994). A corrected version of these volumes plus additional material from C1/69 is now available on a CD-ROM (Kupperman *et al.*, 2000). These represent the best finding aid to these records.

Records after 1688 have been placed in CO 5, and include the original correspondence and entry books (which contain copies of outgoing and some incoming letters, petitions, instructions, etc.) of both the Secretary of State and the Board of Trade, as well as some military and naval despatches, records of land grants and some shipping records. The records are arranged by colony (or province) and then chronologically. CO 5 also includes all the early records relating to the Canadian colonies (Hudson's Bay, Newfoundland, Nova Scotia, etc., including French Canada).

Those papers up to 1739 are calendared in Kupperman *et al.* (2000); no finding aid exists for the remaining records, which run to the early nineteenth century. Stock (1924) provides information on documents relating to proceedings and Acts of Parliament that relate to North America, while Coldham (1985) has abstracted information relating to American emigrants from the archives of the High Court of Admiralty. Many settlers had to sign the 1696 Association Oath Rolls (see Section 17.1 and Gandy, 1922).

TNA: PRO T 47/9–11 contains weekly returns of those emigrating to America between 1773 and 1776, an index to which is available in the Reading Room.

*Published Sources*

The popularity of genealogy within America has led to the production of many historical and biographical publications relating to the early European immigrants. Many of these are specifically aimed at the family history community and may provide much useful genealogical information.

Mackenzie (1907), Hotten (1931), Kaminkow (1966) and Weis (1999) provide general biographical information on early settlers, while Savage (1977) deals with New England settlers, Greer (1960) with Virginia, Goodwin (1995) with Connecticut and Massachusetts, and Tepper (1978) with Pennsylvania. Coldham (1980 and 1992b) provides details on early American estates and on settlers' wills proved in England.

An extract from the association oath roll of 1696 covering New York City. The forty-five signatories on this sheet are a mixture of British and Dutch nationals who had emigrated to America in search of a new life and/or wealth. (TNA: PRO)

Many other published works exist that relate to early American genealogy; for an idea of what is available try consulting the catalogue of the Genealogical Publishing Company (www.genealogical.com), which specialises in books on American genealogy, including reprints of older volumes.

## West Indies and Caribbean

Although they were colonised at around the same time as North America (i.e. early seventeenth century), the Caribbean territories remained British protectorates after American independence in 1776. In fact, many Caribbean territories remained under British control until well into the twentieth century.

The Caribbean territories generated many of the same records and documents as are to be found in England and Wales, including church registers, wills, deeds, legal and civil court records, etc. These documents remain in archives on the islands concerned as well as in the English public records. For a guide to what records are available see Bell and Parker (1926), Pugh (1964), Walne (1973) and Thurston (1995). For documents in European archives, see Matteson (1925).

Within TNA: PRO, records before 1688 are to be found in CO 1 (see notes for North America, above) while later records are to be found in CO 5, arranged by province (again, see North America above). Additional records, mostly of a military nature, are in CO 318 (a finding aid to these exists in CO 326).

The Institute of Commonwealth Studies (27–28 Russell Square, London WC1B 5DS) holds the papers of many senior colonial diplomats and other important figures, especially for southern Africa and the Caribbean.

Published records for the Caribbean are not as advanced as those for North America, but for those researching their family history from outside the Caribbean, a good starting point is the *Caribbeana* volumes (Oliver, 1910–19), which contain the transcriptions of many historical records relating to all the Caribbean territories, including many parish registers, probate and court records. Beyond this, most of the individual islands or groups of islands have had detailed histories published which contain information about long-standing colonial families (e.g. Long, 1970). Most islands have their own historical societies or individuals who have produced volumes of use to family historians; for example, Sanders (1979–81) has produced summaries of all the wills and administrations held on Barbados.

As pertains records held in England, the association oath rolls of 1696 (see Section 17.1 and Gandy, 1922) contain lists of colonists forced to swear allegiance to the Crown. Also, many Caribbean colonists would send their children to England to be educated at school and university (see Chapter 9) or to undergo training in the legal or medical professions; some also chose to have their wills proved at the PCC (see Section 4.2).

My wife's family history has a branch that, through university records and association with the Methodist Church, was traced back to the Caribbean island of

Antigua, where they were plantation owners. My wife's direct ancestor Nathaniel Gilbert was permanently moved from Antigua to Britain in the 1760s, leaving us with the problem of trying to trace his Caribbean ancestry. Fortunately many of the records we needed had been published in *Caribbeana*, such as this 1799 Bill of Complaint and Answer from the Court of Chancery, Antigua, which gives an outline of the debts owed by Nathaniel Gilbert's estate. More importantly, it tells us that his father was also called Nathaniel and that he died around 1761.

> Bill of complaint of Thomas Oliver, Michael Lovell, and others. In *re* the estate of Nathaniel Gilbert the Elder deceased. Nathaniel Gilbert the Elder owed on 25 April 1761 to Richard Oliver the Elder £3205 and Richard Oliver the Elder being grown old and infirm took into partnership with himself and Richard Oliver the Younger and gave him a mutual interest with himself in the business . . .
>
> Answer of James Gordon formerly Brebner Defendant to the Bill of Complaint of Thomas Oliver and others. Richard Oliver came to this Island to settle the affairs of his co-partnership with Richard Oliver the Elder and further sums were advanced by Richard Oliver the Younger and Thomas Oliver to Nathaniel Gilbert the Younger and Nathaniel Gilbert executed a bond in £13,808 sterling and judgement was obtained and the estate was placed in the hands of Trustees for the creditors and Nathaniel Gilbert the younger induced his father's Trustees to take over the estate . . .

## 15.2. THE EAST INDIA COMPANY

The long period of British rule over what now comprises India, Pakistan and Bangladesh has its roots in a bold commercial venture. The British had no political or military interest in India and the Orient, but the wealth of these regions had drawn the attention of various merchants. In the late sixteenth century English traders found themselves in competition with other Europeans, and so in order to facilitate trading, a number of investors formed a joint-stock company which they named the East India Company (it is sometimes nicknamed the 'John Company'). The EIC was awarded a Royal Charter by Elizabeth I on 31 December 1600, which gave it a monopoly on all trade in the East Indies. Over the coming two centuries the EIC engaged in pitched battles with the French and others over control of individual ports and provinces. It also took advantage of the infighting between (and the political ambitions of) India's Mogul leaders and so began to occupy and administer the continent of India, piece by piece. By 1800 the EIC had control not only of all India but of almost all the trade taking place in the Far East and the Orient. They even laid claim to all the waters of the Pacific Ocean, creating tension with whalers and the new North American colonials.

Within India, its main powerbase, the EIC effectively became a government in its own right and had a large standing army. Civil unrest, the loss of its trading monopoly and questions over the EIC's administrative methods led the British government to take over its administrative functions in India in 1858. India gained independence from Britain in 1947.

From the late eighteenth century onwards the EIC employed thousands of people, both as civil servants and for its military ventures. Starting a new life in India was a popular choice for down-at-heel British men and women, as it offered the prospect of good pay, fast promotion and adventure. It was also a popular choice for the middle classes, who could expect to land civil service jobs that were beyond their reach at home. Many left to start farming or other business ventures. Consequently modern British families of all types and classes may find that they have ancestors who spent all or part of their time abroad working for the EIC.

In addition to Baxter (2004), a more general guide to Indian ancestry can be found in *Genealogists' Magazine* (vol. 21(5), 1984, pp. 150–4).

Although called the EIC, it should be borne in mind that the company also had interests in (and therefore also records relating to) the following places:

- Cape of Good Hope (before 1836);
- Zanzibar, Somalia and Ethiopia (mostly nineteenth century);
- St Helena (before 1834);
- Arabia, including the Gulf States, Iraq and Iran (early 1600s to 1947);
- Cental Asia including Afghanistan, Russia and Tibet, Nepal and Bhutan (late eighteenth century to 1947);
- Sri Lanka (*c.* 1750–1802);
- Malaysia and South-East Asia (before 1870);
- Indonesia (before 1825);
- China (early 1600s to 1947);
- Japan (mostly seventeenth century).

## General Sources

The greater majority of original documents and manuscripts relating to the EIC and Britain's involvement with India and the Orient are held in the Oriental and India Office Collections of the British Library. The oldest of these records date to 1600, but many sources are patchy until the late eighteenth century. The standard guide to the India Office's records is known as *Baxter's Guide* (Baxter, 2004), copies of which are obtainable from the British Library. Those undertaking family research in India and the EIC's associated trading regions should first buy or consult a copy of *Baxter's Guide* as it provides a comprehensive list of family history resources for these archives. Alternatively, a list and description of the Oriental and India Office's collections is available on the British Library's website (www.bl.uk/collections/iorarrgt.html).

Many of the EIC's records are subdivided geographically, usually based on its three large administrative provinces in India: Bengal (northern India, Burma and some south-east Asian provinces), Madras (east and south India) and Bombay (west India). This subdivision has been applied retrospectively to some older documents. It is therefore helpful (but not essential) to have a rough idea of where in India your ancestors were living.

Probably the most useful documents in the Oriental and India Office Collections are the ecclesiastical returns (classified in the British Library under IOR/N), which record the baptisms, marriages and burials of those British working and living under the EIC's jurisdiction. These provide the same information as is found in English and Welsh parish registers (see Section 4.1) and run from 1698 to 1947. They are relatively complete from around 1800 but are very patchy before then. There are three separate name indexes to these (for Bengal, Madras and Bombay) in the British Library which will allow you to find the original registry entry on microfilm. Both the indexes and microfilm are on open access; copies are also available through the Mormon Church's Family History Centres. The open-access nature of these records makes them quick and easy to use. The ecclesiastical records should give you an idea as to the sort of career that your ancestor was following; you can then use the records to find out further biographical information.

Alternatively, try *The Asiatic Journal and Monthly Register for British India and its Dependencies* (1816–45), which has news sections, including births, marriages, deaths, civil and ecclesiastical appointments, passengers on ships, and military appointments and promotions. It has name indexes in vols 1–6 (1816–18) only. The *Asiatic Annual Register* (1800–12) contains births, deaths and marriages, and civil and military appointments but no indexes.

In addition to the Oriental and India Office Collections, the Centre of South Asian Studies (Cambridge University, Laundress Lane, Cambridge CB2 1SD) holds the private papers of many British civil servants and others who worked in India and the Middle East. See Carter and Bateson (1995) for details.

Using the civil registration records, I discovered that my great-grandmother had been born in India. Using the ecclesiastical registers at the Oriental and India Office (British Library) I discovered that I had a considerable heritage in India, with some of my ancestors having emigrated there in the early nineteenth century. For example, the ecclesiastical registers alone were able to tell me that my ancestor Juliana Margery Lemmon had been born on 11 March 1842 in Etawah, West Bengal, to John and Caroline Lemmon. She married (aged fourteen) Michael Halloran, a sergeant in the army who died of delirium tremens in 1862 and then, in 1864, married my ancestor Thomas Cuerden. Using further records I was to find out that Juliana's father John was a fife major in the 11th Regiment of Native Infantry who married Caroline Highbert in West Bengal on 11 September 1823.

## Military and Naval Records

The majority of British subjects who ended up in India did so because of their involvement in the EIC's army. The army did not just require foot soldiers; it also employed doctors, nurses, engineers, administrators, chaplains and many others. Farrington (1982) and Baxter (2004) give a detailed breakdown of the records (which date from 1708), most of which are in IOR: L/MIL.

For privates and non-commissioned officers the registers of recruits are to be found in IOR: L/MIL/9, but these date only to 1801. Before this there are muster rolls and registers (IOR: L/MIL/10–12), some dating to 1708, and ship embarkation lists (IOR: L/MIL/9), but these can be tedious to search unless you know your ancestor's regiment and dates of service.

Officers in the Indian Army have been better catered for by historians. Appointment records, which may include details of birth and education, may be found in IOR: L/MIL/9, as may the cadet records. Annual lists of officers and details of any change in their career can be found in the *Bengal Army List* (from 1819), *Madras Army List* (from 1810) and *Bombay Army List* (from 1823) held in IOR: L/MIL/17.

There are many published biographical collections of Indian Army officers' careers. These can save a lot of time and provide useful family history information. The best general resources include Philippart (1823–6), Dodwell and Miles (1838) and Hodson (1927, 1947), but other more restricted biographical dictionaries also occur and can be found in the British Library.

Appointment records relating to medical officers and surgeons may be found in IOR: L/MIL/9; these may contain much biographical information including birthplace, parents and names of sponsors. Published biographies include Dodwell and Miles (1839a–d) and Crawford (2002).

Records pertaining to the EIC's navy are in IOR: L/MAR (again, see Baxter, 2004); there are no published biographies although India Office (1896) contains indexes of names of mercantile ship captains from 1605 to 1856.

The death certificate of my ancestor John Murray told me that he was a retired surgeon-general in the Bengal Army. Using the ecclesiastical registers in the Oriental and India Office I was able to find the baptism, marriage and other records relating to John Murray's family in India. However, the most interesting information came from the army records, which gave me details of his career from his entry as an assistant surgeon in the Bengal Horse Artillery through to being the surgeon-general for the Bengal Army. Of particular help were his examination papers made on his entry into the army on 11 July 1832, as these contained a certificate confirming his baptism details. It gives his date and place of birth and the name and occupation of his father. Using this I was able to further the family tree using Scottish records. As an aside, I came across references to John Murray's prowess as a photographer – in fact, he turned out to be a photographic pioneer responsible for producing the oldest surviving images of India, the originals of which now sell for vast sums.

BAPTISM: Dec 4 1809
PARISH: Peterhead, Aberdeen
NAME: Alexander Murray, farmer in Blackhouse had a son named John baptised.
WITNESSES: Dr John Murray, uncle

## Civil Service

Before 1858 the EIC was such a large organisation that it required its own civil service to administer it. Again, Baxter (2004) provides a detailed breakdown of the available records, most of which begin in the mid- to late eighteenth century. Records of appointments and lists of staff can be found in IOR: B, while details of salaries are in IOR: H/362.

Published annual records include *The Asiatic Journal and Monthly Register for British India and its Dependencies* and *The Asiatic Annual Register* (see earlier), which list appointments and promotions, as well as the better-known *East India Register and Directory* (1800–44), which contains the most complete listing of the civil, military and ecclesiastical establishment for India and Burma. Also worth checking is the *Royal Kalendar* (Section 19.2).

Published biographies of civil servants include Dodwell and Miles (1839b, c and d), Prinsep and Doss (1844) and Prinsep (1885). In 1805 the EIC founded Haileybury College for the training of its covenanted civil servants. Danvers (1894) has a biographical register of the students who attended between 1806 and 1857. Farrington (1976) provides a detailed guide to Haileybury's archives and those of its successor, the East India College.

## Other Resources

Biographical information on the members of the EIC's board, its directors, commissioners and staff can be found in many of the published biographies that deal with the civil service (see above) and in India Office (1919).

Within TNA: PRO references to the activities of the EIC may be found among the Privy Council records in PC 1 and Admiralty Records (use the Admiralty Index and Digest in ADM 12).

## 15.3. IMMIGRANTS

Although it is easy to think of Britain as historically quite a self-contained island, it has always received immigrants from Europe, Asia and elsewhere. In medieval times many of these immigrants were merchants or specialist manufacturers (e.g. weavers) looking for work or business opportunities. In more recent centuries people have arrived in Britain to escape persecution, revolution or war in their home countries, sometimes in large numbers (e.g. the French Revolution). Consequently many people living in modern England are descended from ancestors who arrived here within recorded history. If you find or suspect that an ancestor was an immigrant, it may be possible to trace his or her origins using the available records.

Foreigners (commonly referred to as 'aliens' in the records) were of interest to the authorities because some were distrusted (especially Catholics), but also because many were seen as a source of money (e.g. aliens were often charged at a higher rate than others). For further information about UK immigration and citizenship records see Kershaw and Pearsall (2004).

### General Immigrant Resources

The most useful publications have generally been produced by the Huguenot Society of Great Britain and Ireland. They have transcribed many records, including the registers of many foreign churches operating in Britain and abstracts from tax and other records. A full list of their publications, many of which are available on CD-ROM, can be seen on their website: www.huguenotsociety.org.uk. (*Note*: Huguenots were French or Dutch Protestants who fled to Britain to escape persecution during the sixteenth to eighteenth centuries; most lived in communities in London, Norwich, Canterbury, Southampton, Bristol and Plymouth.)

Many immigrants headed straight for London or the nearest large city. In this respect especially useful resources are Kirk (1900–8) and Scouloudi (1985), which list aliens resident in London whose names are mentioned in the State Papers (see Chapter 16), Exchequer subsidy rolls (E 179) and other resources between 1529 and 1605 plus 1627, 1635 and 1639.

Those immigrants seeking denization (permission to remain) may have had their names recorded among the state papers, many of which have been calendared (see Chapter 16) or, if naturalisation was granted, among the patent rolls (see Section 17.2) and close rolls (Section 17.3). During the years 1708–11 foreigners were able to gain naturalisation by undertaking an oath of allegiance and producing a sacrament certificate to confirm their Protestantism (see Section 17.1). The resulting certificates are filed in TNA: PRO KB 24/2 and E 169/86. Indexes to the aliens listed in these records may be found in Shaw (1911, 1923) and Minet and Minet (1932).

As well as state records, many aliens (especially Huguenots) established and worshipped at their own churches. The registers of these non-parochial churches, some of which date back to the sixteenth century, may provide baptism, marriage and burial records for generations of immigrants and their descendants. A list of these non-parochial registers and other associated records can be found in List and Index Society (vol. 42), but many have been published by the aforementioned Huguenot Society. In addition the Huguenot Society has published records from a variety of other sources concerning foreign hospitals, church courts and pensioners (see their website for details).

Among those records that as yet have no published indexes are the proceedings of the French Refugees' Relief Committee in TNA: PRO T 93. These concern correspondence and other records relating to refugees who fled from the French Revolution and who afterwards applied for financial help. The scope of these records is given in List and Index Society (vol. 46).

From 1789 those seeking denization or naturalisation had to apply through the Home Office. The records, including general correspondence, denization papers and naturalisation papers, are to be found in TNA: PRO HO 1. No published finding aids exist, but details of the applicant's name, place of origin and date of application can be searched or browsed using the TNA: PRO online Catalogue.

Britain's Jewish population has historically not been as large as in some other European countries, but influxes from the Mediterranean countries and, later, from Eastern Europe meant that by the nineteenth century London was playing host to thousands of Jewish merchants and traders. Aside from the denization and naturalisation records mentioned above, there are no separate resources concerning Jewish immigrants of which I am aware. The Jewish Historical Society of England has published many articles on Anglo-Jewish history within its journal, a list of which is available through their website: www.jhse.org. As well as England, some Jewish communities were set up in Britain's colonies, especially the New World; see Section 15.1.

The example below is taken from the marriage register of St Martin Orgars Huguenot Church in London (Huguenot Society of London, vol. 37), which gives the place of origin of many of the brides and grooms, as well as their parish of residence within London:

PETIT – JONQUIERE
1727, 27 Juin. Sr. Henry Petit, natif d'Uzez en Languedoc – Martha Jonquières, née à Berne depuis la refuge, l'un et l'autre à présent de la par. de Stepney; mar. par moi, David Durand. Licence 26 Juin. Téms. Etienne Fanc, Claudine Fanc.

# CHAPTER SIXTEEN

# STATE PAPERS

By late medieval times both Parliament and the Crown had built up a network of officials and civil servants to assist with the day-to-day running of the country. The state papers are an archive of the mountainous paperwork produced by the many secretaries and other officials held in the employ of the government.

The state papers mostly relate to home affairs; however, most areas of government business are covered, including personal and official correspondence, treaties, draft bills, reports and minutes. The state papers contain the names of thousands of people who, for a myriad of reasons, needed to correspond with or who came to the attention of the government. Most correspondents were part of the country's wealthy elite, but this was not always the case; the names of many ordinary citizens can also be found within these archives.

The largest collection of state papers may be found at TNA: PRO, where they have been divided into those of a domestic nature (i.e. matters concerning home affairs) and those of a foreign nature (i.e. dealings with foreign governments, monarchs, etc.). In addition to the archive held at TNA: PRO, state papers may be found in the collections of many other institutions, especially the British Library.

In the nineteenth century a number of printed calendars were produced that cover all or part of the domestic state papers from the reigns of various monarchs. These calendars included not just those papers from TNA: PRO but also those from other major collections as well. These volumes are indexed and as such they represent the most convenient means of searching the state papers for ancestral references. For an introduction to the state papers and the records they hold, consult Atherton (1994).

## James I to George III, 1603–1782

The printed calendar for the reign of James I (1603–25) was edited by Lemon and Green (1856–72) but is now considered to be out of date. However, it remains the best finding aid to the domestic papers.

The calendar for the reign of Charles I (1625–49) was edited by Bruce *et al.* (1858–97). It also contains some of the state papers generated during the Commonwealth (see below).

The calendar for the reign of Charles II (1660–85) was edited by Green *et al.* (1860–1947) and includes some select state papers foreign.

The calendar for the reign of James II (1685–9) was edited by Timings (1960–72) and also includes some select state papers foreign.

The reign of William III (1689–1702) is covered by Hardy and Bateson (1895–1937), with the exception of those papers in class SP 33, which remain without a calendar.

Anne's reign (1702–14) is covered by Mahaffy (1916–25). Class SP 34 is also covered by the List and Index Society (vols 258, 259 and 260, 1995).

The reigns of George I (1714–27) and George II (1727–60) have yet to be calendared but the List and Index Society (vol. 224, 1987) has produced a guide to the records relating to ministerial meetings held in the reign of George I. Unpublished finding aids covering classes SP 35/77 and SP 36 (up to 1745, indexed to 1744) are available at TNA: PRO.

The years 1760–75 within the reign of George III (1760–1820) have been calendared by Redington and Roberts (1878–99). An unpublished descriptive list referring to class SP 37 is available at TNA: PRO.

The classes at TNA: PRO that correspond to the monarchs' reigns are as follows. The majority are available on microfilm only. Within each class the papers are generally arranged in chronological order, with larger documents sometimes being separated into a separate class.

| | |
|---|---|
| James I | SP 14 (domestic); SP 15 (addenda) |
| Charles I | SP 16 (domestic); SP 17 (large documents) |
| Charles II | SP 29 (domestic); SP 30 (large documents) |
| James II | SP 31 (domestic) |
| William III | SP 32 (domestic); SP 33 (large documents) |
| Anne | SP 34 (domestic) |
| George I | SP 35 (domestic) |
| George II | SP 36 (domestic) |
| George III | SP 37 (domestic) |

In addition to the above there are a host of other miscellaneous documents held in classes SP 8, 9, 38, 39, 40, 41, 42, 43, 44, 45, 46 and 87. Many of these are calendared in the above-mentioned publications. For a fuller explanation of the scope of the documents in these classes consult TNA: PRO 'Domestic Records Information Leaflet 20'.

## The Commonwealth, 1642–60

Most of the Commonwealth domestic state papers (1649–60) are calendared by Green (1875–86), including papers from the Council of State (general state papers), Derby House Committee (state papers relating to business with Scotland) and

Committee and Commissioners for Indemnity (a commission to absolve soldiers from any acts they committed during the war).

The Committee for the Advance of Money (which concerns the raising of money for Parliament) is summarised in Green (1888).

The Committee for Compounding with Delinquents (this concerns surveys of the estates of Royalists and the amount of money they were required to pay the government to pardon them for their support of the King) is found in Green (1889–93). A selection of papers is also published in vols 21 and 22 of Bruce *et al.* (1858–97), and an index of surnames (A–F only) can be found in Phillimore (1889). An unpublished finding aid exists in TNA: PRO ZBOX 1/79/2 and ZBOX 1/79/3.

Also published in Green (1889–93) are the papers of the Sequestration Committee, which details those estates confiscated from Royalists during the war. Additional finding aids may be found in TNA: PRO ZBOX 1/71/3, ZBOX 1/79/1 and ZBOX 1/79/4.

The Committee for Plundered Ministers was set up to find money and new positions for priests and ministers who had been affected by the Royalists. An unpublished calendar exists in TNA: PRO ZBOX 1/71/1 and ZBOX 1/77. Those papers relating to Lancashire and Cheshire have been published by the Lancashire and Cheshire Record Society (vols 28 and 29, 1894 and 1896).

Records of the Trustees for Crown Lands and Fee Farm Rents concern the sale of Crown lands. A finding aid exists in TNA: PRO ZBOX 1/71/2.

The Commonwealth Exchequer Papers are a collection of warrants issued by army officials on behalf of Parliament. Included are some muster rolls and petitions relating to various campaigns. No finding aids exist.

The list of corresponding classes at TNA: PRO runs as follows:

| | |
|---|---|
| Council of State | SP 18 (1649–60); SP 25 (Books and Accounts); SP 27 (parchment documents) |
| Committee for the Advance of Money | SP 19 (1642–56) |
| Sequestration Committee | SP 20 (1643–53) |
| Derby House Committee | SP 21 (1644–9) |
| Committee for Plundered Ministers | SP 22 (1642–53) |
| Committee for Compounding with Delinquents | SP 23 (1643–56) |
| Committee and Commissioners for Indemnity | SP 24 (1647–56) |
| Trustees for Crown Lands and Fee Farm Rents | SP 26 (1650–60) |
| Commonwealth Exchequer Papers | SP 28 (1640–74) |

In addition, the following published volumes may be of help: Firth and Rait (1911), Powell and Timings (1963) and Aylmer and Morrill (1979).

## George III to William IV, 1783–1837

After 1782 the domestic state papers are catalogued within the Home Office's archive. The domestic correspondence for George III (class HO 42) has not been indexed or published but an unpublished index for class HO 44 does exist at TNA: PRO. There is a series of indexes relating to the Home Office entry books for the years 1782–92 (TNA: PRO IND 8913), after which each individual volume has its own index.

No finding aids exist for the papers relating to the maintenance of public order (riots, disturbances, demonstrations, political actions, etc.).

| | |
|---|---|
| Maintenance of Public Order | HO 40 (1812–55), HO 41 (1815–1916) and HO 52 (1820–50) |
| Domestic Correspondence (George III) | HO 42 (1782–1820) |
| Domestic Entry Books | HO 43 (1782–1898) |
| Domestic Correspondence | HO 44 (1773–1861) |

## State Papers Foreign

The state papers relating to foreign matters are likely to be of less use to English genealogists unless a particular ancestor was a diplomat or foreign minister. Between 1577 and 1782 the state papers foreign are catalogued by geography and are to be found in classes SP 60 to SP 110.

The Irish state papers between 1509 and 1704 are calendared in Mahaffy (1860–1910) although this is now thought to be out of date. None of the other post-Tudor era foreign records have been calendared although some (especially the Irish ones) may be referred to in the domestic calendars given above. A detailed list of the state papers foreign catalogues can be found either on the TNA: PRO website or in Atherton (1994). State papers colonial are dealt with in Section 15.1.

# CHAPTER SEVENTEEN

# CHANCERY RECORDS

The Chancery was the secretarial office of the king's court that dealt with the issue of writs, the dispensation of equity (covered in Chapter 14) and detailed record keeping. The Chancery was headed by the Chancellor and by the early modern era it had become highly organised with many professional scribes and lawyers to be found within its employ. Record keeping was a vital part of the Chancery's business and as a consequence its archive was highly organised and great care was taken to preserve the documents within. Many of the most important records have been published as calendars and may contain information of use to the genealogist, including details of people's interaction with the state. For further details on the genealogical uses of the medieval Chancery rolls see Chambers (2005) and for general information on the Chancery see Maxwell-Lyte (1926). Information on the medieval charter rolls (which ceased in 1620) and fine rolls (which ceased in 1641) is not included in this book; see Chambers (2005) for details. For Parliament rolls see Section 18.1.

## 17.1. OATH ROLLS

Faced with perceived threats from abroad and from various religious and political factions, it was not unusual for Parliament to request that particular groups of people swear an oath of allegiance to the Crown, the Church of England and/or Parliament. The oath was normally solemnised by the person having to sign a roll as a record of their allegiance. The resulting oath rolls can be a useful source of information for the family historian searching for ancestors who worked as officials for the government or military or who were Catholic or Quakers (see also Section 4.5).

### Protestation Returns, 1642

The Protestation of 1641 took place at exactly the time when Charles I and Parliament were parting company with one another as a prelude to civil war. The Protestation was supposed to be an oath of loyalty to the King by every adult male, but MPs subverted it to become an oath to Parliament. The oath was taken in February/March 1642 and the returns were often made at the same time as those relating to the Collection in Aid of Distressed Protestants in Ireland.

Survival of the Protestation returns varies from total in counties like Devon and Dorset to non-existent in London, Norfolk and others. Gibson and Dell (1995) list the whereabouts of all surviving Protestation returns and include details of any that have been transcribed and published.

The example below is taken from the Protestation Return of Lincolnshire. It provides little information other than the names of those who signed the oath and the parish in which they were living:

**Salmonby**
*Taken Wednesday, 16th March 1641*
*Householders*
Kinge, Edward, gent
Richardson, Thomas
Hodgson, Edward
White, Simeon
. . .

*Other Inhabitants*
Walles, William
Walles, John
Richardson, William
. . .

## Royal Navy Oath Rolls, 1660

The oldest surviving oath roll dates to 1660 and concerns an oath of allegiance taken by all officers and crew of the Royal Navy following the restoration of King Charles II. The roll is in TNA: PRO C 215 and is taken ship by ship. In the same class are other rolls concerning oaths taken by navy personnel between 1673 and 1713.

## Association Oath Rolls, 1696

In 1696 the discovery of an assassination attempt against King William III led to the establishment of an oath roll that had to be signed by all the Crown's office holders. This included MPs, freemen, court officials, judges, all military and naval officers, lawyers and barristers, royal courtiers, doctors, clergymen and the landed gentry. In addition, the adult population of entire colonies was asked to sign the roll, including Bermuda, Barbados, the Leeward Islands, New York, Virginia, Jersey and Guernsey and various merchants based in Europe.

The original 1696 oath rolls are to be found in TNA: PRO C 213, where they are generally arranged by county and then by hundred or borough. Gibson (1996) provides a list of these rolls. Local history societies have transcribed and published some of these rolls; for example, Webb (1989) contains the Surrey association oath rolls while Gandy (1922) contains the names of those who signed in Barbados,

Virginia, New York, the Bermudas, Antigua, Nevis, Montserrat, Antego, St Christopher's, Rotterdam, The Hague, Malaga and Geneva.

The following example comes from the 1696 Association Oath Roll for New York, which contains the names of dozens of (mostly male) settlers, including some Dutchmen and other foreigners, some of whom could only sign by using a mark:

| | |
|---|---|
| Willem Hyer | Claes Burger |
| Johannijs Nijs | Johannes Burger |
| Hendryck Hermer | T. Mashol |
| Wm Huddleston | Jan bos Langestrad |
| Issack Stontenburgh | Barnardus Shardenbroek |
| Jacob Vandeuer X | Johanes Shardenbroek |
| Jacob Vantilburgh | Adraien Man |
| Johannes Vangeldern | James Prefost X |

## Other Oath Rolls

Between 1673 and the late nineteenth century there were a variety of other oaths and allegiances to which various classes of people were required to swear in order to take up an official post or to comply with Parliamentary Acts.

The Test (or Popish Recusants) Act of 1672 required all government officials (civil servants and Crown and military officers) to submit a 'sacrament certificate', sworn before a judge, confirming that they had taken communion in an Anglican church (this was essentially a ploy to exclude Catholics and others from official posts). This requirement ran until 1828, after which a declaration that the individual would not harm the Protestant Church was required. Sacrament certificates and declarations are to be found in TNA: PRO C 214 and C 215, with most of those relating to London and its immediate surroundings being in the court records of the Chancery (C 224), Exchequer (E 196) and King's Bench (KB 22). Outside of London the majority of these certificates were solemnised at the quarter sessions, and so references can sometimes be found among the court records (see Section 12.2).

A series of other oath rolls, including those relating to abjuration (the denial of James II's son's right to the throne), to solicitors' rights to practise and Catholic and Quaker affirmations may be found in TNA: PRO C 215 and KB 24; see the TNA: PRO online Catalogue for descriptions of the oath rolls in these classes.

## 17.2. PATENT ROLLS

Letters patent were a means by which the monarch could grant some form of liberty or privilege to an individual, family, organisation or community. Such grants could be spontaneous gifts or rewards but more often than not they were in response to petitions.

A letter detailing the liberty to be conveyed would be written by the king's Chancellor and made official using the Great Seal of England. However, letters patent were designed to be open documents so that anyone could read them and would then know what privilege was being granted and who was to receive it. As such, rather than closing the letter patent with a wax seal (as was done for the letters close), the wax seal (stamped with the Great Seal) would be attached to the open letter using a thin strip of paper. From the thirteenth century onwards a copy of every letter patent issued was made and then enrolled for storage. The resulting patent rolls were placed in the Chancery's archive and there is a near continuous series of them from the early thirteenth century until the present day.

Although there was no real limit to the type of grants that the king could confer using a letter patent, the sort of information that the rolls contain has changed over the years. The earlier rolls (pre-1700) are likely to contain pardons, grants of land, corporate rights to boroughs and guilds, hereditary titles, judicial commissions, royal appointments, protections, exceptions, etc. After around 1700 their scope becomes more restrictive and mostly concerns privileges granted to nobles and civil servants, such as pensions, titles and honours. Before 1853 they were also used to confirm the intellectual rights to any original inventions or designs (i.e. a patent). In cases where the custody of property was in dispute (e.g. because an heir was under age or a person had been declared a lunatic, a letter patent would be used to confirm who got custody of both land and underage heirs (see Section 13.3). During the interregnum (1645–60) many letters patent were not enrolled and are thus not preserved.

In the early modern era the letters patent are not a widely used genealogical resource as their scope is more restrictive than in earlier times and they are likely only to contain information on wealthy or privileged individuals. Also, the more modern rolls are harder to search than their medieval counterparts. Unless you feel sure that an ancestor of yours had cause to receive a letter patent (e.g. because he was awarded a title), they are probably not worth the effort of searching although in some cases (such as those involving inquisitions post mortem; Section 6.3) they can provide information of genealogical interest. For further information on the originals and genealogical uses of the medieval letters patent see Chambers (2005).

## Finding Aids

All the original rolls relating to the letters patent are to be found in TNA: PRO C 66. The majority of medieval letters patent have been translated and summarised (mostly in the *Calendar of the Patent Rolls* series; see Chambers, 2005 for further details), but no published calendars exist for those rolls produced after 1603. From the early sixteenth century onwards annual calendars of the rolls (which in some cases include indexes of grantees' names) were produced; these are the only finding aids associated with the modern rolls. The manuscript calendars for 1603–14 have been published by the List and Index Society (vols 97, 98, 109, 121, 122, 133, 134, 157), with those from 1615 to 1624 being published as *Chancery Patent Rolls* (Swift Ltd, 1980–9). The contemporary calendars from 1625 to 1932 are on open access at TNA: PRO, with the original manuscript calendars being held in C 274.

Indexes concerning inventions listed in the rolls from 1617 to 1852 (arranged by subject matter and patent title) may be found in Woodcroft (1854a, 1854b).

None of my early modern ancestors were grand enough to be granted a letter patent but they did own a watermill (Le Moulin de Quetivel) on the Channel Island of Jersey, which had initially been in Crown hands but which, in January 1649, was given to Laurens Hampton by the exiled Charles II as a reward for his support during the English Civil War. The letter patent conferring the watermill and other privileges to Laurens Hampton is typically short on genealogical information but it does give details of this man's local importance, wealth and landholdings. The main body of the patent is long, rambling and in French, but the attachment to the seal provides a useful English summary:

> May it please your most Excellent Majestie This Bill containeth a grant from your M[atie] to Laurens Hampton Gent your M[aties] Sheriffe in the Isle of Jersey and to his heirs for ever of five quarters of wheat yearly rent due upon the Franc Fief of St Brelade in the said Island and also of 30 livres tournois and three denies yearly rent to be received upon the Mill of Quetivell in the Parish of St Laurens in the said island; In consideration of the summe of two thousand and fortie livres tournois payd to Sir Edward Walker Knt your M[aties] Receavour Generall for the time being to yr M[aties] use, With a Clause whereby the Mansion House of Him the sayd Laurence Hamptonne and sundry other parcels of Land thereunto adjoining are united and annexed to the premises And made Impartable and descendible to the eldest Heir sonne or daughter of Him the sayd Lawrence Hampton . . . And in consideration of your M[aties] grace and favour, the said Lawrence Hampton and his heirs are to find and maintaine one horse in time of warre for your M[aties] service in this Island.
>
> Signifyed to be yr M[aties] pleasure by Warrant 28 January 1649.
>
> Under your signe manuell: Thom. Coke

## 17.3. CLOSE ROLLS

Whereas letters patent were a form of open communication between the monarch and one of his subjects, if the matter was of a more private nature the letter would be sealed and stamped with the king's Great Seal. Consequently, such communications were known as letters close, and they would be copied into Chancery documents that we know as the close rolls.

The letters would typically contain instructions or orders from the Crown to an individual. The material contained within a letter close could be of great political or strategic importance and the recipients could be anyone from military commanders to foreign monarchs. Equally, letters close could also contain more mundane information, including the issuing of instructions to officials and the enforced settlement of disputes over land and money. A great many private deeds were also copied on to the rolls as a safeguard for wealthy landowners just in case the original deeds should be lost or destroyed.

The oldest surviving close rolls are from 1204. They continued until 1903, when they were replaced by the Supreme Court of Judicature Enrolment Books. From the mid-sixteenth century onwards the close rolls were mostly used for the enrolment of deeds such as those relating to land conveyances, the defining of district boundaries, changes of name (deed poll), charitable trusts and many other uses.

Like patent rolls, the close rolls may contain the names of thousands of people, most of whom are from the middle or upper ranks of society, but for the early modern era their genealogical uses are limited (for their medieval uses, see Chambers, 2005).

## Finding Aids

The original close rolls are all held in C 54, where they are arranged by year and then within the following geographical subdivisions:

B   Anglesey, Brecon, Cornwall, Carmarthen, Caernarvon, Devon, Glamorgan, Middlesex, Somerset, Surrey and the City of London
Y   Bedford, Chester, Derby, Dorset, Hertford, Lincoln, Nottingham, Northumberland, Oxford, Rutland, Stafford, Suffolk, Sussex, Warwick, Westmorland and Berwick upon Tweed
E   Berkshire, Buckinghamshire, Cardigan, Denbigh, Essex, Hampshire, Hereford, Kent, Monmouth, Pembroke, Wiltshire and Haverfordwest
N   Cambridge, Cumberland, Durham, Flint, Gloucester, Huntingdon, Lancaster, Leicester, Merioneth, Montgomery, Norfolk, Northampton, Radnor, Shropshire, Worcester and Yorkshire

Although the majority of medieval close rolls have been translated and published (mostly in the *Calendar of the Close Rolls*; see Chambers, 2005), no published calendars or indexes exist for the post-1603 rolls. However, contemporary indexes for the rolls were made on an annual basis and these can be found in TNA: PRO C 275. For each roll there is normally more than one index (for the later rolls there may be up to seven) covering various topics handled by the rolls. However, the two most important indexes are the Chapel Office series, which contains the names of the grantees, and the Enrolment Office series, which contains the names of the grantors.

# CHAPTER EIGHTEEN

# PARLIAMENTARY RECORDS AND ELECTIONS

## 18.1. PARLIAMENT ROLLS AND RELATED RECORDS

### Parliament Rolls

Acts of Parliament, which include petitions, pleadings and bills submitted by Members of Parliament (MPs), as well as answers to tabled questions, are preserved in the Chancery's archive. Bond (1971) provides a guide to the records of Parliament, but for the purposes of this book, the most important records are the Parliament rolls, held in TNA: PRO C 65. In medieval times the Parliament rolls contained a wealth of interesting material including parliamentary proceedings and private Acts submitted by the public. However, by 1629 they had become pared down and contained only details of public Acts, which limits their use to family historians (unless they are researching the career of a particular MP). An index to the statutes from 1215 to 1714 can be found in *Statutes of the Realm* (Record Commission, 11 vols, 1810–28) and thereafter in *Chronological Table of the Statutes* (HMSO, 1961).

### Parliamentary Proceedings

The general proceedings of Parliament have been covered by a number of publications over the years. The earliest is the *Journal of the House of Commons*, which began in 1547 and continues to the present day; its history and scope is covered by Menhennet (1971). Copies are available at the British Library, House of Commons and on microfilm at some larger university libraries.

Newspapers and magazines (Section 19.1) ought to be a good place to look for details of parliamentary proceedings but there was much tension between government and the media during the late seventeenth and eighteenth centuries, which led to inaccurate reporting or just plain ignorance of Parliament's behaviour. From 1803 Thomas Hansard began printing his authorised *Parliamentary Debates*, which continues to this day. These are indexed and are generally considered to be the best record of parliamentary proceedings.

## Biographies of Members of Parliament

The best biographical guide to members of the House of Commons is the ongoing *History of Parliament* series of volumes being produced by the History of Parliament Trust (e.g. Cruickshanks *et al.*, 2002), which provide detailed biographical notes on all MPs, including their family background and origins. However, not all periods are covered yet, with a gap from 1604 to 1659 and no volumes at all after 1820 although more volumes are currently in preparation.

Those looking for ancestors who may have been politically active but may not have taken a seat in Parliament could try Baylen and Gossman (1979) and Greaves and Zaller (1982), which provide biographies of British political radicals between 1700 and 1914. Many politicians were drawn from the ranks of the legal profession, clergy or the landed gentry and/or may first have taken a university degree (see Chapters 8 and 9 for further information). Writs summoning MPs to Parliament are enrolled in the Parliament Pawns in TNA: PRO C 218. They are not indexed.

## 18.2. POLL BOOKS

One of the fundamentals of modern elections is that the ballot is secret; only the individual should know how he or she voted. However, before 1872 this was not the case and not only was the ballot not secret but the names of individual voters and the people for whom they voted would be entered into a poll book. Furthermore, from the early eighteenth century onwards it was common for private publishers to take the information held in the poll books and print it. Thus, not only was the ballot not secret; it was actually possible to buy printed books that told you exactly how each individual had voted. However, the voters' loss is the genealogist's gain, as the poll books can be a useful source of information.

## Constituencies, Electorate, Elections and Poll Books

In the early modern era elections were not as encompassing or as straightforward as they are today. The members of the electorate were divided into one of three separate constituency types depending on where they lived. County constituencies covered most of England's country parishes, small towns and villages. Borough constituencies covered large towns and cities, although some cities (e.g. Bristol, Exeter and Nottingham) were classified as counties. Finally, university constituencies covered property owned by Cambridge, Oxford and (after 1867) London universities.

People have been entitled to vote since the early fifteenth century, but it is not until the late sixteenth century that the first poll books are preserved. In general, parliamentary elections were held every five years, although this varied somewhat depending on the domestic political situation (see Seaton, 1986 for details).

In county constituencies only adult men (aged twenty-one or over) who held freehold property of 40s value were entitled to vote, although before 1774 they had to be resident in the county to qualify. After 1832 this was revised to include people occupying (including renting) land worth between £2 and £5 or who owned land worth more than £10. With borough constituencies the situation was more complex, with the entitlement to vote being based on local laws and custom. This led to some boroughs having many voters and others almost none at all. In university boroughs the graduates who formed the university's convocation were entitled to vote.

Naturally this means that poll books are not highly representative and usually hold only the names of the wealthier male landowners. For example, in one Cambridgeshire parish that had a population of around 400 people, only 40 names appear in the poll book.

When it came to election time, each county and borough would be represented by two MPs or 'Knights of the Shire' (only one MP in Wales). The electorate would normally have a limited list of only three or four people seeking election. Local officials such as county sheriffs were responsible for compiling poll books, and they would often use tax records to decide who was entitled to vote. Once a list of the potential electorate had been drawn up, the returning officers would note each individual's vote in the poll book, which would then be held by the Clerk of the Peace and open to inspection by anyone. Acts of Parliament in 1696 and 1711 paved the way for publishers to make printed versions of the poll books, many of which were used by commercial companies.

The information that individual poll books may contain and the way that they are organised varies widely. Most published poll books cover a single constituency or geographical area (e.g. a city or town). Before the Victorian era most published poll books are organised geographically by hundred, parish, borough or ward, but I have encountered some that give the voters' names in alphabetical order or by trade.

All poll books will contain a list of entitled voters and the person for whom they voted, but some contain much more information, including whether the voter was entitled to vote through his owning land or a house (or both), where they lived, the name of anyone occupying their land, their occupation and other information. The later poll books tend to give more information than the earlier ones, although this is not always the case.

## Finding Poll Books

Almost all the official manuscript versions of the poll books were destroyed in 1907, although some of the original canvassers' books, from which the poll books would be constructed, survive in CROs. This means that we are reliant on the privately published poll books for our information.

**54**  **HUNDRED OF STAINE.**

| Freeholders and Place of Freehold | Place of Residence | Yorke | Eaton | Townley | Childers |
|---|---|---|---|---|---|
| **SWAFFHAM PRIOR.** | | | | | |
| Allix, John Peter, Esq. | Swaffham Prior | — | — | | |
| Asbee, Charles | ditto | — | — | | |
| Barker, John Rickard, Esq. | Cambridge | — | — | — | |
| Barwick, Rev. Robert | Queen's Coll. Camb. | — | — | | |
| Benson, Thomas | Swaffham Prior | — | — | | |
| Brinkley, Silas | ditto | — | — | | |
| Chambers, Isaac | Swaffham Prior Fen | — | — | | |
| Chambers, Simeon | Swaffham Prior | — | — | | |
| Chapman, John | dit to | — | — | | |
| Clark, Jonas | ditto | — | — | | |
| Crisp, Robert | d itto | — | — | | |
| Cross, Thomas | St. Mary's, Newmarket | — | — | | |
| Danby, Francis | Swaffham Prior | — | — | | |
| Day, John | ditto | — | — | | |
| Downham, Henry | ditto | — | — | | |
| Fitchis, John | ditto | — | — | | |
| Feaks, John | ditto | — | — | | |
| Fennell, Rev. Samuel, clk. | Queen's Coll. Camb. | — | — | | |
| Fuller, Thomas | Swaffham Prior | — | — | — | |
| Galley, Richard | ditto | — | — | | |
| Gallyon, William | Green Street, Camb. | — | | — | |
| Gilbert, Thomas | Bottisham | — | — | | |
| Gunton, John | Swaffham Prior | — | — | — | |
| Harden, Elijah | ditto | — | — | — | |
| Harden, Robert | ditto | — | — | — | |
| Hart, James | ditto | — | — | | — |
| Harrison, Thomas | Swaffham Prior Fen | — | — | | — |
| Haycock, Charles | Gt. St. Andrews, Cam. | | | — | — |
| Holmes, James | Burwell | — | — | | |
| Hubbersty, J. Lodge, L.L.D | Queen's Coll. Camb. | — | — | | |
| Hunt, Robert | Swaffham Prior | — | — | | |
| Hunt, John | ditto | — | — | | |
| Jennings, William | Bottisham | — | — | | |
| Iverson, Thomas | Swaffham Prior | — | — | | |
| Kent, Joseph | ditto | — | — | | |
| King, Joshua, Esq. | Queen's Coll. Camb. | — | — | | |
| Leggett, William | Swaffham Prior | — | — | | |
| Mann, Joseph | ditto | — | — | | |
| Mason, Robert | ditto | — | — | | |
| Newman, John | ditto | — | — | | |
| Phillips, Rev. George, clk. | Queen's Coll. Camb. | — | — | | |

*This Cambridgeshire poll book for 1835 records the names of those residents of Swaffham Prior parish who were eligible to vote. The book records that my ancestor Isaac Chambers was living, not in the main village, but in the remote fens to the north. (Author's collection)*

It is reckoned that there are about 2,000 printed poll books in existence, which represent approximately one-third of the contested elections between 1700 and 1872. The oldest books date to around 1685, but they do not become common until the opening decades of the eighteenth century. Coverage varies greatly, with some constituencies having almost no surviving poll books and others (especially boroughs) being much more complete.

The best sources for printed poll books are CROs, the SoG, the Institute of Historical Research and larger local and university libraries. However, rather than searching randomly, first check Gibson and Rogers (1994), which gives a list of all the surviving poll books and their whereabouts. Sims (1984) has a similar list, but its location list is not as comprehensive as Gibson and Rogers, although it does contain notes about the type of information each poll book holds. Once you have tracked down a poll book, it is then simply a case of searching for your ancestor's name; the majority are not indexed so make sure you know the hundred/parish/ward/etc. in which he lived.

It might be worth checking with the record office covering your ancestor's constituency to see if it holds any original manuscripts relating to the making of the original poll books.

The following example comes from the published 'Poll for the Knights of the Shire for Cambridgeshire' taken at Cambridge on 29 March 1722. The electors in Swaffham Prior parish include several members of the Chambers family, including my direct ancestor George, who is listed as living in Reach, a hamlet to the north of Swaffham Prior village. Interestingly, the majority of the parish voted for Francis Whitchot and Robert Clarke, the two losing candidates.

Candidates:
The Rt. Hon[ble] Edward Lord Harley
Sir John Hinde Cotton
Sir Francis Whitchot
Sir Robert Clarke

| Name, Abode | H. | Cot. | W. | Cl. |
|---|---|---|---|---|
| *Swaffham Prior* | | | | |
| William Ewin, Cambridge, | – | – | | |
| Thomas Edmunds, | – | – | | |
| Thomas Eaton, Wilbraham, | – | – | | |
| Robert Ashley, | – | – | | |
| John Baynard, | | – | – | |
| Peter Allix D.D., | | | – | – |
| William Barnes, | | | – | – |
| George Chambers, Reach, | | | – | – |

| Name, Abode | H. | Cot. | W. | Cl. |
|---|---|---|---|---|
| Thomas Hart | | | – | – |
| John Mendham | | | – | – |
| Samuel Chambers, | | | – | – |
| Edward Eastwell, | | | – | – |
| William Eastwell, | | | – | – |
| Thomas Chambers, | | | – | – |
| John Cokerton, | | | – | – |
| Robert Chambers, | | | – | – |
| Matthew Blinkensop, | | | – | – |

## 18.3. THE PRIVY COUNCIL

In modern Britain the Privy Council has a largely ceremonial function, although it is still the final court of appeal for many Commonwealth countries and also oversees the work of many regulatory bodies and chartered institutions. However, behind its modern embodiment lies a much more important history.

The Privy Council was created in the fourteenth century as an offshoot of the King's Council and had a membership that included the monarch's most powerful and trusted councillors, including the Chancellor. Its core brief was to make judgments on matters that directly affected the king, which in practice meant almost anything from land grants through to foreign policy. However, the Privy Council could also hear criminal cases that impinged upon the monarch, e.g. treason or organised rebellions. It could also accept petitions from the public and was capable of granting pardons. The function and role of the Privy Council changed constantly throughout its history and it later became an important tool in Britain's colonial empire.

The records of the Privy Council begin in 1386 and continue through to the present day. There have been some document losses because of fire and because papers were removed from the public records to become incorporated into other public or private collections (some of the earliest records are held in the British Library).

In among records of the day-to-day work of the Privy Council there are items that may be of use to genealogists. Many people petitioned the Council on matters of local concern, while those suspected of heresy, treason or slander against the Crown would often be victims of the Council's justice. This meant that as well as dealing with the complaints of the rich, it also represented many lesser members of the community, often as a result of some misdemeanour they had committed. Such entries can provide information about a person's location, occupation and sometimes immediate family members (e.g. spouse or son).

## Finding Aids

The most useful records from the Privy Council are the registers, which are to be found in classes PC 1 and PC 2 at TNA: PRO. The TNA: PRO's records begin in 1481, but a substantial quantity of earlier records, back to 1386, is held by the British Library.

The early PRO and British Library Privy Council records up to 1631 have been calendared and published in Nicolas (1834–7) and HMSO (1890–1964); these represent the best means of searching for an ancestor among the Privy Council records.

From the early seventeenth century the Privy Council played an important role in the administration of the British colonies, including setting legislation and hearing appeals. The Privy Council's records are considered a major source for historians of Britain's colonial history, and their colonial papers between 1613 and 1783 have been calendared and published in Grant and Munro (1908–12). Other material relating to colonial matters includes the plantation books in TNA: PRO PC 5, which record brief details of individual acts of the Privy Council, many of which are calendared in more detail in Grant and Munro (1908–12).

The following example is taken from Grant and Munro (1908–12) and concerns Nathaniel Gilbert of Antigua, an ancestor of my wife and daughter. It is one of several entries in the Privy Council records made by the Gilberts, many of which seem to concern their role as the executors to disputed wills.

11 Aug. 1722 Antigua
This day Mr. William Gregson entered an appearance for Nathaniel Gilbert to the appeal of James Parke from the Leeward Islands.

19 Jan 1723
Reference to the Committee of Appeals of the petition of James Parke that, notwithstanding he is four months beyond the time allowed for appeals, a short day may be appointed for hearing his appeal from a decree of the Antigua Chancery, 5 and 6 Aug 1721, in favour of Nathaniel Gilbert, whereby he must surrender to Gilbert a plantation of 20 acres.

# CHAPTER NINETEEN

# PUBLISHED RESOURCES

## 19.1. NEWSPAPERS, MAGAZINES AND PERIODICALS

Printed news-sheets, newspapers and magazines have existed in England and Wales since the mid-seventeenth century, and, although popular with the public, they were often disliked by the establishment because of their readiness to criticise or reveal salacious gossip. Newspapers can be an excellent means of finding information that is unlikely to be recorded anywhere else. There may be stories about events that involved your ancestors, such as shipwrecks, battles or fires, or your ancestors' names may be recorded as part of criminal trials or in the notices section. Although they are a fantastic resource, few newspapers and magazines have been indexed, which makes searching them prohibitively time-consuming. That said, an increasing number of historical newspapers are being made available electronically, which makes searching them much easier (see below). For a general introduction to local newspapers see West (1983) and Collins (2001).

### What can be Expected

Early newspapers were quite a mixed bunch. Some were very formal, others more salacious; some contained only advertisements, shipping news or commodity prices; some contained news from around the country, others only local news.

News items tended to be very abbreviated and (rather irritatingly) the names of central protagonists would often be abbreviated (my name would thus be P——C——s); this was to prevent the proprietors being sued for libel. However, given the lack of indexes associated with these newspapers, unless your ancestors were associated with a specific event the chances of finding their names by random searching are minimal (see below).

The chief use of newspapers for family historians is usually the announcements of births, marriages and deaths, and it is also worth reading the obituaries. These can provide snippets of information that may be useful or help to confirm family connections.

### Newspaper Archives

The fragile nature of newspapers means that very few survive the test of time. That said, there are still some archives that preserve large numbers of early newspapers and periodicals.

Probably the largest and most accessible pre-Victorian archive is the British Library's Burney Collection. This consists of a large number of newspapers that were collected by Charles Burney before his death in 1817. The collection consists of some 700 volumes of papers, the oldest of which date to 1603 and the youngest to 1817. They probably represent the largest collection of pre-Victorian papers in the world.

The Burney Collection is available on microfilm in the Rare Books and Music Reading Room of the British Library at St Pancras, London. Here there is a bound index, which catalogues the newspapers that are available for each year from 1603 to 1817. This catalogue will direct you to the relevant microfilm reel (all are on open access). At the time of writing the contents of the Burney Collection are in the process of being added to the British Library's electronic catalogue.

The British Newspaper Library at Colindale, London, also holds some pre-Victorian titles, although it has very few before 1800. Most must be consulted on microfilm, which can be ordered at about half an hour's notice. The catalogue can be searched on line at www.bl.uk/catalogues/newspapers.html.

Aside from these two major repositories, the Bodleian Library, Oxford, holds a substantial collection of old newspapers, while the Guildhall Library, London, holds a substantial collection of eighteenth-century London newspapers (some are on microfilm). Other potential repositories of local newspapers include large local libraries and some CROs. Collins (2001) provides a guide to British newspaper repositories, while West (1983) and Gibson *et al.* (2002) provide a list of historical newspapers preserved in various archives.

## Searchable Newspapers and Magazines

Very few pre-Victorian newspapers were indexed, which makes searching for random mentions of an ancestor a near impossible task. However, if you know the rough date of a specific event, such as a birth, wedding, death, accident, etc., then it may be worthwhile checking the newspapers for further information. Those periodicals that do have comprehensive indexes are listed below.

### The Times

Several years ago the original printed volumes of *Palmer's Index to the Times: 1785 to 1905* (which are still available in some libraries; e.g. Guildhall Library, London) were digitised and made available on CD-ROM, which was exceedingly expensive. The CD-ROM has since been superseded by *Palmer's Full Text Online*, a web version that allows the reader to summon up any *Times* article written between 1785 and 1870. However, it is only possible to search using the entries from Palmer's original index, something that is much more restrictive than being able to search the text of the articles themselves. *Palmer's Full Text Online* is a subscription service and very expensive; it is generally only available through the British Library and university libraries (see historynews.chadwyck.com for details).

Even more comprehensive is the *Times Digital Archive*, another online service that is generally only available through the British Library and other learned institutions. It is far better than *Palmer's Index* as it is possible to search the newspaper's full text and also to browse individual issues. I have found the *Times Digital Archive* to be excellent when looking for information about people or historical events (see www.galegroup.com/Times).

## Gentleman's Magazine

Founded in 1731, the *Gentleman's Magazine* was a monthly periodical aimed at London's burgeoning middle classes. It was an innovative and cheeky publication that was often a thorn in the side of politicians. It covered the main news of the day as well as carrying announcements of births, marriages, deaths, appointments, etc. It is an especially good resource for information concerning the lives of middle-class professionals such as civil servants, bankers, clergymen, army officers, etc.

The *Gentleman's Magazine* ceased publication in 1907, and many historical libraries (including the Society for Genealogists and the Institute of Historical Research) hold facsimile copies going back to its very beginning. Each volume covers a single year and has an index, but there is also a set of indexes that covers the entire eighteenth and early nineteenth centuries. These include a general index and separate indexes to obituaries and biographies; Ruston (1996) has compiled a list of obituaries and marriage records relating to dissenting ministers. The years 1731–50 are currently available free via the *Internet Library of Early Journals* (see below).

## Annual Register

Published since 1758 (and still going), the *Annual Register* is a yearly summary of British news and events, including some quite gossipy items. Each year has an index with it but recently an online archive has been produced which allows the whole text to be searched; this is a subscription service and generally only available through larger libraries, including the British Library. Some of the earlier volumes are available free through the *Internet Library of Early Journals* (see below).

## Internet Library of Early Journals (www.bodley.ox.ac.uk/ilej)

A project coordinated through Oxford's Bodleian Library. Issues for some early journals are available free on line and can be searched and/or browsed. Titles include: *Annual Register* (1758–78); *Blackwood's Edinburgh Magazine* (1843–63); *Gentleman's Magazine* (1731–50); *Notes and Queries* (1849–69); *Philosophical Transactions of the Royal Society* (1757–77) and *The Builder* (1843–52).

*The Making of America* (cdl.library.cornell.edu/moa)

Coordinated through Cornell University, this free online database contains the full text from a large number of nineteenth-century journals and magazines. It is fully searchable.

*Electronic Archives*

At the time of writing I am aware of only two pre-Victorian newspapers whose contents have been digitised in their entirety. One of these is *The Times* of London, which was first published in 1785, and the other is the *Annual Register*, first published in 1758. Both are available through the British Library and some society and university libraries. Doubtless other newspapers will be made available in time.

The following example comes from the 28 October 1837 edition of the *Cambridgeshire Chronicle* and details an unpleasant incident that involved my great-great-great-great-grandfather Isaac Chambers. The article, which was traced by a fellow researcher in the Cambridgeshire County Record Office, gives a rare insight into Isaac's situation and temperament that would otherwise have been lost to history.

*Daring Attempt at Housebreaking* – On Tuesday night last, about ten o'clock, four men attempted to break into the house of Mr. Chambers, who resides in a lone farm, in Swaffham Fen, in this county. Mr. C. and his family had retired to bed, and upon hearing a noise at the door Mr. C. left his bed, went to the window, and asked them what they wanted, they replied 'the grapes, and we must have them,' they then stripped the vine of its contents, and went away. Mr. C. took the precaution to load his gun in case they should return. About two o'clock the following morning they again made their appearance, and attempted to break into the house, but in vain. After trying sometime, one of them said if the old d——l comes out we will murder him, another said 'if we get in we will murder them all' – Mr. Chambers then took deliberate aim at the villains, but the gun missed fire. Upon seeing the gun they made off for the back part of the house. Mr. C.'s three daughters had previously made their escape the back way. They went into the hen roost, and stole from twenty to thirty fowls, and decamped. Mr. C.'s daughters sent assistance but it was too late, they were gone. Not content with this they rerurned again between four and five, but they could not break open the door – It has been ascertained that a notorious character named Jack Mott, and several others of a gang, had three fowls for supper at a beer-shop at Swaffham; and no doubt is entertained but that before a long time is past the parties will be traced.

## 19.2. DIRECTORIES

A directory is an alphabetical list of names and addresses designed to help us trace people or services for a specific geographical province (think of the modern telephone directory). The earliest directory was published in 1677, but they were not produced regularly until 1734, when the first annual London directories appeared. The majority of these earlier directories concern only London, with many provincial towns and counties not receiving their own directories until the nineteenth century.

Directories can be a valuable aid to the genealogist, especially those searching for an ancestor who held a trade or a position of authority. If you know your ancestor's name and trade, it is often possible to find the address using a directory and then glean further information from tax or other records. Conversely, if you have a name and address, then a directory may be able to tell you what trade your ancestor was in. In addition to trade lists there were other directories that dealt with more specialist areas such as clergy and medics; these are dealt with in the relevant sections elsewhere in the book.

Goss (1932) and Norton (1950) contain detailed lists of the published directories of England and Wales before 1856. The SoG, Guildhall Library, the Institute of Historical Research and the British Library hold many directories, while CROs or large libraries hold local directories. Some directories are commercially available on microfilm or microfiche via local history societies or on searchable CD-ROM through companies such as Drake Software Associates (www.drake-software.co.uk).

Below is a list of the more useful and commonly encountered commercial directories although many others exist.

*The Post Office Directory* (1800 onwards)

Published on a county-by-county basis, each directory gives a topographical and historical introduction to every parish or town, together with information that might be useful to businesses (e.g. the location of post offices, distances to other towns, etc.). It then provides a list of local businesses, farmers, tradesmen, clergymen, gentry and others. The London editions give a street-by-street atlas of businesses, which is useful if you have an ancestor's business address but not their full name.

*Pigot and Co.'s Royal National and Commercial Directory and Topography of the Counties* (1822 onwards)

This is very similar to the Post Office directories and, like them, was published on a county-by-county basis with a topographical and historical introduction to every parish or town, together with business information and lists of local businesses, farmers, tradesmen, clergymen, gentry and others. *Pigot* is noted as a useful resource

---

**Cambridgeshire.**                                                    **Pigot & Co.'s**

ECCLESIASTICAL and CIVIL DIVISIONS, and REPRESENTATION.—Cambridgeshire is naturally divided into two parts by the river Ouse—the most northerly being chiefly composed of the Isle of Ely, in which diocese (excepting fifteen parishes in the eastern part, which are in the diocese of Norwich, and Isleham parish, in that of Rochester,) the county is comprehended. For civil purposes it is divided into seventeen hundreds, namely, Armingford, Chesterton, Chevely, Chilford, Ely, Flendish, Longstow, Northstow, Papworth, Radfield, Staploe, Staine, Threplow, Wetherley, Whittlesford, Wisbeach and Witchford: these contain 162 parishes and five parts of parishes, one city (ELY), one county and borough town (CAMBRIDGE), seven other market towns, and part of the market town of Newmarket. The whole shire returns seven representatives to parliament, viz. two each for the town of CAMBRIDGE and its UNIVERSITY, and three COUNTY members—the gentlemen representing the county are, the Hon. Eliot T. Yorke, R. Jefferson Eaton, Esq., and R. Greaves Townley, Esq.: the votes for county members are taken at Cambridge, Ely, Newmarket, Royston, Whittlesey and Wisbeach.

POPULATION, &c.—By the census for 1831 this county contained 72,031 males, and 71,924 females—total, 143,955: being an increase, since the returns made in the year 1821, of 22,046 inhabitants; and from the census of 1801 to that of 1831, the augmentation amounted to 54,609 persons. The annual value of Real Property in this county, as assessed in April, 1815, amounted to £645,554.

### Index of Distances from Town to Town in the County of Cambridge.

The names of the respective towns are on the top and side, and the square where both meet gives the distance.

*Distance from London.*

|  |  | Distance from London |
|---|---|---|
| | Cambridge ............... | 51 |
| Chatteris ........ | 28 Chatteris............ | 71 |
| Ely............. | 16 12 Ely.. (by way of Cambridge)....... | 67 |
| Linton........... | 11 33 21 Linton......... | 48 |
| March........... | 32 8 19 36 March ............ | 79 |
| Newmarket ..... | 13 25 13 14 26 Newmarket .......... | 59 |
| Royston......... | 13 32 30 15 39 26 Royston .......... | 38 |
| Soham........... | 19 18 6 19 25 8 32 Soham ......... | 69 |
| Thorney......... | 40 18 32 50 14 45 44 39 Thorney ......... | 86 |
| Whittlesea ...... | 30 15 27 41 11 40 39 33 5 Whittlesea ...... | 78 |
| Wisbeach ....... | 43 19 31 50 11 39 51 33 14 19 Wisbeach .... | 90 |

---

## BURWELL,
### SWAFFHAM PRIOR AND SWAFFHAM BULBECK.

BURWELL is a large and populous village and parish in the hundred of Staploe, 13 miles N.E. from Cambridge, 5 s. from Soham, and 3 N.W. of Newmarket. A most attractive ornament to this village is its beautiful church, built in the Gothic style, and scarcely excelled by any village church in Great Britain: it is dedicated to St. Mary; the living is a vicarage, in the patronage of the Earl of Guildford; the present incumbent is the Rev. J. J. Baines. The malting business is carried on here very extensively, and the timber trade is likewise of considerable importance. A dreadful circumstance, which occurred on the 8th of September, 1727, renders this village lamentably memorable:—A great number of persons had assembled in a barn to see a puppet show, and during the exhibition the building accidentally took fire. The rush towards the only passage of egress was tremendous and desperate; unfortunately the door had been affixed so as to open inwardly, and by the pressure from within, this means of escape became impracticable; at length the door was demolished by the crowd that had assembled outside, and the surviving persons were dragged over the dead or expiring victims. Seventy-seven individuals perished, by this appalling catastrophe: the bodies were all interred in one capacious grave on the following day, they being so disfigured as to preclude recognition by their relatives. Population of the parish, in 1831, 1,668.

SWAFFHAM PRIOR is a village and parish in the hundred of Taine, 2 miles s. by w. from Burwell, and between 5 and 6 w. by N. from Newmarket—situated in an agricultural district, noted for the growth of red wheat. In this village are two churches—the one dedicated to St. Cyrie (or St. Cyriac), and the other to St. Mary; the latter has long been in ruins: they are both in the same church-yard, and present a very interesting and conspicuous spectacle. The living of the parish is a vicarage, in the alternate patronage of the bishop and the dean and chapter of Ely. The present incumbent is the Rev. George Jenyns. There is a charity school conducted upon the national plan, which has proved of material advantage to the children of the labouring class. Population of the parish, in 1831, 1,102.

About one mile from and in the same hundred as the above village is SWAFFHAM BULBECK. The trade that it possesses is dependent upon the agricultural population. From the river Cam, which partly bounds the parish, there is a branch called Swaffham Lode, navigable to the village. The church is dedicated to St. Mary; the living is a discharged vicarage, in the patronage of the bishop of Ely and incumbency of the Rev. Leonard Jenyns. A charity school was founded here in 1721, by Mrs. Frances Towers, and endowed with £50. per annum. The remains of a benedictine nunnery are visible here. Population, 727.

POST OFFICE, BURWELL, Michael Bayly, *Post Master.*—Letters from NEWMARKET arrive every morning at eight, and are despatched every evening at seven.

POST, SWAFFHAM PRIOR, *Receiving-House* at Thomas Palmby's.—Letters arrive from and are despatched to NEWMARKET every morning at nine.

**GENTRY AND CLERGY.**
Alix John Peter, esq. Swaffham Prior
Baines Rev. John Johnson, Vicarage, Burwell
Buckpitt Rev. James, Burwell
Casburn Mr. William, Burwell
Doggett Mr. Jeremiah, Burwell
Dunn Mr. Salisbury, Burwell
Ellis Mr. John, Swaffham Bulbeck
Giblin Charles, esq. Swaffham Bulbeck
Giblin Henry, esq. Swaffham Bulbeck
Hawthorn Rev.Robt.Swaffham Prior
Jenyns Rev.George, Swaffham Prior
Jenyns Rev. Leonard, SwaffhamBul.
LucasMr.Thomas(surgeon),Burwell
MulberyMr.John,SwaffhamBulbeck

**ACADEMIES AND SCHOOLS.**
Bayly Michael, Burwell
NATIONAL SCHOOL, Swaffham Prior
—William Shaw, master
Saunders Benjamin, Swaffham Prior

**BAKERS & FLOUR DEALERS.**
Bailey Matthew, Swaffham Bulbeck
Powell Thomas, Burwell
Spalding William, Swaffham Prior
Webb Richard, Swaffham Prior

**BLACKSMITHS.**
Fromant Richard, Swaffham Bulbeck
Hills George, Burwell
Iverson John, Burwell
Iverson Thomas, Swaffham Prior
Stevens William, Swaffham Bulbeck
Waters Thomas, Swaffham Prior

**BOOT & SHOE MAKERS.**
Arber Joseph, Burwell
Clarke Matthew, Swaffham Bulbeck
Day John, Swaffham Prior
Hunt John, Burwell
Mason Joseph, Burwell
Mellor John, Swaffham Bulbeck

**BRICKLAYERS, &c.**
Arber John, Burwell
Gardiner Stephen, Burwell
Hunt Thomas, Swaffham Bulbeck
Watling John, Swaffham Prior
Watling William, Swaffham Prior

**BUTCHERS.**
Bloon Thomas, Burwell
Fuller Thomas, Burwell
Gunton John, Swaffham Prior

**42**

*This entry from Pigot and Co.'s 1839 directory for Cambridgeshire lists the names of many local tradesmen, including Thomas Waters, blacksmith, a distant cousin to my own ancestors. (Author's collection)* for areas outside London. I have found the London editions of *Pigot* generally to be better and more comprehensive than the Post Office directories.

## *The British Almanac* (1828–1914)

These contain lists of civil, military and ecclesiastical officials residing in Great Britain, Ireland and the colonies; some private businesses are also included.

## *Royal Kalendar* (1733–1865)

This is a comprehensive register for the civil, military and ecclesiastical establishment of Great Britain and its colonies. Some private organisations and businesses are also included. Each volume has a table of contents.

## *Boyle's Fashionable Court and Country Guide, and Town Visiting Directory* (c. 1797–1925)

Published in January and April of each year, *Boyle's* is an excellent resource for tracing the addresses of nobles, gentry, ministers and highly fashionable members of society. It is centred on London and lists the names alphabetically with their addresses, but there is also a street index and a directory of public officials, offices, and some organisations and businesses.

Although he was not an ancestor, I was once seeking biographical information on a Mr Carne, who, according to an article in *The Times*, ran the White Lion public house on Vere Street, London, in 1837. I had no success with the 1841 census and so turned to *Pigot's London Directory* for 1838. I could not find Mr Carne under the alphabetical list of traders and so turned to the street index. Under Vere Street the White Lion public house was listed as house no. 44, with the manager being a G.H. Came. Evidently *The Times* had mistaken Carne for Came when copying out his name. Now having the correct spelling, I turned back to *Pigot's* alphabetical list of traders and found this entry: Came, George Hutchings, White Lion PH, 44 Vere Street.

Knowing his full name, I used the Mormons' Internet Family Search facility (see Section 2.1) and was able to find a pedigree relating to George Hutchings Came that revealed him to have been born in 1799 in Devon. The pedigree went back to the seventeenth century, although I have yet to check its accuracy. The FreeBMD website (www.freebmd.org.uk) gave me references to his marriage and death certificates, information that confirmed that the baptism entry given on the Mormon website is correct.

# CHAPTER TWENTY

# HERALDRY

This chapter will offer only a brief introduction to the field of heraldry, which, in truth, is more liable to be encountered by those searching out medieval ancestors (it is rare for a family that held a coat of arms in recent times to have forgotten about it). Those seeking further information about heraldry should consult one of the many books on the subject or read my more detailed account in Chambers (2005).

## A Brief History of Heraldry

The origins of coats of arms is obscure (a favoured explanation is that they result from the designs used on knights' shields and flags in battle), but the use of hereditary coats of arms dates back to at least the twelfth century. By the fourteenth century heraldry (the discipline associated with the study and awarding of arms) had developed its own set of rules and regulations as well as a whole separate language that could be used to describe succinctly a person's coat of arms (see Friar, 1992 for details of heraldry terminology).

By the early fifteenth century heraldry was being roundly abused, and many individuals or families were displaying arms to which they had no right. Since at least the mid-thirteenth century there had been various 'Officers of Arms', officials tasked with policing the heraldry system, but it was not until 1417 that Henry V decreed that only the Crown could award the right to bear arms.

In the following decades the Officers of Arms grew in stature and formed themselves into a hierarchical organisation that consisted of the King of Arms, Heralds of Arms and Pursuivants of Arms. By the early sixteenth century the Heralds of Arms had been tasked with travelling the countryside, seeking out those individuals and families who were claiming the right to use a coat of arms. These people were then asked to provide evidence to back up their claim to arms – if they could not, then the right to bear those arms would be withdrawn. The Heralds' Visitations, as these inspections were known, took place every thirty years or so between 1530 and 1684 and are described in more detail later on.

In modern times the administration of arms has been handed to the College of Arms, based in London. Here, thirteen Officers of Arms assess individual claims to hold arms but also award entirely new coats of arms to those people who meet their criteria. The Officers of Arms also have a ceremonial function during the State Opening of Parliament.

It is a common mistake to believe that, because coats of arms are attached to a surname, anyone bearing that surname is entitled to use those arms. In reality a coat of arms will have been awarded to a particular individual and it is only the heirs (usually male) of that individual who will be entitled to display those arms. Thus a coat of arms is attached not to a surname but instead to a particular family's bloodline, and in order to be able to display a coat of arms it is first necessary to prove that you have a direct link (usually through the male line) to an ancestor who was himself awarded the right to bear arms.

The Internet is awash with companies offering to sell you certificates, paperweights, ashtrays and other objects emblazoned with the coat of arms that, according to them, belongs to your family. Unfortunately, the complex rules associated with heraldry and the awarding of coats of arms almost certainly mean that you will not be legally entitled to use any coat of arms sold to you by mail order.

To the genealogist heraldry is more than just a status symbol. Because the right to bear arms was hereditary, finding an *armiger* (someone who has the right to bear arms) in the family tree can open up an avenue into a new and productive field of genealogical research that can take a family tree way back into the medieval era.

The next section deals with the techniques and resources for finding an armigerous ancestor. The remainder of this section will deal with some of the peculiarities associated with the laws and language of heraldry.

## Law of Arms

In England and Wales the right to use arms is determined by a strict set of rules policed by the College of Arms. The central tenet of these laws is that a lawfully awarded coat of arms can be passed down to the next generation only through the male line. The only circumstance under which arms may pass through a female line is when the daughter of an armiger has no male heirs or brothers. In these circumstances the woman is entitled to display her father's arms. If she then marries a man who is himself an armiger, then her father's coat of arms may be included in the shield of her husband and male children.

Where several male heirs occur, each brother may add a cadency mark to his shield to reflect whether he is the eldest, second, third, etc. son. Cadency marks (for these see the references listed in the terminology of armory below) follow a set pattern and can be useful in reconstructing family relationships. Other family relationships, such as illegitimacy, can also be determined using the coat of arms.

It is still possible to apply for a coat of arms through the College of Arms, but in order to be awarded one you will have to have an ancestral connection with England or Wales and will also usually have had to have distinguished yourself in some way. Recently politicians, businessmen and celebrities have been awarded the right to bear arms.

## Discovering Armigerous Ancestors

Given the importance and status conveyed by a coat of arms, it is unlikely that an individual family that was entitled to one would forget about it. The best that most of us can hope for is to discover that some of our ancestors along the female lineages were arms-bearers. While this will not entitle us to bear the arms ourselves, it can be a door to a wealth of additional genealogical information, especially if the family occurs in the Heralds' Visitations.

Discovering an armigerous ancestor is, in my experience, mostly a matter of luck. Of the three armigerous families from whom I am descended, all three were discovered by chance. In each case I discovered the connection to the family through conventional genealogical research and only later discovered that they held arms. In two instances I discovered the arms by looking through the published Heralds' Visitation volumes for the county where they resided (see below). In the other instance it was through a footnote written in a published transcription of a seventeenth-century forced loan. The footnote described my ancestors' coat of arms. Then, using armorials, Heralds' Visitations and other records, I managed to uncover several more generations of the family going back to medieval times.

I know of other people who have discovered armigerous ancestors by having found the coat of arms displayed on a funeral monument (brasses are especially good for this) or through mention being made of a family's coat of arms in publications such as the VCH or in local history volumes. It may also be worth checking the churches in which your ancestors were likely to have been buried, as some better-off families would pay to have their arms carved into the walls or incorporated into stained-glass windows. On visiting a Suffolk church I was greatly surprised to find that my armigerous ancestors had had their coat of arms incorporated into the top of the church's bell tower so that they were visible from the surrounding countryside.

However, if you have not been lucky enough to stumble across a chance reference to a coat of arms belonging to an ancestor and you want to know whether they were armigerous, then there are a number of avenues open to you. These are described below.

## The College of Arms

The College of Arms is the only corporation that has the right to award arms within England and Wales (separate corporations exist for Scotland and Ireland). Their address is: Queen Victoria Street, London EC4V 4BT (tel: 020 7248 2762; www.college-of-arms.gov.uk).

The College has been incorporated since 1484 and contains the original registers of grants of arms, funeral certificates, the records of Heralds' Visitations as well as numerous other official records related to heraldry. Their library also contains a

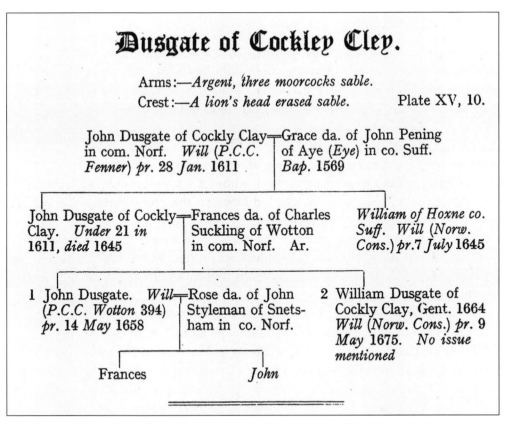

# Dusgate of Cockley Cley.

Arms:—*Argent, three moorcocks sable.*

Crest:—*A lion's head erased sable.* Plate XV, 10.

John Dusgate of Cockly Clay=Grace da. of John Pening
in com. Norf. *Will (P.C.C.* | of Aye (*Eye*) in co. Suff.
*Fenner) pr.* 28 *Jan.* 1611 | *Bap.* 1569

John Dusgate of Cockly=Frances da. of Charles | *William of Hoxne co.*
Clay. *Under 21 in* | Suckling of Wotton | *Suff. Will (Norw.*
1611, *died* 1645 | in com. Norf. Ar. | *Cons.) pr.* 7 *July* 1645

1 John Dusgate. *Will*=Rose da. of John | 2 William Dusgate of
(*P.C.C. Wotton* 394) | Styleman of Snets- | Cockly Clay, Gent. 1664
*pr.* 14 *May* 1658 | ham in co. Norf. | *Will (Norw. Cons.) pr.* 9
 | | *May* 1675. *No issue*
 | | *mentioned*

Frances John

*A tree for the armigerous Dusgate family of Norfolk taken from* The Visitation of Norfolk, 1664 *(Harleian Society, vol. 85). Although such pedigrees are not always entirely accurate, the information gathered by the Heralds' Visitations can be very useful.* (Author's collection)

wealth of unofficial material, including pedigrees, wills and other genealogical material that it has gathered over the centuries.

If you believe that you have an ancestor who held arms or that you yourself are entitled to bear arms, then the College of Arms may well be able to confirm this using information held in their archive. The scope of this archive can be seen in Wagner (1952) and also in *The College of Arms Catalogue* (1988).

Unfortunately, the College of Arms' library is out of bounds to the public and any research must be undertaken by the staff for a fee. If you explain your research needs in writing (by letter or via their website), the staff will be able to tell you whether or not they can be of service and, if so, how much the research will cost. However, before contacting the College of Arms it is advisable to have done some groundwork yourself, as this will save you time and money. Some of the more useful information held within the archive has been published, especially by the Harleian Society. Consulting these publications should give you an idea as to whether or not you have any armigerous ancestors (see below for details).

An alternative to the College of Arms is The Heraldry Society (PO Box 772, Guildford, Surrey GU3 3ZX; tel: 01483 237373; www.theheraldrysociety.com), whose library is accessible to members. Contact the Society for further details.

## Armorials

To see whether or not there are arms associated with a surname, the first place to check are the many 'armorials' that exist on the subject. Armorials are an alphabetical list of surnames that are legally entitled to hold a coat of arms; they will also usually include a description and/or picture of the arms plus additional information such as where in Britain the family bearing them lived and when the arms were awarded.

The largest and most famous armorial is Burke (1884, but reprinted many times since) which, although it is old, is still the most comprehensive work on the subject containing several tens of thousands of entries. Below is a typical entry:

> **Barentine.** (Lord mayor of London, 1398 and 1408). Sa. an annulet or, betw. three eagles displ. or.
> **Barentine.** Sa. three eagles displ. ar. armed gu. *Crest* – An eagle displ. ar. betw. the attires and scalp of a stag or.

However, while it is comprehensive, Burke is not always correct and contains many coats of arms that have been taken from dubious sources. Additions and corrections have been made in Humphrey-Smith (1973).

Other armories worth consulting are Fox-Davies *et al.* (1883, reprinted many times since), whose 1929 edition is generally considered to be accurate, and the earlier Berry (1828–40) and volume two of Edmondson (1780), which contains an armory.

## Ordinaries

If you find yourself in the situation of having a coat of arms but no surname to go with it, you will need to consult an ordinary. Ordinaries are publications that enable us to identify a coat of arms using the charges that appear on the shields.

The largest and most famous of these is Papworth (1874, but reprinted many times), which lists the charges in alphabetical order. To identify a coat of arms using an ordinary you will need to have a description of the coat of arms using the correct terminology (see terminology of armory). Then use the ordinary to look up the charges on the shield, e.g. if there are three swans on the shield, turn to the BIRDS section of the ordinary and then find the section relating to three swans. There will often be several entries under the same heading. You will have to use the other features of the shield to identify the coat of arms.

**BIRDS.          3 EAGLES**

Sa. three eagles displ. arg. BARANTYNE, BARENTINE or BARENTYNE. Co. Buckingham, and co. Oxford. William BARANTINE, or BARENTIN, E. William de BARANTINE, F. Dru BARNTIN, G. And with an annulet in the centre for difference or, Sir Drew BARENTINE, Lord Mayor of London, 1398, W., and 1408.

Fairbairn *et al.* (1905) may also be of use when trying to identify a coat of arms. If you have a motto with your arms and want to know more about it, consult Elvin (1971).

Once you have identified a coat of arms, try looking for further information in the other resources listed here.

## The Heralds' Visitations and the Harleian Society Publications

The Harleian Society was founded in 1869 with the objective of publishing 'the Heraldic Visitations of Counties, and any manuscripts relating to genealogy, family history, and Heraldry'. In the years since its foundation the Society has lived up to this objective, publishing over one hundred volumes, many of which are an invaluable resource for the genealogist.

The core of the Harleian Society's publications are their Heralds' Visitations volumes taken directly from the archives of the College of Arms. The Heralds' Visitations publications are among the most useful heraldry records and it is through them that many people are able to discover that they had armigerous ancestors.

The Heralds' Visitations were a series of inspections carried out by the College of Arms roughly every thirty years (once a generation) between 1530 and 1684. Each visitation would see a Herald of Arms despatched into the countryside with the express aim of seeking out those people who claimed to have the right to bear arms. These individuals would be asked to provide genealogical evidence linking them to a known arms-bearer.

If a connection could be proved, the right to bear arms would be confirmed. If a genealogical link could not be proved, the right to bear the arms would be denied, but often the individual was given the chance to submit further evidence to back up his claim. Sometimes the Heralds would impose corrections on the arms.

The result of each visitation would be a large number of annotated pedigrees, some of which contain dozens of names and go back several generations or more. These were entered into the College of Arms' archives, where they currently form the Library of Visitation Books.

The visitation records can be a genealogical goldmine but until the founding of the Harleian Society few of these records had found their way into print.

Over the last 130 years the Harleian Society has managed to print the majority of the Heralds' Visitations on a county-by-county basis. A list of these published volumes is available on the Harleian Society's website (harleian.co.uk) and they can be found in many large institutional libraries, but some of the older ones are also available on CD-ROM (see the Harleian Society's website). Some authors have mentioned differences between the published visitation records and the originals in the College of Arms.

Each visitation volume consists of dozens of pedigrees produced by the individuals claiming the right to bear arms. Many of these pedigrees stretch back into the medieval era and can provide information that is difficult to come by otherwise, such as a wife's maiden name or where an ancestor lived. The volumes are fully indexed and so even if your ancestors do not have a pedigree devoted specifically to them, they may still be mentioned as part of another person's pedigree.

It is definitely worth checking the volumes that relate to the county (or the neighbouring counties) where your ancestors lived. Through these I have found a number of genealogical connections that would otherwise have gone unnoticed. In my experience the published Heralds' Visitations are the most useful heraldry resource and are worth taking the time to consult. Some other visitation records have been published by local history societies.

In addition to the Harleian Society volumes, a list of the visitation records held in the College of Arms can be found in Wagner (1952). A catalogue of visitation records, including an index to the named pedigrees, can be found in Humphrey-Smith (1997).

The following summarised example comes from the Visitation of Cambridgeshire in 1619 and concerns the Backus (Bacchus) family to whom I am indirectly related:

### Backus
ARMS – *Ermine, on a bend gules three eagles displayed or.*

John Backus of Swapham priory = Catherine d. of . . . Houlte

I

Edward Backus of Swapham priory = Margerett d. of . . . Sawyers of Sandwich in Kent

I

Barthelmew Backus of Trumpington in Com. Cambridg 1619 = Elizabeth d. of John Ware of Foulborne

In addition to the Heralds' Visitations, the Harleian Society has also published many other volumes that contain information relating to heraldry; for a list of these see the website.

It should be noted that a certain amount of caution must be used when it comes to heraldry records, especially those from medieval or early modern times. At the time that many of the records were being created (in the sixteenth and seventeenth centuries) there was a great deal of emphasis on genealogy and family status. For this reason many pedigrees submitted to the College of Arms were inaccurate, either through deliberate manipulation, bad memory or honest errors that had been passed down through the generations. It can be very difficult to identify and rectify such mistakes on these pedigrees unless, by fortune, additional information (such as a will) is available.

# CHAPTER TWENTY-ONE

# EXISTING PEDIGREES

The advent of the Internet means that it is now much easier to find information relating to your own ancestry either through library catalogues or through other researchers who may be working on the same family tree as you. Finding a pre-existing pedigree that connects with your own family tree can potentially save a great deal of research time. With diligent searching it is often possible to find connections to existing pedigrees that stretch back into the medieval era. It hardly needs adding that any pedigrees that you find should be regarded with suspicion until you have verified the information they contain for yourself.

## Unpublished Pedigrees

A fascination with one's ancestry is not just a modern phenomenon. In the past many families, especially the better-off ones, have sought to trace their ancestry. This was especially true in late Tudor and early Stuart times, and in the Victorian era when many family trees were researched often with the sole intention of finding a direct connection to royalty or to Norman aristocracy. Many of these pedigrees were written down and have subsequently found their way into various archives.

The British Library holds many such historical pedigrees (try searching their online manuscripts catalogue at www.bl.uk/catalogues/manuscripts.html), as do the SoG and the College of Arms (whose collections are closed to the public; see Chapter 20). Other good resources can be CROs and local history societies.

Copies of some of these unpublished manuscripts are to be found in privately produced volumes, a large collection of which is held by the SoG and the British Library. Others may be referred to or reproduced in local history volumes. For example, Blomefield's eleven-volume *An Essay towards a Topographical History of the County of Norfolk* contains dozens of previously unpublished local family genealogies, as do many of the VCH volumes.

## Published Pedigrees and Family Histories

In addition to a mass of unpublished pedigrees, there are a great many standard published volumes that can be of assistance in tracing your ancestors. Most of these concern the more wealthy members of society, but they may also contain information on some of the less wealthy families into which many younger sons and daughters often married.

For peers and their relations, the standard reference for the ancestry of living or recently deceased peers is *Burke's Peerage* and *Debrett's Peerage*. However, more comprehensive is *The Complete Peerage* (Cokayne, 1910–59), which holds information on all those who have held peerages, alive and deceased; an alternative source is Burke (1996), while for lesser members of the aristocracy there are Cokayne (1900–6) and Burke (1937).

It is the hope of many genealogists that they will discover a connection between themselves and a member of royalty. Statistically this is not as unlikely as it may at first seem, especially given the number of illegitimate children that some kings produced. Most kings acknowledged their children (both legitimate and illegitimate) by giving them hereditary peerages and a certain amount of wealth. Thus, in order to discover a royal connection it is first usually necessary to find a direct connection to a peer or noble, many of whom are distantly descended from the lesser sons and daughters of various kings and queens. Realistically speaking, the odds of being descended from one of the post-Tudor monarchs without already knowing about it are extremely remote. Even Charles II, who fathered a number of illegitimate children, ensured that they knew about their parentage. For example, Captain Robert FitzRoy, who was in charge of the voyage that took Charles Darwin around the world, is descended from a family whose lineage begins with an illegitimate son of Charles II, a fact that is acknowledged both in his name (FitzRoy means 'son of the king') and his coat of arms.

For more humble families try local history publications (especially the VCH volumes), as these can contain invaluable biographical information about people or families who live in a region. Check local libraries and CROs for details.

## Magazines and Journals

National or international genealogical magazines and journals, such as *Family Tree Magazine* or *Genealogists' Magazine*, are unlikely to have genealogies that connect to your family tree published within them, and searching through their annual indexes (assuming that they have them) can be a frustrating process. The same is true of national magazines such as *Notes and Queries*, although this can be worth the effort if you have a famous (or infamous) ancestor.

Local history magazines and journals may often contain information that will be of relevance. A search through the archive of *The East Anglian* produced a number of references to my research. However, some of these local magazines have not been indexed, which makes them almost impossible to search with any effectiveness. The SoG and the Institute of Historical Research are good sources for local history material of this nature.

# COUNTY RECORD OFFICES

This is a list of the main CROs of England and Wales. Some counties have subsidiary or regional record offices which have not been listed; contact the central offices for further details.

## ENGLAND

Bedfordshire Record Office
County Hall, Caldwell Street, Bedford MK42 9AP
Tel: + 44 (0)1234 228833
Website: www.bedfordshire.gov.uk

Berkshire Record Office
9 Coley Avenue, Reading, Berks RG1 6AF
Tel: + 44 (0)118 901 5132
Website: www.berkshirerecordoffice.org.uk

Centre for Buckinghamshire Studies
County Hall, Walton Street, Aylesbury HP20 1UU
Tel: + 44 (0)1296 382587
Website: www.buckscc.gov.uk/archives

Cambridgeshire CRO
Shire Hall, Castle Hill, Cambridge CB3 0AP
Tel: + 44 (0)1223 717281
Website: www.cambridgeshire.gov.uk

Cheshire Record Office
Duke Street, Chester CH1 1RL
Tel: + 44 (0)1244 602574
Website: www.cheshire.gov.uk

Cornwall Record Office
County Hall, Truro TR1 3AY
Tel: + 44 (0)1872 323127
Website: www.cornwall.gov.uk

Cumbria Record Office
140 Duke Street, Barrow-in-Furness, Cumbria LA14 1XW
Tel: + 44 (0)1229 89437
Website: www.cumbria.gov.uk

Derbyshire Record Office
County Education Department, County Offices, Matlock DE4 3AG
Tel: + 44 (0)1629 580 000
Website: www.derbyshire.gov.uk

Devon Record Office
Bittern Road, Exeter EX2 7NL
Tel: + 44 (0)1392 384253
Website: www.devon.gov.uk

Dorset CRO
9 Bridport Road, Dorchester DT1 1RP
Tel: + 44 (0)1305 250550
Website: www.dorsetcc.gov.uk

Durham CRO
County Hall, Durham DH1 5UL
Tel: + 44 (0)191 383 3253
Website: www.durham.gov.uk/recordoffice

Essex Record Office
Wharf Road, Chelmsford CM12 6YT
Tel: + 44 (0)1245 244644
Website: www.essexcc.gov.uk

Gloucestershire Record Office
Clarence Row, Alvin Street, Gloucester GL1 3DW
Tel: + 44 (0)1452 425295
Website: www.gloucestershire.gov.uk

Hampshire Record Office
Sussex Street, Winchester SO23 8TH
Tel: + 44 (0)1962 846154
Website: www.hants.gov.uk/record-office

Hereford & Worcester Record Office
Harold Street, Hereford H41 2QX
Tel: + 44 (0)1432 260750
Website: www.herefordshire.gov.uk

Hertfordshire Record Office
County Hall, Pegs Lane, Hertford SG13 8DE
Tel: + 44 (0)1438 737333
Website: www.hertsdirect.org

Huntingdonshire
See Cambridge CRO

Isle of Wight Record Office
26 Hillside, Newport PO30 2EB
Tel: + 44 (0)1983 823820
Website: www.iwight.com/library/record_office

Centre for Kentish Studies
County Hall, Maidstone ME4 1XQ
Tel: + 44 (0)1622 694363
Website: www.kent.gov.uk

Lancashire Record Office
Bow Lane, Preston PR1 2RE
Tel: + 44 (0)1772 533039
Website: www.lancashire.gov.uk

Leicestershire Record Office
Wigston Magna, Leicester LE18 2AH
Tel: + 44 (0)116 2571080
Website: www.leics.gov.uk/museums/records

Lincolnshire Archives Office
St Rumbold Street, Lincoln LN2 5AB
Tel: + 44 (0)1522 525158
Website: www.lincolnshire.gov.uk

London Guildhall Library
Aldermanbury, London EC2P 2EJ
Tel: + 44 (0)20 7332 1863
Website: www.history.ac.uk/gh

London Metropolitan Archives
40 Northampton Road, London EC14 0HB
Tel: + 44 (0)20 7332 3820
Website: www.cityoflondon.gov.uk

Middlesex
See London Guildhall Library and Metropolitan Archives

Norfolk Record Office
Martineau Lane, Norwich NR1 2DQ
Tel: + 44 (0)1603 222599
Website: www.norfolk.gov.uk

Northamptonshire Record Office
Wootton Hall Park, Northampton NN4 9BQ
Tel: + 44 (0)1604 762129
Website: www.northamptonshire.gov.uk

Northumberland Record Office
Melton Park, North Gosford, Newcastle-Upon-Tyne NE3 5QX
Tel: + 44 (0)191 2362680
Website: www.swinhope.myby.co.uk/NRO

Nottinghamshire Archives Office
Castle Meadow Road, Nottingham NG1 1AG
Tel: + 44 (0)115 958 1634
Website: www.nottinghamshire.gov.uk/libraries/Archives

Oxfordshire Record Office
St Luke's Church, Temple Road, Oxford OX4 2EX
Tel: + 44 (0)1865 398200
Website: www.oxfordshire.gov.uk

Rutland
See Leicestershire Record Office

Shropshire Records & Research Centre
Castle Gates, Shrewsbury SY1 2AQ
Tel: + 44 (0)1743 255350
Website: www.shropshirearchives.co.uk

Somersetshire Archive & Record Service
Obridge Road, Taunton TA2 7PU
Tel: + 44 (0)1823 337600
Website: www.somerset.gov.uk/archives

Staffordshire Record Office
Eastgate Street, Stafford ST16 2LZ
Tel: + 44 (0)1785 278379
Website: www.staffordshire.gov.uk

Suffolk Record Office
Gatacre Road, Ipswich IP1 2LQ
Tel: + 44 (0)1473 584541
Website: www.suffolkcc.gov.uk/sro

Surrey History Service
130 Goldsworth Road, Woking GU21 6ND
Tel: + 44 (0)1483 518737
Website: www.surreycc.gov.uk/surreyhistoryservice

East Sussex Record Office
The Maltings, Castle Precincts, Lewes BN7 1YT
Tel: + 44 (0)1273 482349
Website: www.eastsussexcc.gov.uk

West Sussex Record Office
County Hall, West Street, Chichester PO19 1RN
Tel: + 44 (0)1243 753600
Website: www.westsussex.gov.uk

Warwickshire CRO
Priory Park, Cape Road, Warwick CV34 4JS
Tel: + 44 (0)1926 738959
Website: www.warwickshire.gov.uk/countyrecordoffice

Westmorland
See Cumbria Record Office

Wiltshire Record Office
County Hall, Bythesea Road, Trowbridge BA14 8JG
Tel: + 44 (0)1225 713709
Website: www.wiltshire.gov.uk

Worcester Public Library
County Hall, Spetchley Road, Worcester WR5 2NP
Tel: + 44 (0)1905 763763
Website: www.worcestershire.gov.uk

East Riding of Yorkshire Archive Service
County Hall, Beverley HU17 9BA
Tel: + 44 (0)1482 393939
Website: www.eastriding.gov.uk

North Yorkshire CRO
Malpas Road, Northallerton DL7 8SG
Tel: + 44 (0)1609 771658
Website: www.northyorks.gov.uk/archives

West Yorkshire Archive Service
Newstead Road, Wakefield WF1 2DE
Tel: + 44 (0)1924 305980
Website: www.archives.wyjs.org.uk

# WALES

Anglesey (Ynys Môn) County Record Office
Shire Hall, Glanhwfa Road, Llangefni, Anglesey LL77 7TW
Tel: + 44 (0)1248 752080
Website: www.anglesey.gov.uk

Brecknockshire (see Powys)

Caernarfon (Gwynedd) Record Office
Swyddfa'r Cyngor, Caernarfon LL55 1SH
Tel: + 44 (0)1286 679095
Website: www.gwynedd.gov.uk

Cardiganshire (Ceredigion) Archives
County Offices, Marine Terrace, Aberystwyth, Ceredigion SY23 2DE
Tel: + 44 (0)1970 633697
Website: archifdy-ceredigion.org.uk

Carmarthenshire (Sir Gaerfyrddin) Archive Service
Parc Myrddin, Waun Dew, Carmarthen, Carmarthenshire SA31 1DS
Tel: + 44 (0)1267 228232
Website: www.carmarthenshire.gov.uk

Denbighshire (Sir Ddinbych) Record Office
Ruthin Gaol, 46 Clwyd Street, Ruthin, Denbighshire LL15 1HP
Tel: + 44 (0)1824 708250
Website: www.denbighshire.gov.uk

Flintshire (Sir y Fflint) Record Office
The Old Rectory, Hawarden, Flintshire CH5 3NR
Tel: + 44 (0)1244 532364
Website: www.flintshire.gov.uk

Glamorganshire (Morgannwg) Record Office
The Glamorgan Building, King Edward VII Avenue, Cathays Park, Cardiff CF10 3NE
Tel: + 44 (0)29 2078 0282
Website: www.glamro.gov.uk

Merionethshire (see Powys)

Monmouthshire (Gwent) Record Office
County Hall, Cwmbran, Gwent NP44 2XH
Tel: + 44 (0)1633 644886
Website: www.llgc.org.uk/cac/cac0004.htm

Montgomeryshire (see Powys)

Pembrokeshire (Sir Benfro) Record Office
The Castle, Haverfordwest, Pembrokeshire SA61 2EF
Tel: + 44 (0)1437 763707
Website: www.pembrokeshire.gov.uk

Powys County Archives Office
County Hall, Llandrindod Wells, Powys LD1 5LG
Tel: + 44 (0)1597 826088
Website: archives.powys.gov.uk

Radnorshire (see Powys)

# A LIST OF REGNAL YEARS

The following is a list of regnal years for the early modern period.

**James I**
   1. 24 March 1603–23 March 1604
   2. 24 March 1604–23 March 1605
. . .
23. 24 March 1625–27 March 1625

**Charles I**
   1. 27 March 1625–26 March 1626
   2. 27 March 1626–26 March 1627
. . .
24. 27 March 1648–30 January 1649

**The Commonwealth**
31 January 1649–28 May 1660
Although he did not officially rule during the Commonwealth, Charles II's reign is deemed to have begun on the date of his father's death.

**Charles II**
12. 29 May 1660–29 January 1661
13. 29 May 1661–29 January 1662
. . .
37. 30 January 1685–6 February 1685

**James II**
   1. 6 February 1685–5 February 1686
   2. 6 February 1686–5 February 1687
. . .
   4. 6 February 1688–11 December 1688

**Interregnum**
12 December 1688–12 February 1689

**William and Mary**
   1. 13 February 1689–12 February 1690
   2. 13 February 1690–12 February 1691
. . .
   6. 13 February 1694–27 December 1694

**William III**
Continues after Mary's death
  6. 28 December 1694–12 February 1695
  7. 13 February 1695–12 February 1696
. . .
14. 13 February 1702–8 March 1702

**Anne**
  1. 8 March 1702–7 March 1703
  2. 8 March 1703–7 March 1704
. . .
13. 8 March 1714–1 August 1714

**George I**
  1. 1 August 1714–31 July 1715
  2. 1 August 1715–31 July 1716
. . .
13. 1 August 1726–11 June 1727

**George II**
  1. 11 June 1727–10 June 1728
  2. 11 June 1728–10 June 1729
. . .
34. 22 June 1760–25 October 1760

**George III**
  1. 25 October 1760–24 October 1761
  2. 25 October 1761–24 October 1762
. . .
60. 25 October 1819–29 January 1820

**George IV**
  1. 29 January 1820–28 January 1821
  2. 29 January 1821–28 January 1822
. . .
11. 29 January 1830–26 June 1830

**William IV**
  1. 26 June 1830–25 June 1831
  2. 26 June 1831–25 June 1832
. . .
  7. 26 June 1836–20 June 1837

# REFERENCES

Addison, W.I. (1898), *A Roll of the Graduates of the University of Glasgow, 1727–1897*, MacLehose and Sons

Admiralty (1760–4), *A General List of the Lieutenants of his Majesty's Fleet, with the Dates of their First Commissions*, Admiralty Office, 5 vols

Alcock, N.W. (2001), *Old Title Deeds: A Guide for Local and Family Historians*, Phillimore

Allen, D.H. (1974), *Essex Quarter Sessions Order Book, 1652–1661*, Essex County Council

Anderson, R.C. (1964), *List of English Naval Captains, 1642–1660*, Society for Nautical Research

Andrews, C.M. (1912 and 1914), *Guide to the Materials for American History, to 1783, in the Public Record Office of Great Britain*, 2 vols, Carnegie Institution of Washington

Anstruther, G. (1968), *The Seminary Priests: A Dictionary of the Secular Clergy of England and Wales, 1558–1850*, 4 vols, Ushaw College

Arber, E. (1875–94), *A Transcript of the Registers of the Company of Stationers of London, 1554 to 1660*, privately printed

Atherton, L. (1994), *Never Complain, Never Explain: Records of the Foreign Office and State Paper Office 1500 to c. 1960*, Public Record Office

Atmore, C. (1801), *The Methodist Memorial*, Richard Edwards

Aylmer, G.E. and Morrill, J.S. (1979), *The Civil War and Interregnum Sources for Local Historians*, Bedford Square Press

Baach, J. (1962), *A Directory of English County Physicians 1603–1643*, Dawsons of Pall Mall

Baildon, W.P. (1896), *The Records of the Honourable Society of Lincoln's Inn*, 2 vols, London

Baker, D.E., Reed, I. and Jones, S. (1812), *Biographica Dramatica or, A Companion to the Playhouse*, 4 vols, Longmans

Baker, R.L. (1961), *The English Customs Service 1307–43: A Study of Medieval Administration*, The American Philosophical Society

Barlow, D. (1968), *The Records of the Forfeited Estates Commission*, PRO

Baxter, C.J. (1987a), *General Muster of New South Wales 1814*, Society of Australian Genealogists

Baxter, C.J. (1987b), *General Musters of NSW, Norfolk Island and Van Diemen's Land, 1811*, Society of Australian Genealogists

Baxter, C.J. (1988a), *Muster and Lists of New South Wales and Norfolk Island, 1800–1802*, Society of Australian Genealogists

Baxter, C.J. (1988b), *General Muster and Lands and Stock Muster of NSW, 1822*, Society of Australian Genealogists

Baxter, C.J. (1989), *Musters of New South Wales and Norfolk Island 1805–1806*, Society of Australian Genealogists

Baxter, C.J. (1999), *General Muster List of New South Wales 1823, 1824, 1825*, Society of Australian Genealogists

Baxter, I.A. (2004), *Baxter's Guide: Biographical Sources in the India Office Records*, Families in British India Society

Baylen, J.O. and Gossman, N.J. (1979), *Biographical Dictionary of Modern British Radicals*, 3 vols, Harvester Press

Beard, G. and Gilbert, C. (1986), *Dictionary of English Furniture Makers, 1660 to 1840*, Furniture History Society

Beckerlegge, O.A. (1968), *United Methodist Ministers and their Circuits: 1797–1932*, Epworth Press

Beech, G. and Mitchell, R. (2004), *Maps for Family and Local History*, The National Archives

Bell, H.C. and Parker, D.W. (1926), *Guide to British West Indian Archive Materials, in London and in the Islands, for the History of the United States*, Carnegie Institution of Washington

Bendall, S. (1997), *Dictionary of Land Surveyors and Local Mapmakers of Great Britain and Ireland, 1530–1850*, 2 vols, British Library

Berry, W. (1828–40), *Encyclopaedia Heraldica*, 4 vols, London

Bevan, A. (2000), *Tracing Your Ancestors in the Public Record Office*, Public Record Office

Bevan, J. (1985), *Index and Finding List to Joseph Gillow's Bibliographical Dictionary of the English Catholics*, John Bevan

Bloom, J.H. and James, R.R. (1935), *Medical Practitioners in the Diocese of London*, Cambridge University Press

Bourne, S. and Chicken, A.H. (1994), *Records of the Medical Professions – A Practical Guide for the Family Historian*, Susan Bourne

Breed, G.R. (1995), *My Ancestors were Baptists*, Society of Genealogists

Brown, R. (1986), *The English Baptists of the Eighteenth Century*, Baptist Historical Society

Bruce, J., Hamilton, W.D. and Lomas, S.C. (1858–97), *The Calendar of State Papers Charles I*, 23 vols, HMSO

Bryant, M. (1903), *A Biographical and Critical Dictionary of Painters and Engravers*, 5 vols, Bell and Sons (originally published 1816)

Bryant, M. and Heneage, S. (1994), *Dictionary of British Cartoonists, 1730 to 1980*, Scolar Press

Burke, B. (1884), *The General Armory of England, Scotland, Ireland and Wales*, Wm Clowes and Sons (reprinted many times since)

Burke, B. (1937), *A Genealogical and Heraldic History of the Landed Gentry*, London

Burke, B. (1996), *A Genealogical History of the Dormant, Abeyant, Forfeited and Extinct Peerages of the British Empire*, London (originally published 1831)

Burtchaell, G.D. and Sadlier, T.U. (1924), *Alumni Dublinenses*, Williams and Norgate

Camp, A.J. (1974), *Wills and their Whereabouts*, Anthony Camp

Campbell, J. and Stevenson, W. (1917), *Lives of the British Admirals*, London

Carter, L. and Bateson, D. (1995), *Principal Collections of Papers in the Cambridge South Asian Archive*, Centre for South Asian Studies

Chambers, P. (2005), *Medieval Genealogy*, Sutton

Chapman, C.R. (1992), *Ecclesiastical Courts, their Officials and their Records*, Lochin Publishing

Chapman, C.R. (1999), *Using Educational Records*, Federation of Family History Societies

Chapman, J. (1992), *Guide to Parliamentary Enclosures in Wales*, University of Wales Press

Charnock, J. (1794–6), *Biographia Navalis, or, Impartial Memoirs of the Lives and Characters of Officers of the Navy of Great Britain: From 1660 to the Present Time*, London

Clifford, D.J.H. (1997), *My Ancestors were Congregationalists in England and Wales*, Society of Genealogists

Cockburn, J.S. (1959), *Somerset Assize Orders*, Butler & Tanner

Cockburn, J.S. (1972), *A History of English Assizes, 1558 to 1714*, Cambridge University Press

Cockburn, J.S. (1973–95), *Calendar of Assizes Records*, 14 vols, HMSO

Cockerell, H.A.L. and Green, E. (1994), *The British Insurance Business, 1547–1970*, Sheffield Academic Press

Cokayne, G.E. (1900–6), *The Complete Baronetage*, Pollard and Co.

Cokayne, G.E. (1910–59), *The Complete Peerage of England, Scotland, Ireland, Great Britain and the United Kingdom*, 14 vols, St Catherine's Press (republished by Sutton, 1998)

Coldham, P.W. (1980), *English Estates of American Colonists: American Wills and Administrations in the Prerogative Court of Canterbury, 1610–99; 1700–99*, Genealogical Publishing Company

Coldham, P.W. (1985), *English Adventurers and Emigrants, 1609–60 and 1661–1733: Abstracts of Examinations in the High Court of Admiralty with Reference to Colonial America*, 2 vols, Genealogical Publishing Company

Coldham, P.W. (1988), *The Complete Book of Emigrants in Bondage, 1614–1775*, Clearfield Company

Coldham, P.W. (1992a), *Supplement to the Complete Book of Emigrants in Bondage 1614–1775*, Genealogical Publishing Company

Coldham, P.W. (1992b), *American Wills Proved in London, 1611–1775*, Genealogical Publishing Company

Coldham, P.W. (2002), *More Emigrants in Bondage: 1614–1775*, Genealogical Publishing Company

Coldham, P.W. (2005), *British Emigrants in Bondage, 1614–1788*, Genealogical Publishing Company

Cole, J.A. (1997), *Wiltshire Militia Courts Martial, 1759 to 1770*, Wiltshire Family History Society

Collinge, J.M. (1978), *Navy Board Officials, 1660–1832*, University of London

Collinge, J.M. (1979), *Foreign Office Officials, 1782–1870*, University of London

Collins, A. (2001), *Basic Facts About Using Colindale and Other Newspaper Repositories*, Federation of Family History Societies

Colvin, H. (1995), *A Biographical Dictionary of British Architects, 1600 to 1840*, Yale University Press

Colwell, S. (2002), *The Family Records Centre: A User's Guide*, Public Record Office

Cooke, W.H. (1877), *Students Admitted to the Inner Temple*, Clowes and Sons

Copeman, W.S.C. (1983), *The Worshipful Society of Apothecaries of London: A History*, Wellcome Institute

Cornwall, J. (1993), *How to Read Old Title Deeds, 16th–19th Centuries*, Federation of Family History Societies (originally published 1964)

Crawford, D.G. (2002), *Roll of the Indian Medical Service: 1615–1930*, Families in British India Society (originally published in 1930)

Cruickshanks, E., Handley S. and Hayton, D.W. (2002), *House of Commons, 1690–1713*, History of Parliament Trust

Culling, J. (1999), *An Introduction to Occupations: A Preliminary List*, Federation of Family History Societies

Cumbria Family History Society (2002), *Window Tax for Whitehaven and Hensingham also Land Tax for Whitehaven Preston Quarter 1770*, Cumbria Family History Society

Dalton, C. (1892–1904), *English Army Lists and Commission Registers: 1661–1714*, 6 vols, Eyre & Spottiswoode

Dalton, C. (1910–12), *George the First's Army: 1714–1727*, Eyre and Spottiswoode

Danvers, F.C. (1894), *Memorials of Old Haileybury College*, Constable and Company

Desmond, R. (1994), *Dictionary of British and Irish Horticulturalists*, Taylor and Francis

Dietz, F.C. (1964), *English Government Finance, 1558–1641*, University of Illinois

Dodwell, E. and Miles, J.S. (1838), *Alphabetical List of Officers of the Indian Army: 1760 to 1834*, London

Dodwell, E. and Miles, J.S. (1839a), *Alphabetical List of Indian Medical Officers: 1764 to 1838*, London

Dodwell, E. and Miles, J.S. (1839b), *Bengal Civil Servants: 1780 to 1838*, London

Dodwell, E. and Miles, J.S. (1839c), *Madras Civil Servants: 1780 to 1839*, London

Dodwell, E. and Miles, J.S. (1839d), *Bombay Civil Servants: 1780 to 1838*, London

Downie, R. (2000), *Who's Who in Davy Jones' Locker: A Biographical Directory of Pirates, Buccaneers and Privateers*, Southgate Books

Duckett, G.F. (1889), *Naval Commissioners from 12 Charles II. to 1 George III., 1660–1760, Compiled from the Original Warrants and Returns*, Printed for the author

Edmondson, J. (1780), *A Complete Body of Heraldry*, T. Spilsbury

Edwards, R.F. (1898), *List of Officers of the Corps of Royal Engineers from 1660 to 1898*, Royal Engineers Institute

Edye, L. (1893), *The Historical Records of the Royal Marines*, Harrison

Ellis, M. (1994), *Using Manorial Records*, Public Record Office

Elvin, C.N. (1971), *A Handbook of Mottoes*, Heraldry Today (originally published 1860)

Emden, A.B. (1963), *Biographical Register of the University of Cambridge*, Cambridge University Press

Emden, A.B. (1974), *Biographical Register of the University of Oxford*, Clarendon Press

Emmison, F.G. and Gray, I. (1967), *County Records*, The Historical Association

Eyre, B. (1913–14), *A Transcript of the Worshipful Company of Stationers from 1640 to 1708*, P. Smith (reprinted 1967)

Fairbairn, J., Jack, T.C. and Jack, E.C. (1905), *Book of Crests*, London

Faithfull, P. (2002), *Lunacy in England and Wales for Family Historians*, Federation of Family History Societies

Farrar, M. (1994), *Genealogical Sources in Cambridgeshire*, Cambridgeshire County Council

Farrington, A.J. (1976), *The Records of the East India College, Haileybury, & other Institutions*, HMSO

Farrington, A.J. (1982), *Guide to the Records of the India Office Military Department*, India Office Library

Farrington, A.J. (1999), *A Biographical Index of the East India Maritime Service Officers: 1660–1834*, British Library

Fidlon, P.G. and Ryan, R.J. (1981), *The First Fleeters*, Australian Documents Library

Filby, P.W. and Meyer, M.K. (1981), *Passenger and Immigration Lists Index: A Guide to Published Arrival Records of about 500,000 Passengers who came to the United States and Canada in the Seventeenth, Eighteenth and Nineteenth Centuries*, Gale Research Co.

Firth, C.H. and Rait, R.S. (1911), *Acts and Ordinances of the Interregnum, 1642–1660*, HMSO

Fisher, S.W. (1972), *A Dictionary of Watercolour Painters: 1750 to 1900*, Foulsham and Co.

Floate, S.S. (1999), *My Ancestors were Gypsies*, Society of Genealogists

Foster, J. (1889), *The Register of Admissions to Gray's Inn*, Hansard Union

Foster, J. (1890), *Index Ecclesiasticus*, Parker and Co.

Foster, J. (1891–2), *Alumni Oxonienses*, Parker and Co.

Fowler, S. (2003), *Researching Brewery and Publican Ancestors*, Federation of Family History Societies

Fowler, S. and Spencer, W. (2000), *Army Records for Family Historians*, Public Record Office

Fox-Davies, A.C., Fox-Davies, T.C. and Jack, E.C. (1883), *Armorial Families*, T.C. and E.C. Jack (reprinted many times since)

Friar, S. (1992), *Heraldry*, Sutton Publishing

Fry, E.A. (1904), *Index to Chancery Proceedings (Reynardson's Division) Preserved in the Public Record Office*, British Record Society

Gandy, M. (1993a), *Catholic Parishes in England, Wales and Scotland: An Atlas*, Michael Gandy

Gandy, M. (1993b), *Catholic Missions and Registers: 1770–1880*, Michael Gandy

Gandy, M. (2001), *Tracing Catholic Ancestors*, Public Record Office

Gandy, M. (2002), *Tracing your Catholic Ancestry in England*, Federation of Family History Societies (revised edition)

Gandy, W. (1922), *The Association Oath Rolls of the British Plantations A.D. 1696: being a Contribution to Political History*, Wallace Gandy

Gerhold, D. (1994), *Courts of Equity: A Guide to Chancery and other Legal Records for Local and Family Historians*, Pinhorns

Gibson, J.S.W. (1974), *Wills and Where to Find Them*, Phillimore Ltd

Gibson, J.S.W. (1982), *Quarter Sessions Records*, Federation of Family History Societies

Gibson, J.S.W. (1989), *Tudor and Stuart Muster Rolls: a Directory of Holdings in the British Isles*, Federation of Family History Societies

Gibson, J.S.W. (1996), *The Hearth Tax and other later Stuart Tax Lists and the Association Oath Rolls*, Federation of Family History Societies

Gibson, J.S.W. (2001), *Bishops' Transcripts and Marriage Licences, Bonds and Allegations: a Guide to their Location and Indexes*, Gibson Guides

Gibson, J.S.W. and Dell, A. (1995), *The Protestation Returns 1641–1942 and other Contemporary Listings*, Federation of Family History Societies

Gibson, J.S.W. and Hampson, E. (1998), *Specialist Indexes for Family Historians*, Federation of Family History Societies

Gibson, J.S.W. and Hunter, J. (2001), *Victuallers' Licences: Records for Family and Local Historians*, Federation of Family History Societies

Gibson, J.S.W. and Medlycott, M. (2001), *Local Census Listings, 1522–1930: Holdings in the British Isles*, Federation of Family History Societies

Gibson, J.S.W. and Medlycott, M. (2004), *Militia Lists and Musters 1757–1876: A Directory of Holdings in the British Isles*, Federation of Family History Societies

Gibson, J.S.W. and Peskett, P. (2001), *Record Offices: How to Find Them*, Federation of Family History Societies

Gibson, J.S.W. and Rogers, C. (1992), *Coroners' Records in England and Wales*, Federation of Family History Societies

Gibson, J.S.W. and Rogers, C. (1994), *Poll Books 1696–1872: A Directory to Holdings in Great Britain*, Federation of Family History Societies

Gibson, J.S.W., Langston, B. and Smith, B.W. (2002), *Local Newspapers 1759–1920: A Select Location List*, Federation of Family History Societies

Gibson, J.S.W., Medlycott, M. and Mills, D. (2004), *Land and Window Tax Assessments*, Federation of Family History Societies

Gibson, J.S.W., Rogers, C. and Webb, C. (2005), *Poor Law Union Records*, 4 vols, Federation of Family History Societies

Giles, J. (1740), *The Compleat Attorney's Practice in English, in the Courts of King's Bench and Common Pleas at Westminster*, Nutt and Gosling

Gillow, J. (1885–1902), *A Literary and Biographical History, or Bibliographical Dictionary of the English Catholics; from the Breach with Rome in 1534 to the Present Time*, Burn and Oates (reprinted since)

Gooder, E.A. (1978), *Latin for Local History: an Introduction*, Longman

Goodwin, N. (1995), *Genealogical Notes: First Settlers of Connecticut and Massachusetts*, Genealogical Publishing Company (originally published 1856)

Goss, C.W.F. (1932), *The London Directories, 1677–1855; A Bibliography with Notes on their Origin and Development*, D. Archer and Co.

Greaves, R.L. and Zaller, R. (1982), *Biographical Dictionary of British Radicals in the Seventeenth Century*, 3 vols, Harvester Press

Graham, N.H. (1980), *The Genealogist's Consolidated Guide to Nonconformist and Foreign Registers, Copies and Indexes in the Inner London Area*, Norman Graham

Grant, W.L. and Munro, J. (1908–12), *Acts of the Privy Council of England; Colonial Series*, 6 vols, HMSO

Green, M.A.E. (1875–86), *Calendar of State Papers Domestic, The Commonwealth*, 13 vols, HMSO

Green, M.A.E. (1888), *Committee for Advance of Money, 1642–1656*, HMSO

Green, M.A.E. (1889–93), *Committee for Compounding with Delinquents, 1643–1660*, HMSO

Green, M.A.E., Daniell, F.H.B. and Bickley, F. (1860–1947), *The Calendar of State Papers Domestic, Charles II*, 28 vols, HMSO

Greer, G.C. (1960), *Early Virginia Immigrants, 1623–1666*, Genealogical Publishing Company

Grenham, J. (1999), *Tracing your Irish Ancestors*, Gill and Macmillan

Grieve, H. (1978), *Examples of English Handwriting, 1150–1750*, Essex Records Committee

Griffin, G. (1946), *A Guide to Manuscripts relating to American History in British Depositories*, The Library of Congress

Guiseppi, M.S. and Griffin, R. (1938), *Appendix to a List of Monumental Brasses in the British Isles*, Headley Brothers

Gunnis, R. (1951), *Dictionary of British Sculptors, 1660 to 1851*, Abbey Library

Hall, J. (1897), *Hall's Circuits and Ministers: 1765 to 1896*, Wesleyan Methodist Book Room

Hardy, W.J. and Bateson, E. (1895–1937), *Calendars of State Papers Domestic, William III*, 11 vols, HMSO

Harrison, B.A. (1991), *Prisoners of the Tower*, Brian Harrison

Harvey, P.D. (1984), *Manorial Records*, British Records Association

Harvey, R. (1998), *A Guide to Genealogical Sources in Guildhall Library*, Guildhall Library

Hawkings, D.T. (1987), *Bound for Australia*, Phillimore

Hawkings, D.T. (1992), *Criminal Ancestors*, Sutton

Hawkings, D.T. (2003), *Fire Insurance Records for Family and Local Historians 1696 to 1920*, Francis Boutle

Hector, H.C. (1966), *The Handwriting of English Documents*, Edward Arnold

Hennessy, G. (1898), *Novum Repertorium Ecclesiasticum Parochiale Londinense*, London

Herber, M. (1998–2001), *Clandestine Marriages in the Chapel and Rules of the Fleet Prison 1680–1754*, 3 vols, Francis Boutle

Highfill, P.H., Burnim, K.A. and Langhams, E.A. (1973), *A Biographical Dictionary of Actors, Actresses, Musicians, Dancers, Managers and other Stage Personnel in London, 1660 to 1800*, Southern Illinois University Press

Hill, J. (1994), *Hertfordshire Militia Lists: Baldock*, Hertfordshire Family and Population History Society

HMSO (1890–1964), *Acts of the Privy Council of England, 1542 to 1631*, 46 vols, HMSO

HMSO (1913), *An Account of the Commissioners of Customs, Excise, Hearthmoney, and Inland Revenue, 1642–1913*, HMSO

HMSO (1967), *Maps and Plans in the Public Record Office: British Isles, c.1410–1860*, HMSO

HMSO (1986), *An Inventory of Nonconformist Chapels and Meeting-Houses in Central England*, HMSO

Hodson, V.C.P. (1927 and 1947), *List of the Officers of the Bengal Army, 1758–1834, Alphabetically Arranged and Annotated with Biographical and Genealogical Notices*, 4 vols, Constable

Hollowell, S. (2000), *Enclosure Records for Historians*, Phillimore

Hone, N.J. (1906), *The Manor and Manorial Records*, Methuen

Horwitz, H. (1995), *Chancery Equity Records and Proceedings: 1600–1800*, Public Record Office

Hotten, J.C. (1931), *The Original Lists of Persons of Quality; Emigrants; Religious Exiles; Political Rebels; Serving Men Sold for a Term of Years; Apprentices; Children Stolen; Maidens Pressed; and Others Who Went From Great Britain to the American Plantations 1600–1700. With their Ages, the Localities Where they Formerly Lived in the Mother Country, the Names of the Ships in which they Embarked, and other Interesting Particulars. from Mss. Preserved in the State Paper Department of Her Majesty's Public Record Office, England*, G.A. Baker

Howell, T.B. (1816–28), *A Complete Collection of State Trials and Proceedings for High Treason and other Crimes and Misdemeanours from the Earliest Period to the Year 1783*, Longman, Hurst, Rees, Orme, and Brown

Hoyle, R.W. (1994), *Tudor Taxation Records: A Guide for Users*, Public Record Office

Humphrey-Smith, C.R. (1973), *General Armory Two*, Genealogical Publishing Co.

Humphrey-Smith, C.R. (1995), *The Phillimore Atlas and Index of Parish Registers*, Phillimore

Humphrey-Smith, C.R. (1997), *Armigerous Ancestors: A catalogue of sources for the study of the Visitations of the Heralds in the 16th and 17th centuries with referenced lists of names*, Family History Books

India Office (1896), *List of Marine Records of the Late East India Company, and of Subsequent Date, Preserved in the Record Department of the India Office, London*, Eyre and Spottiswoode

India Office (1919), *Chronological Lists of Heads of Administration in India and at Home: 1680–1702, 1714–72, 1773–1858*, London

Johnson, C. and Jenkinson, H. (1915), *English Court Hand A.D. 1066 to 1500*, Clarendon Press

Johnson, W.B. (1970), *The English Prison Hulks*, Phillimore

Jones, P.E. and Smith, R. (1951), *A Guide to the Records in the Corporation of London Records Office and the Guildhall Library Muniment Room*, English Universities Press

Jurkowski, M., Smith, C.L. and Crook, D. (1998), *Lay Taxes in England and Wales: 1188–1688*, Public Record Office

Kain, R.J.P. (1986), *An Atlas and Index of the Tithe Files of Mid-Nineteenth-Century England and Wales*, Cambridge University Press

Kain, R.J.P. and Oliver, R.R. (1995), *The Tithe Maps of England and Wales: a Cartographic Analysis and County-by-County Catalogue*, Cambridge University Press

Kain, R.J.P. and Prince, H.C. (2000), *Tithe Surveys for Historians*, Phillimore

Kain, R.J.P., Chapman, J. and Oliver, R.R. (2004), *The Enclosure Maps of England and Wales, 1595–1918*, Cambridge University Press

Kaminkow, J. (1966), *A List of Emigrants from England to America, 1718–1759*, Magna Charta Books

Kealy, A.G. (1905), *Chaplains of the Royal Navy*, London

Kershaw, R. and Pearsall, M. (2004), *Immigrants and Aliens: A Guide to Sources on UK Immigration and Citizenship*, The National Archives

Kirk, E.F. and Kirk, R.E.G. (1900–8), *Returns of Aliens Dwelling in the City and Suburbs of London, 1529–1605*, 4 vols, Huguenot Society (vol. 10)

Kirk, J. (1968), *Biographies of English Catholics in the Eighteenth Century*, Gregg International Publishers (originally published in 1909)

Kitzmiller, J.M. (1988), *In Search of Forlorn Hope: A Comprehensive Guide to Locating British Regiments and their Records*, Manuscript Publishing Foundation

Kupperman, K., Appleby, J.C. and Banton, M. (2000), *Calendar of State Papers, Colonial: North America and the West Indies 1574–1739*, CD-ROM, Routledge

Larn, R. (1995–8), *Shipwrecks of the British Isles*, 4 vols, Lloyd's Register of Shipping

Latham, R.E. (1980), *Revised Medieval Latin Word-list from British and Irish Sources*, Oxford University Press

Laurence, A. (1990), *Parliamentary Army Chaplains, 1642–1651*, Boydell Press

Le Neve, J. (1969–2003), *Fasti Ecclesiae Anglicanae*, Institute of Historical Research

Leary, W. (1993), *My Ancestors were Methodists*, Society of Genealogists

Lemon, R. and Green, A. (1856–72), *Calendar of State Papers, Domestic Series, of the Reigns of Edward VI, Mary, Elizabeth I and James I*, 12 vols, HMSO

Lewis, P. (1999), *My Ancestors were Freemasons*, Society of Genealogists

Long, E. (1970), *The History of Jamaica: or, General survey of the ancient and modern state of that island: with reflections on its situations, settlements, inhabitants, climate, products, commerce, laws, and government*, Cass (originally published 1774)

Lowe, J.A. (1990), *Records of the Portsmouth Division of Marines, 1764–1800*, Portsmouth Record Series, vol. 7, City of Portsmouth

Mackenzie, G.N. (1907), *Colonial Families of the United States of America, 1607 to 1775*, 7 vols, Grafton Press

Mahaffy, R.P. (1860–1910), *Calendar of State Papers relating to Ireland*, 24 vols, HMSO

Mahaffy, R.P. (1916–25), *Calendars of State Papers Domestic, Anne*, 2 vols, HMSO

Manning, P. (1996), *Calendar of Quarter Sessions Records: Session Papers, 1639–1677: Index to Persons*, Rainham

Marshall, J. (1823–30), *Royal Naval Biography: 1760 to the Present Period*, 12 vols, London

Martin, C.T. (1982), *The Record Interpreter*, Phillimore (originally published in 1892)

Matteson, D.M. (1925), *List of Manuscripts concerning American History Preserved in European Libraries and Noted in their Published Catalogues and Similar Printed Lists*, Carnegie Institution of Washington

Maxwell-Lyte, H.C. (1926), *Historical Notes on the Use of the Great Seal of England*, HMSO

Mayhew, H. (1983), *London Labour and the London Poor*, Dover Publications (originally published in 1861)

McArthur, J. (1813), *Principles and Practice of Naval and Military Courts Martial*, A. Strahan

McGowan, A. (1996), *The Winchester Confessions 1615–1616: Depositions of Travellers, Gypsies, Fraudsters, and Makers of Counterfeit Documents, including a Vocabulary of the Romany Language*, Romany and Traveller Family History Society

McKerrow, R.B. (1910), *A Dictionary of Printers and Booksellers in England, Scotland and Ireland, 1557 to 1640*, Bibliographical Society

McLaughlin, E. (1999), *Simple Latin for Family Historians*, Varneys Press

Meekings, C.A.F. (1979), *Analysis of Hearth Tax Accounts 1662 to 1665*, List and Index Society, vol. 153

Meekings, C.A.F. (1980), *Analysis of Hearth Tax Accounts 1666 to 1669*, List and Index Society, vol. 163

Menhennet, D. (1971), *The Journal of the House of Commons: a Bibliographical and Historical Guide*, HMSO

Miller, F.H.H. (1970), *The 282 Protestant Martyrs of England and Wales, 1555–1558*, Educational Publishers

Milligan, E.H. and Thomas, M.J. (1999), *My Ancestors were Quakers*, Society of Genealogists

Minchinton, W. and Harper, P. (1983), *American Papers in the House of Lords Record Office: a Guide*, Wakefield

Minet, W. and Minet, S. (1932), *A Supplement to Dr W.A. Shaw's Letters of Denization and Acts of Naturalization*, Huguenot Society (vol. 35)

Moore, S.T. (2003), *Family Feuds: An Introduction to Chancery Proceedings*, Federation of Family History Societies

Mordy, I. (1995), *My Ancestors were Jewish*, Society of Genealogists

Morris, J. (1989), *A Latin Glossary for Family and Local Historians*, Federation of Family History Societies

Mortimer, I. (1999), *Record Repositories in Great Britain*, Public Record Office

Munby, L.M. (2002), *Reading Tudor and Stuart Handwriting*, British Association for Local History

Munk, W. (1878–1989), *A Roll of the Royal College of Physicians (Munk's Roll)*, 8 vols, University of London

Newdigate, C.A. (1935), *Our Martyrs. A chronological list of those who died for the faith in England and Wales in the 16th and 17th centuries*, Catholic Truth Society

Newman, P.R. (1981), *Royalist Officers in England and Wales, 1642–1660: A Biographical Dictionary*, Garland

Nicolas, H. (1834–7), *Proceedings and Ordinances of the Privy Council of England*, Eyre and Spottiswoode

Norton, J.E. (1950), *Guide to the National and Provincial Directories of England and Wales, Excluding London, Published Before 1856*, Royal Historical Society

O'Byrne, W.R. (1849), *A Naval Biographical Dictionary: Comprising the Life and Services of every Living Officer in Her Majesty's Navy, from the Rank of Admiral of the Fleet to that of Lieutenant, inclusive*, 3 vols, John Murray

Oates, P.J. (2003), *My Ancestors were Inghamites*, Society of Genealogists

Oliver, V.L. (1910–19), *Caribbeana: Being Miscellaneous Papers relating to the History, Genealogy, Topography, and Antiquities of the British West Indies*, 6 vols, Mitchell, Hughes and Clarke

Paley, R. (2001), *Using Criminal Records*, Public Record Office

Pappalardo, B. (2001), *Using Navy Records*, Public Record Office

Pappalardo, B. (2003), *Tracing your Naval Ancestors*, Public Record Office

Papworth, J.W. (1874), *An Ordinary of British Armorials*, London

Parry, G. (1995), *A Guide to the Records of Great Sessions in Wales*, National Library of Wales

Pascoe, C.F. (1901), *Two Hundred Years of the S.P.G.*, Society for the Propagation of the Gospel

Peacock, E. (1983), *The Army Lists of the Roundheads and Cavaliers*, Trotman (originally published in 1863)

Peterkin, A., Johnston, W. and Drew, R. (1968), *Commissioned Officers in the Medical Services of the British Army*, 2 vols, London

Philippart, J. (1823–6), *The East India Military Calendar: containing the Services of General and Field Officers of the Indian Army*, London

Phillimore, W.P.W. (1889), *Index Nominum to the Royalist Composition Papers, First and Second Series*, London

Phillimore W.P.W. and Fry, E.A. (1889–1904), *Calendar of Chancery Proceedings, Bills and Answers, Charles I*, 4 vols, British Record Society

Phillimore W.P.W. and Fry, E.A. (1905), *An Index to Changes of Name: Under Authority of Act of Parliament or Royal Licence, and Including Irregular Changes from I George III to 64 Victoria, 1760 to 1901*, Phillimore

Plomer, H.R. *et al.* (1907), *A Dictionary of Printers and Booksellers who were at Work in England, Scotland and Ireland from 1641 to 1667*, Oxford University Press

Plomer, H.R. *et al.* (1922), *A Dictionary of Printers and Booksellers who were at Work in England, Scotland and Ireland from 1668 to 1725*, Oxford University Press

Plomer, H.R. *et al.* (1932), *A Dictionary of Printers and Booksellers who were at Work in England, Scotland and Ireland from 1726 to 1775*, Oxford University Press

Powell, J.R. and Timings, E.K. (1963), *Documents Relating to the Civil War 1642–1648*, London

Power, D. (1930–81), *Plarr's Lives of the Fellows of the Royal College of Surgeons*, 7 vols, London

Price, J.E. (1886), *A Descriptive Account of the Guildhall of the City of London*, Blades, East and Blades

Prinsep, H.T. (1885), *Record of Services of Madras Civilians: 1741 to 1858*, London

Prinsep, H.T. and Doss, R. (1844), *Register of Bengal Civil Servants: 1790 to 1842*, London

Pugh, R.B. (1964), *The Records of the Colonial and Dominions Offices*, HMSO

Pyle, A. (2000a), *The Dictionary of Seventeenth Century Philosophers*, Thoemmes Press

Pyle, A. (2000b), *The Dictionary of Nineteenth Century Philosophers*, Thoemmes Press

Raimo, J.W. (1979), *A Guide to Manuscripts relating to America in Great Britain and Ireland: a Revision of the Guide Edited in 1961 by B.R. Crick and Miriam Alman*, Mansell

Ralfe, J. (1828), *The Naval Biography of Great Britain: Consisting of Historical Memoirs of those Officers of the British Navy who distinguished themselves during the Reign of His Majesty George III*, 4 vols, Whitmore & Fenn

Raymond, S. (1997), *Occupational Sources for Genealogists: A Bibliography*, Federation of Family History Societies

Raymond, S. (2004), *Words from Wills and Other Probate Records*, Federation of Family History Societies

Redington, J. and Roberts, R.A. (1878–99), *Calendar of Home Office Papers of the Reign of George III*, 4 vols, HMSO

Rickard, G. (1995), *Vagrants, Gypsies and Travellers in Kent 1572–1948*, G. Rickard

Rodger, N.A.M. (1998), *Naval Records for Genealogists*, Public Record Office

Rogal, S.J. (1997), *A Biographical Dictionary of 18th Century Methodism*, E. Mellon Press

Rose, E.A. (1981), *A Checklist of British Methodist Periodicals*, WMHS

Ruston, A.R. (1993), *My Ancestors were English Presbyterians/Unitarians*, Society of Genealogists

Ruston, A.R. (1996), *Obituaries and Marriages of Dissenting Ministers in the Gentleman's Magazine in the 18th century*, Alan Ruston

Ryan, R.J. (1982), *The Second Fleet Convicts*, Australia

Sainty, J.C. (1971), *Officers of the House of Lords, 1485–1971*, House of Lords Record Office

Sainty, J.C. (1972), *Treasury Officials, 1660–1870*, Athlone Press

Sainty, J.C. (1973), *Officials of the Secretaries of State 1660–1782*, University of London

Sainty, J.C. (1974), *Officials of the Boards of Trade, 1660–1870*, Institute of Historical Research

Sainty, J.C. (1975a), *Home Office Officials: 1782–1870*, Athlone Press

Sainty, J.C. (1975b), *Admiralty Board Officials, 1660–1870*, Athlone Press

Sainty, J.C. (1976), *Colonial Office Officials: Officials of the Secretary of State for War 1794–1801, of the Secretary of State for War and Colonies 1801–54, and of the Secretary of State for Colonies 1854–70*, University of London

Sainty, J.C. (1983), *Officers of the Exchequer*, Swift

Sainty, J.C. and Bucholz, R.O. (1997 and 1998), *Officials of the Royal Household 1660–1837. Department of the Lord Chamberlain and associated offices. Departments of the Lord Steward and the Master of the Horse*, Institute of Historical Research, 2 vols

Sainty, M.R. and Johnson, K.A. (1980), *The 1828 Census of New South Wales*, Australia

Salmon, T. (1730), *A Complete Collection of State-Trials, and Proceedings for High-Treason, and other Crimes And Misdemeanours: from the Reign of King Richard II. to the End of The Reign of King George I.*, J. Walthoe

Sanders, J.M. (1979–81), *Barbados Records: Wills and Administrations*, 3 vols, Sanders Publications

Savage, J. (1977), *A Genealogical Dictionary of the First Settlers of New England*, Genealogical Publishing Company (originally published in 1873)

Schurer, K. and Arkell, T. (1992), *Surveying the People: The Interpretation and Use of Document Sources for the Study of Population in the Later 17th Century*, Leopard's Head Press

Scottish Record Office (1976), *List of American Documents*, Scottish Record Office

Scouloudi, I. (1985), *Returns of Strangers in the Metropolis, 1593, 1627, 1635, 1639*, Huguenot Society (vol. 57)

Seaman, P. (2001), *Norfolk Hearth Tax Exemption Certificates, 1670–1674*, British Record Society (vol. 117)

Seaton, J. (1986), *English Constituency Histories, 1265–1832*, HMSO

Sharp, H. (2000), *How to Use the Bernau Index*, Society of Genealogists

Shaw, W.A. (1911), *Letters of Denization and Acts of Naturalization for Aliens in England and Ireland, 1603–1700*, Huguenot Society (vol. 18)

Shaw, W.A. (1923), *Letters of Denization and Acts of Naturalization for Aliens in England and Ireland, 1700–1803*, Huguenot Society (vol. 27)

Shearman, A. (2000), *My Ancestor was a Policeman*, Society of Genealogists

Sims, J. (1984), *A Handlist of British Parliamentary Poll Books*, University of Leicester

Skempton, A.W. (2002), *A Biographical Dictionary of Civil Engineers in Great Britain and Ireland*, Institute of Civil Engineers

Smellie, W. (1752), *A Treatise on the Theory and Practice of Midwifery*, D. Wilson and T. Durham

Spencer, W. (1997), *Records of the Militia and Volunteer Forces: 1757 to 1945*, Public Record Office

Steel, D.J. (1973), *Sources for Nonconformist Genealogy and Family History*, Phillimore

Stell, C.F. (1991), *An Inventory of Nonconformist Chapels and Meeting-Houses in South-west England*, HMSO

Stell, C.F. (1994), *An Inventory of Nonconformist Chapels and Meeting-Houses in the North of England*, HMSO

Stephenson, M. (1926), *A List of Monumental Brasses in the British Isles*, Headley Brothers

Stewart, B. and Cutten, M. (1997), *The Dictionary of Portrait Painters in Britain up to 1920*, Antique Collectors' Club

Stock, L.F. (1924), *Proceedings and Debates of the British Parliaments respecting North America*, Carnegie Institution of Washington

Stow, J. (1734), *A Survey of the Cities of London and Westminster, Borough of Southwark, and Parts Adjacent: being an Improvement of Mr. Stow's, and Other Surveys*, 3 vols, J. Read

Stuart, D. (1992), *Manorial Records*, Phillimore

Stuart, D. (2000), *Latin for Local and Family Historians*, Phillimore

Sturgess, H.A.C. *et al.* (1949–78), *Register of Admissions to the Honourable Society of the Middle Temple*, 5 vols, London

Syrett, D. and DiNardo, R.L. (1994), *The Commissioned Sea Officers of the Royal Navy, 1660–1815*, Scolar Press (originally published in 1954)

Tarver, A. (1995), *Church Court Records: an Introduction for Family and Local Historians*, Phillimore

Tate, W.E. (1969), *The Parish Chest: A Study of the Records of Parochial Administration in England*, Cambridge University Press

Tate, W.E. (1978), *A Domesday of English Enclosure Acts and Awards*, University of Reading

Taylor, E.G.R. (1956), *The Mathematical Practitioners of Tudor and Stuart England*, Cambridge University Press

Taylor, E.G.R. (1966), *The Mathematical Practitioners of Hanoverian England: 1714 to 1840*, Cambridge University Press

Taylor, G. (1978), *The Sea Chaplains*, Oxford Illustrated Press

Tepper, M. (1978), *Emigrants to Pennsylvania, 1641–1819*, Genealogical Publishing Company

Thomas, G. (1995), *Records of the Royal Marines*, Public Record Office

Thurston, A. (1995), *Sources for Colonial Studies in the Public Record Office, Volume 1: Records of the Colonial Office, Commonwealth Relations Office and Commonwealth Office*, HMSO

Timings, E.K. (1960–72), *Calendar of State Papers Domestic, James II*, 3 vols, HMSO

Timperley, C.H. (1889), *A Dictionary of Printers and Printing*, H. Johnson

Trebilcock, C. (1985 and 1998), *Phoenix Assurance and the Development of British Insurance*, 2 vols, Cambridge University Press

Turner, W.H. (1878), *Calendar of Charters and Rolls preserved in the Bodleian Library*, Clarendon Press

Valentine, A.C. (1970), *The British Establishment, 1760–1784; An Eighteenth-Century Biographical Dictionary*, University of Oklahoma Press

Venn, J. and Venn, J.A. (1922–54), *Alumni Cantabrigienses: a Biographical List of all known Students, Graduates and Holders of Office at the University of Cambridge, from the Earliest Times to 1900*, Cambridge University Press

Wagner, A.R. (1952), *The Records and Collections of the College of Arms*, College of Arms

Wallis, P.J., Wallis, R.V., Whittet, T.D. and Burnby, J.G.L. (1988), *Eighteenth-Century Medics (Subscriptions, Licences, Apprenticeships)*, Project for Historical Bibliography

Walne, P. (1973), *A Guide to Manuscript Sources for the History of Latin America and the Caribbean in the British Isles*, London

Watts, C.T. and Watts, M.J. (2004), *My Ancestor was a Merchant Seaman*, Society of Genealogists

Webb, C. (1989), *Association Oath Rolls for Surrey 1695*, West Surrey Family History Society

Webb, C. (1996–2002), *London Livery Company Apprenticeship Registers*, 41 vols, Society of Genealogists

Weis, F.L. (1999), *Ancestral Roots of Certain American Colonists Who Came to America before 1700*, Genealogical Publishing Company

Wenzerul, R. (2000), *A Beginner's Guide to Jewish Genealogy in Great Britain*, Jewish Genealogical Society of Great Britain

West, J. (1983), *Town Records*, Phillimore

White, B.R. (1983), *The English Baptists of the Seventeenth Century*, London

Wood, T. (1999), *Basic Facts About Using Record Offices for Family Historians*, Federation of Family History Societies

Woodcroft, B. (1854a), *Subject Matter Index of Patents of Invention: from March 2 1617 (14 James I) to October 1, 1852 (16 Victoriae)*, Queens Printing Office

Woodcroft, B. (1854b), *Titles of Patents of Invention: Chronologically Arranged from March 2, 1617 (14 James I.) to October 1, 1852 (16 Victoriae)*, Queens Printing Office

Wright, A. *et al.* (1879), *Court-Hand Restored: The Student's Assistant in Reading Old Deeds, Charters, Records, etc.*, London

Yolton, J.W., Price, J.V. and Stephens, J. (1999), *The Dictionary of Eighteenth-Century Philosophers*, Thoemmes Press

Young, S. (1890), *The Annals of the Barber-Surgeons of London, compiled from the Records and Other Sources*, London

Zubatsky, D.S. and Berent, I.M. (1984), *Jewish Genealogy: a Sourcebook of Family Histories and Genealogies*, England

Zupko, R.E. (1968), *A Dictionary of English Weights and Measures from Anglo-Saxon Times to the Nineteenth Century*, University of Wisconsin Press

# INDEX